MY COLOURFUL LIFE
by Juliet Pannett M.B.E., F.R.S.A.

Unicorn Press • London

First published by Unicorn Press 2006

Unicorn Press
76 Great Suffolk Street
London
SE1 0BL

www.unicornpress.org
email: unicornpress@btinternet.com

ISBN 0 906290 90 2

Printed and bound in Slovenia for Compass Press Limited

Contents

	Foreword	5
	Acknowledgements	6
Chapter one	My Passion, My Art	7
Chapter two	Sussex Types: Old Codgers	8
Chapter three	Foreign Trips & Boyfriends	10
Chapter four	Ancestors & Early Life	13
Chapter five	The Man of my Life	17
Chapter six	After the Blitz	22
Chapter seven	East Africa	24
Chapter eight	Portrait, Yes, Please	28
	Portrait Techniques: Charcoal	30
Chapter nine	The Valiant Years	32
Chapter ten	Qantas trip	37
Chapter eleven	Public Figures	42
Chapter twelve	Academics	47
	Techniques: Water Colours	50
Chapter thirteen	New York & Canada	52
Chapter fourteen	Stage, Film & Television	54
Chapter fifteen	Medicine	56
Chapter sixteen	Ballet Dancers	58
Chapter seventeen	Sports	60
Chapter eighteen	Lectures, two cities and Rick's sad death	62
	Factories	64
Chapter nineteen	Israel	65
Chapter twenty	House of Commons, House of Lords	68
Chapter twentyone	Literary Figures & Explorers	72
Chapter twentytwo	Musicians	75
Chapter twentythree	The Legal Profession	87
	Techniques: Oil Painting	93
Chapter twentyfour	Artists	94
Chapter twentyfive	Buckingham Palace	95
	Drawing Children	96
	Epilogue	104
	Who's Who	105
	Juliet of a Thousand Faces	106
	Partial List of Portraits	107
	Index	111

Foreword

Juliet Somers Pannett, Chronicler of her Times.

In this day and age it seems hardly surprising when we read of a woman who has achieved the heights, in spite of her sex and her circumstances. My aunt's story, spanning almost all of the 20th century, is of a strong will, backed by an unusual talent – which for many years she had stifled, weighed down by the drudgery of her early married life, one child constantly sick; and there seemed to be no future on the horizon. It was only when she hit the bottom, and was in despair, that her doctor gave her the spark of determination that started her on her way.

Her childhood friend Biddy Hutchinson Tugwell had the idea of a biography and worked with Juliet on a first draft of this book, which I have had the pleasure of reworking with my enthusiastic aunt, and my long-suffering husband.

Between her generation and ours, there have been six painters in the family, often into forms of painting quite different one from the other; but the most famous of course was Juliet. And her resolve to pick herself up from the depths, and work her way up, is what this book is all about. She puts it all so matter-of-factly one tends to lose sight of the circumstances and the courage of overcoming timidity and fear, time and time again. There are also many tips for the painter that will unlock some of the secrets of drawing, and painting watercolours and oils. Throughout the book are the portraits, landscapes and interiors most of which she created in a feverish 30-year period. (She drew over a 1000 portraits!) For her, "Life Begins at 40" really was true.

Several years before her death in 2005, Juliet discovered she had macular degeneration in both eyes. She felt suicidal at the beginning of that disease but later became more philosophical. In fact her only complaint was not being able to do her passion – her art.

Vanessa Somers Vreeland

Acknowledgements

JULIET KATHLEEN SOMERS PANNETT – IMPORTANT PEOPLE IN MY LIFE

May Somers - my mother, for her eccentricity and role model of survival and perseverance in hardship.

Rick - my wonderful husband, for giving me his encouragement, support and so much freedom to travel and paint.

Phoebe - my sister, who was my best friend and support after Rick died. Painter.

Denis Pannett - my dear son, fellow watercolourist, I greatly appreciated the photographs he took at Buckingham Palace [front cover, and pages 100 and 103]

Liz Pannett - my dear daughter and abstract artist who helped with this book.

Brice Somers – my talented brother of whom I'm so proud.

Biddy Hutchinson - my good friend (later Tugwell, still later Hutson) who helped me in writing the first draft.

Miss Trist - my inspirational art teacher and mentor at school - grandaughter of one of the Pre-Raphaelites, but I can't remember which.

Doctor Stephens from Croydon - for encouraging me to resume my art career when at a low ebb.

Sir Bruce Ingram - Editor of Illustrated London News, for giving me my big break, which opened so many doors and sent me on interesting assignments at home and abroad, including the first Woman´s Press Seat in the Houses of Parliament.

Eileen Joyce - the pianist, for being a great friend during the 50's and 60's and handing on some of her beautiful clothes that I could never have afforded!

Vanessa Somers Vreeland and Freck Vreeland - my niece and her husband, for giving me the tape recorder to record my memories when my eyesight failed, that became the basis for this book, and all their tireless dedication in its research and editing.

Nick Gould M.A. (Oxon) - for his professional assistance with research and archiving work over many years and all his help in producing this book.

Mr Forsyth - Head of the Cardiology Department, Royal Sussex County Hospital, Brighton, my heart surgeon who gave me a new lease on life in May 2004 with a replacement aortal pig's valve.

Sue Botha - for her inspirational and dedicated cheerfulness, care and encouragement over the last difficult years.

Sandy Nairne - Director of the National Portrait Gallery, London, who gave me a superb show in 2004-2005, and whose words of introduction touched me deeply.

Ambassador Sir Stephen and Lady Egerton.

Anthony Fagin - for his memories of my sittings with Sir W. Thesiger and Sir L. van der Post.

Emma Palmer - for all her help with the book

Leo Zampa who helped tremendously with the page layout of this book.

Many thanks to the Chartered Insurance Institute for giving me the tremendous opportunity to paint HM The Queen.

And of course so many thanks to Daler-Rowney, Windsor & Newton, and Cotman; Arches Paper, Whatman Paper and Greens Pasteless Board.

Images of portraits by Juliet Pannett in the National Portrait Gallery, London, have been reproduced from the Artist's own colour transparencies.

Dame Laura Knight, a famous painter of circuses, was busy painting the scene. Only six, I stood behind her, fascinated, and gradually drew closer and closer to where she was working on her large canvas. Suddenly she spun around and barked at me: "Will you get further back, please; you're interfering with my work." I felt like a worm!
She was the first artist I had ever seen and luckily her admonition did not put me off my life's work.

From my earliest infancy, even left in my pram, I was always happy with a pencil in my hand, and I remember my first attempt at doing a portrait. On Armistice Day, at the end of the First World War. a little girl was standing on the promenade at Hove, clutching a Union Jack. I remember the thrill of achievement I felt when I drew her. It was the first time I knew that I was trying to reproduce a likeness and the first time that I had the encouragement of praise. I was seven.

Chapter one

My Passion, My Art

Life class in second year

I left school when I was sixteen and received a scholarship to Brighton College of Art. I adored it. Although my mother had been left without a penny by my wastrel father, she never suggested that I take up another career, one in which I would have earned some welcome money. I went daily from home, which was three miles from the art college. I quickly discovered that there was a lorry which

Juliet Somers at 17, by Lucy Walpole

took the same route as I did when I bicycled to classes every morning. The driver slowed down when I hung on and then hotted up the engine and went fast all the way along Brighton Front, slowing down again to let me off at the art school opposite the Royal Pavilion. We got there in four or five minutes. It was extremely dangerous, but exhilarating.

At college, I worked hard at those subjects which interested me and ignored the rest, never bothering to take any exams. My art master was Louis Ginnett and I admired him enormously. I loved his classes and when he painted I found him very inspiring.

It was so lovely spending all my time doing what I really liked. But we were considered too young to do naked bodies in life classes until the second year, and I hated illustration classes with Mr Rendell who wanted us to use our imagination. Being a literal person, I had to have the subject in front of me.

Sussex sheperd, me at 18

1934

I never had a regular job. I never joined a studio. By the time I was eighteen, I knew I wanted to do portraits. I thought that if I drew old fishermen and shepherds — all sorts of old codgers with lots of character — perhaps I could sell them to some paper or magazine and get paid. So that is what I did.

I managed to get an appointment with Arthur Beckett, Editor of the *Sussex County Magazine*. He looked at my work and said, "I think it is rather a good idea; we'll do six and see how we go."

Chapter two

Sussex Types: Old Codgers

He asked me to go round different parts of Sussex and find craftsmen, shepherds and fishermen. I did nearly 50 and thoroughly enjoyed it.

I became rather fond of an old fish net maker and his wife who lived in Hove. On one visit I had to help them lift their bed out of the rotten floorboards as they were so pathetic and old that they couldn't pick it up themselves.

There was the blacksmith at Rottingdean whom I had known since I was very small. He was one of my first subjects and gave me two old horse brasses, which I still have — beautiful little barrels.

Also, there was George Mitchell, a 93-years-old crookmaker at Pycombe. The shepherd's crook from Pycombe was well known in Sussex. I went over with my sister Phoebe to draw him, and some weeks later I came back to give him a copy of the magazine. He clapped his hands and pointed to the picture and said. "My wife won't reckernize this 'ere." "Why not?" I asked disappointedly, "It's a good likeness." "Waal," he replied, "she won't reckernize it 'cos she'm been dead this twenty year." He chuckled with glee at his joke and capered about the room like a wizened old gnome. I still have the crook he made me — a treasured possession in much demand for nativity plays.

William Brazier of Southwick, a Crimean War veteran 99 years old, had been present at the fall of Sebastopol. When I arranged with his daughter to come, he was sitting up in bed leaning back on pillows, wearing his Crimean medals. I went close up to him after a time. He perked up and smiled and said "you're a beauty." I don't think he could see me until I came close. He died just before his hundredth birthday.

I also did "Strawberry Nose", the fat red-faced cabby who had driven his horse cab around Hove for fifty years. Everyone knew toothless George Elliot, and he never lost the opportunity to relate at length how he had once driven Edward VII, as Prince of Wales. He was very proud of that. He sat up high, wearing a bowler hat, and his big bulbous nose was wonderful to draw.

Then there was a corporation boatman who claimed he had saved over a hundred people from drowning; and a saddler and

harness maker who lived in Tarring. He gave me a beautiful 18th-century buckle off a Christ's Hospital shoe.

One interesting character was Stumpy Arnold, from Burpham, a rabbit catcher who supplied the local meat market — this was before we had heard of myxomatosis. He told me he caught four thousand rabbits a year but lived on pork, whisky and tea.

"Old Drip" of Sompting was another of my favourites. Once he took me to see some ruins behind Sompting church, and said darkly, "This were done during the war." "Really?" I said in surprise, "How is that possible?" Old Drip considered my remark and spat thoughtfully before replying, "Cromwell and his men did it."

William Brazier of Southwick

Stumpy Arnold, rabbit catcher

One day I was in the Royal Pavilion where my art club was having an exhibition. Emperor Haile Selassi was brought to see the exhibition and I rather cheekily asked if I could do a drawing of him. He said, "Yes, when I am in England longer, but I have got to go back to Ethiopia tomorrow." Still, it was interesting just to meet him. I don't think he ever came back to Britain.

In July 1932, when I was just 21, I had my first exhibition, in the Hove Public Library. Arthur Beckett observed "Oh dear, nothing over two guineas?" The most expensive of my watercolours and drawings was in fact priced at three guineas — a watercolour of West Blatchington Mill, which he bought. I sold 26 of the 41 pictures.

In 1934 I was elected a member of the Society of Graphic Artists, and started teaching at a girls' school near Crawley. One of my pupils was Pamela Mountbatten, daughter of the Admiral.

In 1937 I acquired my first studio, in a mews in Hove. Its steep, rickety steps were in the last stages of wood rot, but luckily none of my friends or models broke their necks. I also had my first mention in the national press. *The Observer* reported "a small head in silverpoint, of Miss Judy Campbell, an actress, by Juliet Summers [sic], should not be missed."

John Mackie, writer

My first show, 1932

Chapter three

Charles Job

Foreign Trips & Boyfriends

M y family was desperately poor, but somehow I managed to get abroad at regular intervals in search of the local colour I loved so much. Our house never lacked foreigners since to make ends meet we took in paying guests, mostly visitors from the Continent, so I had plenty of contacts abroad.

Thinking back, I feel I was probably young for my age, and took no interest in my appearance. Mostly I went about dressed in an ancient mackintosh. There was no money to spare for clothes and I was quite content with whatever anybody chose to give me.

Despite my lack of interest in my looks, by the age of seventeen I had two devoted suitors. One was the Colonel, who was thirty years older than I was, the other a young airman called Charles Job. The Colonel worried me considerably. He was so wildly in love that he made me nervous, and I asked Mother for help. Unfortunately she only made matters worse by advising me to treat the Colonel kindly in case he might do something desperate.

In 1929 I had my first trip abroad, the excitement of which was shrouded in distressing circumstances. In my absence, Mother received a telegram from Liege, Belgium, saying that my older brother Willie had had a bad motorbike accident. The Colonel was visiting her at the time, trying to persuade her to influence me on his behalf, and he took charge of the situation and made arrangements for Mother's departure.

She left the same night, but I knew nothing since I was staying with Mrs Job and her son Charles at Battle. The Colonel arrived there next day, to conduct me to my mother in Liege. Mrs Job was naturally suspicious when this middle-aged man wanted to take me abroad, but after a long argument she reluctantly let me go.

It seemed that Willie, who had a fractured skull, was left lying in the road while a crowd looked on with interest. An English boy scout, who happened to be passing, got an ambulance, had Willie taken to a clinic, and sent the telegram. Mother and I stayed in the clinic and the Colonel went to a nearby hotel.

Willie was unconscious for a week. A young doctor looked after him with great care, while my mother watched wide-eyed as he removed the dirty, bloodstained dressings from the wounds, and threw them out of the window into the garden. Willie recovered consciousness, and got better slowly, but for the rest of his life he continued to have blackouts, remaining unconscious for a couple of hours during which his legs kicked violently. I was there once and it was frightening.

The visit to Belgium had finally made the Colonel realise the hopelessness of his situation, and he took himself off on a trip round the world. Six months later, we read the announcement of his engagement in *The Times*.

My friendship with Charles Job came to a tragic end. His plane failed to return from a flight to Paris, and it was presumed he was lost in a storm over the Channel. Day after day, Mrs Job and I waited for news that never came. Nobody ever found out exactly what happened.

Among the friends I had made at art school was Mary Prince whose parents were music hall artistes — her father was said to be the best ventriloquist of the day — and money was plentiful. The enormous Buick in which Mary drove to school every day caused something of a stir. At tea one day, Mrs Prince, in the tone of one saying she'd like to take a stroll, remarked out of the blue:

"I think perhaps we'll go to Spain to-morrow."

"Good idea," Mary agreed. "Can we take Juliet too?"

"Yes of course, if she'd like to come."

I was too astonished to say anything, and could only listen while arrangements were made.

Hardly had we left than there were a couple of hitches: we lost our passports, and all the luggage fell off the back of the car without our noticing. We got to Spain though, and I was enchanted. This was before the Civil War and I enjoyed drawing the Basque people in their berets.

Canoodling Couple, Grinzing Vienna

Charley Hutchinson

The 1930s were turbulent years for me, as for the world, filled with decisive and unexpected turns of events. I made months-long visits to both Germany and Italy, the nations that were soon to become our enemies.

At 19 I became engaged to Charley Hutchinson, a music student at the Royal College of Music. His parents opposed the marriage because he too was only 19. Over the next couple of years, the engagement gradually fizzled out. In the summer of 1932 we all found ourselves roaming around Italy and bumping into each other every now and then: me with Betty Willis, Charley with a school friend. The break with Charley was so gradual that it was hardly noticeable, and there was no ill feeling on either side. In Capri, I was surprised to run into the Blums. They didn't know that they would never again see their beautiful house in Vienna. Hitler marched into Austria, and they went straight from Italy to the United States. Lucy and her husband escaped and joined them there. Herr Blum died soon after their arrival, but I kept in touch with Frau Blum until her death twenty-five years later.

My mother had gone to finishing school in Germany in the 1890s with the mothers of both of David's future wives, Hilda Supper and Betty Willis — and these were the young ladies I visited in Germany and Italy. I was 20 when my brother David and I visited the Supper family, soon after Hilda had been with us as a paying guest, and had nursed David back to health from a violent attack of pneumonia. On her next trip to England she stayed long enough to become his wife. In 1937 I made a trip to Italy with my good friend Betty Willis who was fated to succeed Hilda as David's second wife. Hilda, so beautiful, was wild and flirtatious, cruel and kind. She wanted to marry an Englishman to get away from her provincial hometown. Betty was vivacious, and quite pretty when she was young. David probably married her on the rebound from the unfaithful Hilda.

I went to Vienna one Easter holiday just before the War to visit Lucy Blum who had stayed with us while her parents were in America. They had been preparing for the day when trouble for the Jews would inevitably come to Austria and they would need an escape route. The Blum house in Vienna was a four-storied mansion, in a big garden surrounded by railings with a locked gate. A fierce Alsatian dog was let loose at night, and when Herr Blum went out, he kept the blinds drawn in the back of his chauffeur-driven car. Members of the family collected at the house for secret meetings, when they would shut themselves up behind a steel door to discuss their plans. I spent six weeks with them, and had a happy time in spite of the tension. Lucy's engagement was celebrated, and I made the acquaintance of Professor Cisek, a well-known Austrian art master. He let me attend his classes and I learned a great deal which I was able to use later when I started teaching.

Juliet in the Thirties

Around this time I led quite a hectic social life, and such things as trips to London, dances, theatres and cinemas took up a lot of my time. I had many friends — both women and men — and life was something of a jigsaw puzzle into which I fitted as many pieces as possible in a day. I sometimes stayed up all night. My diary records the menu of one party that took place in a caravan: "Baked beans, sherry, raspberries, beer, whisky" — in that order. The evening ended in a violent quarrel, but it must have been at least partially patched up in the small hours, for there were ten of us in one car going home, including my escort, Peter Cranmer, captain of the English rugger team.

Chapter four

Ancestors & Early Life

My Mother's Family

May in 1898

My mother, May, was from an old family of yeoman stock. Somewhere dim in the family tree was a relationship to Shakespeare through his wife Anne Hathaway, as well as to the noted 19th Century children's illustrator Kate Greenaway. Mother's mother, Lizzie Relph, married William Brice whose family bred horses in Essex. He left for the big city and founded a successful company called Brice Palmer & Co. They made "mantles" – cloaks which were very fashionable at the turn of the 19th century. Each morning he took his carriage from his Chiswick mansion to his warehouse opposite St Paul's. He rose to be a Sheriff in the City of London, With Lord Dewar he owned a string of racehorses, one of which won the Derby the year the king's horse killed a suffragette. May's sister, Kathleen Clare Watson, was a painter and book illustrator. They attended a boarding school in Brighton so strict that the girls were fined for even looking out of the window, in case "the sight of a male should outrage their modesty." On leaving this austere atmosphere, May was ready to fall in love with the first man she met, who happened to be a handsome but penniless curate. She was so besotted with him that she collected and treasured his cigarette butts. Almost suicidal when he was transferred to another parish, her broken heart was healed before long by my father's lavish presents and invitations. She married him in 1898 when she was a very immature nineteen. My father was 35, a professional gambler, obsessed with horses and cards. Her parents considered him a wastrel and did everything to dissuade her. Even in the carriage going to the wedding, her father said to her "It is still not too late to pull out." But she was strongly independent, already somewhat eccentric, and her willfulness won out.

My Father's Family

My paternal grandfather, Laurence Somers, died before I was born. He had married a beautiful Jewish girl, Phoebe Lyons, who would scream at her Irish maid and then, remorseful, give her a sixpence to light a candle in church. I was frightened of her eruptions but fascinated by her blue eyes and frizzy blonde hair.

My father Charles had two brothers: Uncle Henry, a veterinary surgeon, following in his father's footsteps, looked after cab horses in London; and Uncle George, who gambled at the racetrack, and influenced my father to do the same. I was fond of Uncle George; he gave me my first beautiful sable paintbrushes, which I still have.

His two sisters were Annie, who painted big masses of flowers in thick impasto oils, and Kate. One of Annie's children, Esther, was the second woman ever to earn a Master Degree in Surgery at St Mary's Hospital. Mother was fond of Esther, who did all the operations for the family, including when mother was seriously ill and Esther saved her life by chopping out eight inches of her intestines.

Charles Somers loved small children and was a doting father to his own — as long as they were under seven. When they got older he lost interest, and used to carry bags of sweets for other people's children. I was his favourite daughter and he even allowed me to see his record collection. He was really quite nice to me but not to the other children, and my sister Phoebe hated him.

When he was seven my oldest brother Willie built a tall castle of bricks and was rather proud of it. My father came in and kicked it down. Wasn't that dreadful? Since he didn't understand children at all, I don't know why he had so many.

Growing Up

This ill-assorted couple set up house in Hove, Sussex, and had their first four children in just over three years. This was heavy going for Mother, hardly compensated by her having two nannies and a cook.

First came Eileen, who succumbed to meningitis when she was five. Mother grieved terribly about her death.

Willie won the engineering prize at St Paul's and then did his City & Guilds to get his Engineering Degree. In the First World War, at the age of 17 he joined the Navy as a hydrophone listener for enemy submarines and quite enjoyed his time on a destroyer. Keen on Beethoven, he would sit with the curtains closed listening to the gramophone — very very loud! On one school holiday he took me to hear a lady friend playing Beethoven piano concertos and God I was bored: I was too young for Beethoven! The family saw him as solid, sensible and conventional until we heard that he and his wife had joined a nudist colony, carrying out the principle in their own home as well. Even mother was a little shocked by the news that, when visitors came, Willie's wife answered the front door in her birthday suit!

Then my favourite, David, who always remembered my birthday. He had a strong sense of responsibility, and when finally Mother persuaded Father to leave home, he took over helping the family financially, to the extent that his meagre salary as a young Chartered Surveyor would allow. One high point came in 1926 during England's General Strike when he drove a bus to help keep the public services going, and thoroughly enjoyed it. He was a good dancer and took me to my first hops.

Next was Phoebe, strong personality and gifted artist, who taught art in England and then moved to Kenya when it was still a colony, saying she "preferred teaching little black faces to little white ones." All her African sketch books were recently bought by the Pitt-Rivers Museum in Oxford.

I was born on July 15th 1911, nine years after David and five years before Brice, who was very musical. He was christened Stanley, because Mother had a lot of towels with "S" on them. After the Second World War he became known as Brice — mother's maiden name.

Eight years later, when my eldest brother was 25, came my sister Leonore, unexpected and a little unwanted. She had great difficulty being happy. Her older sister Phoebe bullied her, not letting her go to art school; so little "Leo" finally escaped by emigrating to Canada. She ended up as a practising artist, married to an inventor called Fuhrer, and living in San Diego where she died in a car crash in 1985.

Sadly, by 1920 family life in Hove had become more and more strained. I remember it wasn't unusual for Father to throw plates about, and once, he threw a knife at Phoebe, cutting her on the hand. I also remember one awful occasion when Brice put salt on father's grapefruit on April Fool's Day. The resulting storm was terrifying to witness. Grapefruit was a regular feature at breakfast. Father was the only one to enjoy the luxury, and all the others looked on while he consumed it with lingering pleasure. Long afterwards, Phoebe and David admitted to licking the sugary juice from father's grapefruit, without either of them knowing that the other did this too! Father also brought home a juicy chop every evening, which he cooked for himself and ate before our envious eyes.

If Father's alarming rages upset the days, the nights were disturbed by the piercing screams of delicate Brice having nightmares. Finally, cousin Esther operated on his stomach, removing a knot of tubercular glands which she said were like a bunch of bananas.

When Mother's father died, she inherited quite a little bit of money, though I don't know exactly how much. Father proceeded to take it all, saying everything was going so badly for him that he had to borrow it. In spite of the windfall, shortly after the outbreak of World War I, Father, who, had led a chancy but prosperous life, suddenly found his luck had run out. We moved to a horrid house in Ealing so that Willy and David could be day boys at St Paul's School, where David had won a scholarship. My chief recollection of that house is of a vast, damp basement, with big white slugs in the sink and a squirming pattern of black beetles on the floor.

Mother did her best to preserve some sort of family unity, and rose above her poverty in a dignified way even though she lived perpetually on the fringe of a nervous breakdown. With three daughters growing up to be artists and our shady father turning up at odd moments from his nefarious activities, the Bohemian stage was set – rather like the family in *The Constant Nymph*. In 1925 when I was around 14 we moved back to a cheaper house in Hove. One day I remember Mother saying that Father had taken her to London and given her a nice lunch out — which was most unusual. After lunch they went to a solicitor's office and she had to sign over to Father all the household furniture.

Juliet Somers with a portrait of her mother

Mother

Then, Father went bankrupt. Far from breaking Mother, it relieved her, and she finally persuaded him to go and live in one of his gambling clubs, the Compton Club in Hove. They gave him a room in return for organising the bridge and other gaming tables.

With characteristic courage, Mother merely laughed when most of the furniture was taken away by his creditors. Before the movers came she had sneaked out of sight his favourite feather mattress and this she sent to the club after him, to ensure that he did not come back. Thereafter, he was always referred to within the family as "Compton", the name of his club, so that outsiders should not know whom we were discussing. I used to have breakfast with him there once a week, which I enjoyed because I was mildly fond of him.

For £50 a year, we rented the house in Rutland Gardens, which became a centre where all comers were welcome. Willie, David and Phoebe, now young adults, often spent weekends there, usually bringing friends with them. Brice came home for the holidays from Malvern School, where David was paying for his education. At weekends, the first to arrive had beds, the rest slept where they could, even in a tent in the garden. Sometimes there was enough to eat, and sometimes there wasn't.

Mother disliked anything in the way of housework or cooking, and meals were erratic to say the least. Our domestic staff had been reduced to one unemployed ex-army batman called Cobb, who came every day for a negligible wage. He was scrupulously honest, according to his lights, and when certain sums of money disappeared — as they frequently did — there was always a polite little note left on the table: "Dear Madam, I regret that I have had to borrow 10/- in order to pay my rent, which I will let you have back next week." Which he did.

After Cobb came Ada, elderly, fat and puce of face. She wore a man's cap and frightened everybody except Phoebe, who was never frightened. Ada despised us, and continually stressed the fact that she was used to being in "*good* service", with its obvious implication. The worst servant we ever had was Mrs Bishop in Ealing, who always wore a hat. I remember when she finished working one day she adjusted her hat as she was leaving, sending raisins and sugar cubes cascading down her face.

Mother was an eccentric. She was often extremely rude to people she didn't like, but when she chose she could be charming, witty and excellent company. She gave the appearance of being easy-going, but we were brought up to have high ideals in important matters. We all idolised her, and were guided in everything by what she said. Her natural instinct was to be lazy and let other people wait on her, so it is all the more to her credit that the household was such a happy one, and that she managed to run it on almost nothing.

How did she do this? By taking in paying guests, mostly the children of German friends she had made in 1898 at her Wiesbaden finishing school. We had a house with five bedrooms in which we put as many as three or four at a time and occasionally even had some sleeping on mattresses on the floor.

Keen on antique furniture, Mother befriended a lovely old dealer in Ship Street, Brighton, named Mr Fox. Once when she had managed to save a little money Mr Fox produced a beautiful Sheraton shell-fronted sideboard which he let her have for £30. Some years later when she needed the money, he took it back... at the same price.

Hilda (David's fiancée), sister Phoebe, brother Brice and Juliet. Leo off camera

Mother indulged in a craze for planchette and table turning, and even the skeptical joined in. She had a way of dramatising all that she did, which made the most trivial things seem exciting and important. Sometimes other elements helped to provide atmosphere for her spooky sessions, such as the collapse of the ceiling or the fusing of all the lights. No repairs were ever carried out until after a calamity had occurred.

Mother was a keen atheist, and refused to have us baptised when we were babies. Later she admitted that perhaps there was something in it, but she stoutly maintained that the proper time for baptism was when children were old enough to think for themselves. Really, religion played very little part in my childhood. In order to be like my school friends, I was baptised at the age of 17 on 30th April 1928 at St Paul's Church, Brighton, at 6.15 pm by Mr Mann, a family friend. Six months later, there is a note in my diary that Mr Mann said I *must* learn my catechism and go to church on Sundays — which I regarded as a bit of a nuisance.

Mother tried to convert everybody to atheism. Years later when I had a family of my own, and Mother was living with us, one Sunday just before church she called my son Denis into her room. After she talked to him he would no longer go to church with my husband Rick, saying "Grandma has told me the truth. She has told me religion is a lot of rubbish, and has caused many wars and all sorts of things." This of course is true, but it was rather naughty of her because it hurt Rick's feelings very much and Denis refused ever to go to church. Nevertheless, Rick was very patient and good about it.

Typical of life with Mother was what was organized for my 21st birthday party. Thirty of us set out in convoy for Chanctonbury Ring. Abandoning the cars at the foot of the Downs, we climbed up the slope to have a picnic supper by the dewpond, one of those golden occasions that stick in one's memory. The bare outlines of the Downs were made soft and mysterious by the moonlight, and we all felt as if drawn into a magic circle.

Chapter five

The Man of my Life
and the Eclipse of my Art

In the summer of 1937 I went to stay with Betty Willis, who lived in Grafton Manor, an extraordinary Elizabethan mansion near Birmingham where King Charles I had stayed. A friend of Betty's invited us to tea at Bromsgrove School close by. Little did I think that this was to be such an important day in my life: for that was when I met Captain Pannett, ex-soldier, and bursar of the school — salary £200 per year. In six weeks we were engaged.

I hadn't fallen violently in love, but he was such a wonderful reliable human being, so mature (13 years older than me) and so different from my own father, that I said "yes" when he popped the question, much to his mother's annoyance. A typically military man with clipped moustache and the glamour of being half French.

His full name was Maurice Richard Dalton Pannett. I didn't like Maurice, nor Dalton (just a family name). Rather than Richard, Dick or Dickie I settled for Rick, and that was what he was affectionately called.

Rick's great grandfather was French and came to London in the Huguenot exodus. He started a little jewellery factory in Soho Square — T.D. Pannett and Son — which went on for 100 years.

His mother, Amelie Goyard, was Parisienne. Her family made silver plate for all the best hotels in Paris, as well as a line of chic luggage with their initials emblazoned on it. Louis Vuitton uses the same colours today. When she was young, she came to stay with Rick's family to learn English in exchange for teaching them French. She was about 18 and Rick's father soon proposed to her.

Rick Pannett by Juliet Pannett, 1960

Rick had started his army career at Sandhurst in 1916, after which he went to France with the Devonshire Regiment. He survived the terrible Battle of the Somme, in which many of his friends were lost. He was shot right through the face, the bullet passing in one cheek and out the other. By a miracle it only passed through flesh, not even harming bone or teeth. He was always so grateful that he hadn't lost his eyesight, that for the rest of his life he contributed to St Dunstan's charity and even left them money in his tiny will. After the Great War he was posted for several years to India, which he thoroughly enjoyed.

We planned our wedding for the following October, 1938, but these were anxious days: Chamberlain's uneasy peace, following the Munich crisis, threatened the outbreak of war. Rick, as a reserve officer, would have to rejoin his regiment at twenty-four hours notice. Luckily, as we had planned, exactly a year after becoming engaged, we were married on October 4th, 1938.

Ours was a quiet wedding at Newtimber Church, on the Sussex Downs, followed by a small reception. I wore a blue dress and hat (costing 30 shillings each!) and carried a bouquet of roses. My mother, who could be relied upon to be unorthodox, was at her gayest and most witty; it was the bridegroom's mother who spent the afternoon in copious tears. This formidable

French lady terrified me, and had ruined Rick's army career by forcing him to leave active service when he was posted to India for the second time ("Or you won't find me here when you get back!").

After the wedding, our send-off was enthusiastic, if not exactly stylish. We went to Brighton station in a decrepit car to which my brothers had attached a fair quota of tin cans and old boots. A honeymoon was out of the question, so we spent one night in London, with a celebration dinner at Quaglino's.

Poverty in Suburbia - Early Married Life

For nearly a year we lived in a sterile little flat at Purley, with barely enough money to survive. I desperately tried to conform to Rick's conservative tastes in everything and now realize that this denial of my own personality was the cause of various sicknesses and despondency during those years. The lucky thing is that somehow my inner spark was never extinguished by these grinding years in suburbia.

The first year of my married life was uneventful, except for the delayed honeymoon in March, spent at Villefranche. After that I stayed at home to await the arrival of my first baby. It soon became clear that war was inevitable. Sandbags sprang up everywhere. Gas masks were issued. Finally London was evacuated and, with the baby due any day, I was advised by my doctor to leave at once.

Mother was with me, and a friend drove us down to Hove. The doctor had given me a strong sedative and mother, not to be outdone, had demanded the same for herself, with the result that we were both a bit dazed when we arrived at midnight. Brice was fast asleep in the sitting room, so we didn't disturb him but went straight through to the other room. The bed was occupied, and all we could see was a tuft of dark hair sticking out.

"Good God, Phoebe's home!" exclaimed Mother, and shook the sleeping figure. "Get up, Juliet must go to bed immediately."

The bedclothes were heaved back with a snort, and we found ourselves looking into the startled face of one of Brice's friends. Mother pushed him out of the bed so that she and I could get in.

Next morning, while we were all hovering round the radio, the first air-raid warning sounded. All hospitals and maternity homes were full after the evacuation of London, and it was only thanks to a doctor friend that I was squeezed into a dingy nursing home where my son Denis was born on September 7th.

Rick was unable to come to me. At the outbreak of War there were seven hundred men at his training centre, who had to be dispatched to different units all over the country. As soon as that job had been completed, Rick had to report to the depot of the Devonshire Regiment at Exeter, the regiment with which he had served during his days in the Regular Army.

I stayed in the nursing home for a fortnight. We were unprepared for the blackout, and had no proper curtains, so I wasn't allowed light to read at night. I reached a low ebb at this time, lying in the semi-darkness, feeling ill and miserable. I was worried about Rick, who might be sent overseas at any moment, and about the baby, who was constantly sick and cried most of the time. The war was difficult for everyone. I accepted gratefully when some Exeter friends invited us to go and live in their house.

A year later we received the news of my oldest brother Willie's death. He had joined the Bristol Aeroplane Company and worked up to the end on a device he had invented that was being mounted in every Blenheim bomber. He only went into hospital for a check-up on account of a slight but persistent pain. Cancer was diagnosed, but it was too late for anything to be done and he was sent home, where his wife nursed him with great devotion and courage all through the Bristol Blitz. He died six weeks later at the age of 40, leaving four little children under five.

My next move was to Cumberland, where I developed my love of mushrooms and fungi. These were useful in supplementing our meagre rations. David had divorced Hilda and remarried Betty Willis. They were moderately happy. Betty and David sent Hilda's daughter Vanessa off to boarding school when she was barely four, and later even had her spend her holidays with me and my family up in Cumberland.

Soon afterwards Mother had a severe heart attack and was in hospital for six weeks. Baby Denis, too, was causing a great deal of worry, constantly sick and running a high temperature.

When the war ended, it was some time before Rick, now a Major, could join us. Being bilingual, thanks to his French mother, he was busy instructing units of the Belgian Army in Northern Ireland and could not be spared. Although I was happy

to have the comfort of his presence, when Rick was finally released from the Army, this brought with it a major financial worry. His gratuity dwindled away with frightening rapidity and he could not find a job. I took up teaching art again, but earned very little, and for a while the outlook was black.

However, in the autumn Denis was well enough to leave hospital, and Rick got a job as bursar and part-time French master at Rose Hill, a small prep school in Alderley, Gloucestershire, where Denis, then six, became a pupil.

The journey there was ghastly. I had caught Denis' mumps and was transported all the way to Gloucestershire lying on a sack in the back of the removal van. The cold was intense; we broke down once and lost our way twice. After midnight when we finally reached Alderley, I was very ill indeed. The headmaster's wife isolated me immediately at the top of the building and did all the nursing herself.

Rose Hill School

While Rick was teaching I started to get commissions to do portraits of the boys, which I hadn't done since the beginning of the war. This meant I was happy and, at £2 per portrait, I was finally earning a little bit of money. One of the boys I was asked to draw was named Stewart Clarke, who was older than Denis. It was strange, because years and years later, when I was perhaps 70, I had an appointment with a surgeon at King Edward VII Hospital, Midhurst. I was taken to see the chief consultant of the hospital, who said "Mrs Pannett, you and I have met before — do you remember me?" Well, I had to admit I didn't. "My name," he said, "is Stewart Clarke, and you did my portrait when I was fourteen!" I ring him when I want medical advice. I still see him although he has retired from the hospital. Over the years, he operated on me several times and has become a really good friend.

Rose Hill was a school of great character and my little family was at once absorbed into its happy atmosphere. The school community was like a big family, with. T.G. "Tiggy" Hughes, the wonderfully dedicated headmaster, as *pater familias*.

"In a school of this kind," he said "it is essential for me to have a nucleus of boys of my own choosing, whether their parents can afford to pay the fees or not."

He was certainly a personality, even eccentric in some ways, but he was a kind and generous friend. The school had a free and easy atmosphere, ideal for me. Rick's salary was not large, but we were housed and fed and Denis was educated.

One local inhabitant of the kind I love to draw was old Jack Rodway, who had been born and lived all his life in the same cottage. When he sat for me, he was wearing a navy blue suit, red tie and brown trilby hat, saying that he wanted to be "took in his best." I hadn't the heart to tell him how much I would have preferred the hand-made smock of his working days. He had never travelled farther afield than the next village but said he liked to have things from "furrin parts", and the parlour was crammed with Gosse china ornaments. His treasures included a stuffed fox, and a red velvet heart as big as a soup plate with "I love you" written on it in beads. His wife said it took three hours to dust the room.

During these post-war years I suffered three miscarriages and Denis seemed to go from one bout of bad health to another. But finally Elizabeth was born on May 31st, 1947, a healthy baby with fair curly hair like mine, and dark blue eyes. She gave no trouble.

The little boys were always desperately hungry as food was so scarce after the war. Sniffy, the dear old butler at the school, would push the enormous double trolley with the remains of the staff supper very slowly down the corridor so that the line of boys could grab the remains on the plates to get a little extra food.

Visitors to Rose Hill were allowed to wander at will into the kitchen, the dormitories, the bathrooms, at any hour. No special preparations were made for outside eyes, so anybody could see things just as they were. Everyone in the school community had meals with the boys, and shared the same fare. Tiggie Hughes' kindly influence set the tone, in which Rick and I were entirely happy. One of the masters used to say that Rose Hill had everything other schools had, plus something no other school had.

But just when things seemed settled in a more or less permanent way, we received a rude shock. The blow fell at half-term in the spring of 1949, when Mr Hughes told us that the school was to be enlarged, family accommodation must be cut down, and Rick had to be replaced by an unmarried bursar who would require only one room. This news came as a complete surprise. It seemed totally unlike the headmaster to treat us in this way, but as it turned out the poor man was going through hell, since his wife and his business partner had run off – together! So Tiggie's little world was in shambles. Some time afterwards he told us he had allowed himself to be talked into getting rid of us, and had bitterly regretted it ever since. At the end of term we went to live with the family of the school matron, and in due course Denis returned alone to Rose Hill as a boarder, while Rick set about the disheartening business of seeking a new job. Food was so scarce, we seemed to live on spam. And we had to turn out the lights at 9 pm.

At first we were optimistic, but as time went on Rick found that he got the same answer to all his applications. He was too old at fifty, and he had no degree. With Lizzie to look after, I had no time to earn anything, and things looked bad. There were too many ex-service men out of a job. Rick had been trying for three months before one of the scholastic agencies notified him of a vacancy at Coombe Hill House, Croydon. This time he was engaged on the spot, to teach French and Geography and help with games. We began house hunting, and in July we moved to Sydenham Road, Croydon.

41 Sydenham Road

A time of excessive domesticity started for me. We were very poor. Rick's tiny salary was the same as at Rose Hill, £300 per year, but we no longer had free board and lodging. Like my mother, I had to cram the little house full of paying guests in order to make out. I had no time at all for art or making new friends, but devoted myself entirely to shopping, looking after Lizzie and cooking meals for everybody.

There was a brief respite in August 1950. Claire-Lise, the sister of my Swiss friend, had come to England as a break from her unhappy married life. It was then that she met my brother Brice; they fell in love and, some time later were married. At the end of that visit Claire-Lise took Lizzie back to Geneva with her; so I went out there for a fortnight and then brought Lizzie home. After this short holiday, the drudgery began again.

It wasn't long before I felt the strain of overwork and of leading a life that was thoroughly uncongenial to me. I carried on for another nine months. But then, I felt too tired and ill to cope any more, and for six weeks I lost my voice entirely. The doctor said there was nothing really wrong with me. I was suffering from what he called a "functional illness", due to lack of any opportunity for expressing myself. He urged me to take up art again as the only way to recovery.

People rallied round to help. One of the paying guests took Lizzie to her home in Zurich for three months to give me a rest, and at the doctor's instigation, our unoccupied garage was converted to a studio. Phoebe organised me to go to classes in silk-screen printing.

As a means of self-expression, silk-screen was a dead loss. It took me nearly a year to make one set of curtains, and I got bored with them. They were a hideous maroon with wine glasses and squiggles. Still, I had taken the first step towards getting out of my rut.

Transition

Christmas Card Design

Bosham Mill

Denis progressed to Uppingham School. Rick and I could only go one at a time to visit him because of the expense of the fare and a night at a hotel.

Most important, Lizzie started at Croydon High School next door, which gave me time to paint. I joined the Croydon Art Society, and began showing my pictures at exhibitions in Croydon, Brighton and London. I was often worried in the early years that I was neglecting my children, but my youngest, Lizzie, always said "I never felt left alone, in fact I think of Ma as a wonderful role model. She used to bring back little canapés for me after parties, which made me feel included."

I was busy taking in boarders and caring for my parents. My father was ill in a hospital in Brighton for more than a year and died at the age of 95. Mother came to live with me again and I nursed her at home.

Money was still very short, but I carried on, putting my efforts into my painting, on the strength of which we had a telephone installed. Rick was against this extravagance, but I was able to pay for it out of my own earnings.

Mother was often too ill to see people, but when she was well enough, quite a crowd would collect and sit on her bed or on the floor and all her former wit and charm would keep us entertained for hours at a time. In spite of her many and serious illnesses, she got up and moved about the house and garden when not bed-ridden. At one time she lived on opium pills. She was never one to go in for petty ailments or petty cures.

Except for David, my brothers and sisters had scattered, but my house provided a base whenever they came to England. After leaving school, Denis went into the timber trade and worked at Lewes, coming home for weekends.

In 1958 I surprised Rick by organizing a holiday, staying with a former paying guest in the south of France. I told Rick nothing in advance, because, as a great home and garden lover, he was always reluctant to move. Presented with a *fait accompli*, he found the surprise a pleasant one.

From our friend's house in Toulouse, we visited Van Gogh's house at Arles and the pathetic, white-washed room at Saint-Remy, where the great painter spent the tortured hours of his madness. Also, there was the Toulouse-Lautrec collection at Albi. We went to a bullfight in Nimes, where we saw Dominguin perform. I tried to concentrate on the colour and the graceful movements, and couldn't help admiring the courage of the matadors, in spite of feeling sorry for the bulls, and more especially the horses. I was glad to have seen a bullfight, but didn't think I'd want to go again.

It was back in Croydon that I again took the plunge into journalism. I went to the local paper, *The Croydon Advertiser*, with six portraits I had done of local characters. They commissioned a series on well known Croydonians, including a road sweeper and a beautiful old woman in an alms house. After this I worked for the *Croydon Times* and the *Kentish Times*, for both of whom I painted series of interesting people. The papers sent a reporter around to interview them. Frequently my sitters would suggest other subjects and so my series grew and grew.

Chapter six

After the Blitz
the ILN

St. George's Hospital after the doodle bug hit

I loved painting London after World War II, in the aftermath of the Blitz, when so many bombs had been dropped. Though it was terrible for England it was, to the artist's eye, all broken up and interesting, with distant views of St Paul's. So I sent pictures to many of the exhibitions in London, and finally had three accepted in the late 1950's for the Britain in Watercolour Show. To my delight, a few days later I had a telephone call from Luke Hermann the Art Editor of one of my favorite magazines, "I have been to your exhibition and like your work very much. If you are interested in working for the *Illustrated London News* our Editor, Sir Bruce Ingram will see you." Sir Bruce was the oldest and most respected editor in London. He was 87, and he had been the youngest at 19. Of course, I said, "Yes, please! Wonderful!"

I had some pictures of musicians at work – well known conductors and orchestras — so I got my portfolio ready and took them up. I had a set of four: Sir Malcolm Sargent conducting the BBC Symphony Orchestra; Sir Adrian Boult with the London Philharmonic; Sir Thomas Beecham; and Sir John Barbirolli with the Hallé Orchestra – which they later published as "The Knights of the Baton."

Sir Bruce was a bit frightening. He was a ferocious figure and had an enormous desk in front of him, rather like a dining table, completely empty. I had a lot of drawings with me to show and he spread them out on this table. We looked at them and he said, "I think we will give you a chance. You can come and do the installing of the first baroness in the House of Lords. We will get you put up in the gallery and see how you do with it." I came up to London the week after and the drawing went easily with no difficulty at all. Luckily I was not overawed by the House of Lords. I wasn't allowed to work in the Chamber while they were doing the actual investiture, but outside the door I was given a folding desk in the corridor. Sir Bruce was

Hugh Ingram, nephew of Sir Bruce Ingram, Editor of the Illustrated London News

frightfully pleased, and I dared to say, "Can I be one of your special artists?" – meaning that my name would appear under my art works. He said, "Well I think so. Yes, alright." He was a fierce old man but he had a twinkle.

After a while I started doing charcoal drawings of famous people for the *ILN*.

I loved drawing academics – they always have interesting faces. I wrote straightaway to Lord Annan, Master of Kings College Cambridge, and he was the first one I think that was reproduced in the *Illustrated London News*. Later I did Sir Eric Ashby, Master of Clare College Cambridge, then Professor A J Ayer, Professor of Logic, Oxford. I knew he had an interesting face and thought he would be fun to do. I wrote to Sir Maurice Bowra, Master of Wadham College, Oxford. Though less interesting to draw, he was a most amusing man. I just shrieked with laughter for about an hour while drawing him. I did a very interesting Professor of Science, Sir John Cockcroft, Master of Churchill College, Cambridge. I did Lord Fulton, Master of the new University of Sussex.

Of course, I had to arrange all the sittings myself: ring up the people, write to them and see if they were willing; and I only had two refusals ever. Now I was determined to make up for all those years I hadn't painted, so I thought nothing of walking a mile to the Croydon station when I had appointments for sittings in London, sometimes even carrying three big pictures. Money was so tight that I often got a "Workman's Ticket", East Croydon to London Victoria Return for only 2 pence, though I had to leave before 8 am.

If I went away, for instance to Oxford, and the *ILN* had to pay the expenses, then they kept the drawing and only paid me a fee of £20 (they were bad payers). But if I paid my own expenses they paid me that fee for publishing it and I could keep the portrait and sell it. Frequently the subject did buy it, which is always nice. I made a big mistake one time by letting the *ILN* pay my expenses for a trip to Oxford when I drew C.S. Lewis and some other notable Oxonian dons, so I lost a lot of sales. I could have sold C.S. Lewis again and again.

I was a special artist to the *Illustrated London News* for seven years and was often sent abroad to do drawings. One year I went to Israel and another time to East Africa. But the most artistically rewarding trip was with Qantas, when I did over 300 paintings and sketches in three weeks.

C S LEWIS *Theologian and author*

Fascinating and interesting, quick mind; spoke in very formal sentences, assertive and argumentative. Very serious — no small talk.

Awesome experience drawing him. Lovely bells of Magdalen punctuating the afternoon. Large armchairs — strong tea — kind but a bit frightening. Didn't like foreign cooking - liked simple British foods. Didn't look happy.

C.S. Lewis, Oxford Don

Chapter seven

East Africa

In the late 1950s I flew to Tabora, Tanganyika, where my older sister Phoebe was teaching African girls. With numerous stops, it took over ten hours. After the desert area of Khartoum, the landscape gradually became greener until we finally came down at Entebbe, on Lake Victoria: lovely, lush country with tiny islands dotting the vast lake. It was the Garden of Eden — new trees and plants, curious flowers and birds, and strange insects.

Phoebe's house girl, Mwajuma, was a twenty-seven year old grandmother, whose married daughter of twelve already had her first child. Mwajuma danced to any record Phoebe put on the gramophone, and before going to bed we watched her execute an African shuffle-shuffle to Handel's *Messiah*. I was awoken by torrential rain which I feared would destroy the beautiful blossoms on the trees. But the jacaranda and flamboyant trees were even more colourful after the rain, and a carpet of fine, fairy grass of a dazzling green had sprung up overnight.

While exploring we were halted by a thick line of safari ants going to a neighbour's anthill to get eggs for their larder. The soldier ants on either side, each half an inch long, made a bridge with their bodies every time the workers had to cross a rivulet. Ants can destroy walls, undermine foundations and even kill human babies by biting right through them if they are in the ants' path.

To these Africans, death is just the end of a journey, and they don't care what happens to the bodies, sometimes even putting them out for the hyenas. I saw a corpse being taken from the hospital on the back of a bicycle. The Police Chief told me that when out shooting in the bush, he once thought he saw a baboon; it turned out to be an old woman, quite naked, who had been put out to die as she was of no further use to her tribe. He wrapped her up in a blanket and retuned her to her village, where she had a cool reception.

The school where Phoebe taught was mainly for daughters of tribal chiefs: some lived over three hundred miles away and their trek home took them a week. At night three watchmen patrolled the school grounds with bows and arrows because lions roamed around. I did a drawing of Jumo, the oldest guard, who had been a sergeant in the King's African Rifles. "Now everyone in England will see my picture," he said proudly to anybody who would listen to his story.

I attended a *baraza*, a meeting of all the chiefs in honour of a visit from the Governor. Afterwards there was a tribal dance at Itetamia, where Phoebe and I were the only non-Africans. We wandered in and out of the various dances, and were invited to join, but I was too busy sketching the colourful costumes.

Particularly alluring was Chief Kitembe in purple robes with a shell on his head. He agreed to sit for a portrait but when we arrived at his village, he was away settling a tribal dispute. Three of his wives made us welcome with signs and gestures and showed us over their two-storied mud hut. On departure, I stopped to admire the carved doorway, and the wives, with much

giggling, pointed to the figure of a child. They obviously wished me to touch it, and their merriment reached an hysterical pitch when I complied. By touching the carved baby, I had apparently become the chief's new wife!

On a patrol through tsetse fly country with a Game Ranger, we were bitten by these insects. After they painlessly suck your blood, their withdrawal is extremely painful, and they can be infected with sleeping-sickness. While the camp was being set up, the ranger showed us baboons, antelope, giraffes, wart hogs and zebras, as well as cerulean-headed lizards. Some anthills were twenty feet high with trees growing on them, and some were squat, resembling Henry Moore statues. We spurned the ranger's offer of sleeping across the door, but later his wife said she had once had a lion come into her tent. The only thing that kept us awake was the noise of hippos grunting in the nearby river.

After my lecture at the Women's Service League, Phoebe and I went off to spend Christmas with friends. It took us three days by train, bus, and car. Crossing the Rift Valley the earth is red and amethyst, and the baobab trees wave their root-like branches. We only met three other cars.

From more than a hundred miles away we caught our first glimpse of the snows of Kilimanjaro. The top of this vast mountain – round and white like a tennis ball – loomed up enticingly through the clouds. At Arusha, our hosts drove us the last fifty miles to their coffee, maize and banana plantation at Kibuni. Christmas on the slopes of Kilimanjaro, was my first away from our family. I did a portrait of my host, Jock Taylor, but while I drew he told me the story of a trek he had made across Australia prospecting for gold, and it was so exciting my hand trembled. Aborigines attacked them, and only seven of the nineteen on the expedition lived to tell the tale.

Except in cases of serious illness, the Taylors distributed medicines to the Africans on their estate. I would sit by the medicine cupboard at the appointed hour sketching the people in the queue. Cice Taylor ran the health service with great efficiency, but Jock was more haphazard in his remedies. One girl said she was constipated, and he dosed her with a tumbler of salts, to which he added a large spoonful of red diarrhoea medicine. "They like a bit of colour in it," he explained to me. "They think it does them more good that way." I wasn't surprised to see the girl back in the queue again the following day.

Phoebe and I visited a village high up on Kilimanjaro, where there was a well-known maker of wood bowls for *Pombe*, the native beer, brewed from millet seed with a great deal of spittle. Under his shelter of banana leaves, hee held the bowls with his feet, using a sharp knife and a scoop to fashion their exquisite shape; his output was two a day. We bought sixteen bowls, and left with much shaking of hands.

One of Phoebe's schoolgirls, the daughter of the village headman, invited us to her father's hut. Two tiny rooms contained five chairs, thirteen framed examination certificates and six hymnbooks. Father, mother and uncle stood in a row to receive their guests, and a two-year old sister greeted us by kneeling before us with bowed head. As soon as the formalities were over, the uncle announced that he was an Evangelist, handed us hymnals, and we joined in singing "Rock of Ages" in the Chagga language. After that there was no refusing a drink, and I had to swallow my *pombe* with the rest.

I was keenly interested in the scenery and wild life around me in Kibuni, and my favourite occupation, after painting, was to lie on my back under a tree, watching the bright yellow weaver birds build their nests. Each bird builds several in one tree and there were at least fifteen birds working on sixty or seventy nests right above my head.. Then they bring their ladies to decide which nest they like best, using the tree as a sort of "Ideal Home Exhibition"; when the lady has indicated her preference, the male flies off with her to another site to build the real nest.

It's not always wise to lie on the ground in Africa, and I suffered for my rashness. Once I felt a stab of pain in my thigh, but took no notice at the time. Two days later a large red lump appeared, and Cice Taylor, said casually: "Oh, that's a mango worm. It will live on you for three weeks or so, until it's ready for you to give birth to it." My leg was extremely sore, but as everybody took it calmly, I didn't dare suggest a trip to the doctor in Moshi. I lay awake at nights with the pain, and though I felt the worm "corkscrewing violently" there was nothing to do.

Returning from one of our excursions, we stopped outside the mosque and Phoebe suggested that we go in. There was no one in sight, so we removed our shoes, washed our feet and went in through the magnificently carved doors. The inside was painted blue and gold, the only ornament being a red tin advertisement for Coca-Cola.

I sketched many of the local Chagga tribe: they were not in the least interested in my drawings, and certainly never recognised themselves. The one exception was a Chagga artist who had lived in England, having won a scholarship to the Slade School. When he reached London, he wrote his father that he had to pay sixpence for a banana (his tribe's staple diet) "If this is true, my son," replied the scandalised father, "come home AT ONCE."

On leaving Paradise, we travelled by bus to Nairobi, a nine-hour drive through Masai country. This fierce tribe constituted one of my biggest artistic delights. These warriors are tall and lean, with ancient Egyptian features and independent to the point of arrogance. They stand on one leg for long periods, leaning on their spears. Their hair, which hangs in tufts, is matted with cow dung and smeared with red ochre, and they wear huge earrings, necklaces and bracelets of beads or coiled copper wire. Apart from milk, their main sustenance is blood, which they drink through bamboo straws from a hole they cut in an animal's neck. At the next bus stop Phoebe and I followed three Masai into a shop: they wore only short red cloaks which came down to their armpits, large bead earrings, and copper bracelets! They haughtily refused our request to be drawn. How I would love to have painted them. Simply beautiful — red-ochred all over, with their legs painted in blue and black ribs like knitted stockings. Their lower front teeth had been removed, as with all Masai, so that they could still eat if they got lockjaw.

Phoebe's friends in Nairobi took us to the town rubbish dump to watch marabou storks. "What disgusting birds," I remarked to Phoebe. "Look at their evil eyes and pink, flabby necks. They're like dirty old men." While Phoebe laughed I felt a searing pain in my leg. There was now an angry excrescence like a big boil in my thigh. At that moment the mango worm was born. It was a revolting maggot, half an inch long, but it might have been much worse, so I was lucky. One woman I met had twenty-eight of the nauseating things round her waist, and everybody seemed quite unconcerned.

In Nairobi, I did a series of drawings of coffee processing. An elderly Englishman, senior taster for Kenya, began tasting standing at the far end of a long bench, with a small oil drum about three feet high and one foot wide in front of his feet. He bent over as if bowing to the Queen, dipped a spoon into one of many sample coffees, put it to his outstretched lips, and swooshed it in with a really frightful noise to the back of his palate, slapping it against his tonsils After three seconds of this, the lips were stretched out again and the liquid accurately ejected into the drum. Then he shuffled the drum forward an inch or two with his knees, and started on the next sample. It was very hard not to laugh.

From Nairobi, we went to Nyeri, for a visit to the famous Treetops Hotel, first in Land Rovers, then on foot, leaving our luggage for the porters. The white hunter went first, rifle at the ready. Every few yards the trees had slats of wood nailed to them in the form of a rough ladder, in case we should have to make a hasty escape from dangerous animals. He told us that one party had had to wait in the trees for three hours until a herd of fifty elephants moved away.

This Treetops, built high in the branches of massive trees, was a new one, the original having been burnt down by the Mau Mau in 1954. A year before that, Princess Elizabeth was there with the Duke of Edinburgh when she received the news of her father's death, and had to hurry home as Queen of England. Shortly after my trip, the Queen Mother also visited. It only holds twelve people at a time, and we were warned to take coats and sweaters. Although it is on the Equator, nights are very cold 6000 feet up in the Aberdare Mountains.

From Treetops we looked out on a mass of pink Cape chestnut trees in flower, and a lovely glade which stretched down to a pool and a natural salt lick. Age-old elephant paths led from the forest to the water's edge. It was only early afternoon, but some baboons and three families of wart hogs were already in the glade, and also some water buck. Phoebe and I had tea on the roof, and were entertained by the efforts of a tame mother baboon and her baby to steal our food.

The animals in the glade were quite unconscious of people watching them, since Treetops is too high for them to smell human beings, and all visitors are requested to keep very quiet and to wear bedroom slippers instead of shoes. Salt is put down to attract the animals, and every evening at twilight the ladders are drawn up and an arc lamp was lit to act as an artificial moon focused on the salt lick.

Blind beggars in Tabora.

26

No one slept much that night. As soon as it was dark, I saw the glowing eyes of what seemed like hundreds of animals, creeping slowly through the forest towards the water. Buffalo, giant wart hog and rhinoceros came down to drink throughout the night, and at one time there were eleven rhinos rocking the hotel with their snorting. All the animals left before dawn. *ILN* later published the sketch of Treetops that I did (guarded by a white hunter with gun) from the far side of the pool.

Sir Eldred Hitchcock, the millionaire sisal and tea planter, wanted some drawings of his estate and factory near Tanga. During the hundred-mile drive through the heart of Mau Mau country to his tea farm in Kwamkoro, three thousand feet up in the Usambara Mountains, the car broke down and I was frightened for the first time. There was a Kikuyu village nearby, and soon the car was surrounded by tribesmen thrusting their heads in the window to peer at my face. Some were carrying long, curved knives, and looked anything but friendly. There wasn't another car in sight, and it was rapidly getting dark. An hour passed, and I feared I would have to spend the night in that lonely, hostile place. (It was during the Mau Mau uprising.) After nearly two hours, a Land Rover came by, driven by a European agricultural officer with four Africans in the back. Between them they managed to repair our car and I got to Nairobi three hours late. The following morning a bottle of French scent arrived from the owner of the hire car with a card reading: "For artist lady, hoping not inconvenienced."

I returned to London with forty watercolours and three full sketchbooks. My portrait of Sir Eldred Hitchcock was the first of my works published in the *Times*. It was shortly followed by double page spreads in The *Illustrated London News* of my drawings of Tabora School, and later Treetops.

ERE THE QUEEN MOTHER WILL WATCH WILD GAME: THE UNIQUE AND FASCINATING TREETOPS HOTEL, KENYA, NOW REBUILT AFTER DESTRUCTION BY MAU MAU.

th the Queen Mother is to spend a night in one of the most ..els in the world, during her visit to East Africa in February. Hotel, Kenya, was the idea of Mr. E. Sherbrooke Walker, who .e an enormous tree in the forest, from whose branches visitors he movements of wild game which came by night to a nearby n this "Wendy" house that the Queen, then Princess Elizabeth,

was staying with the Duke of Edinburgh on February 5, 1952, when she became Queen of England on the sudden death of King George VI. The hotel was burned down in 1954 by the Mau Mau, and on the tree now rests an inscribed plaque commemorating the event. A new Treetops Hotel has now been constructed nearby. Mrs. Juliet Pannett, who has just returned from a visit to East Africa, spent two nights at the new Treetops, and made the

drawing which we have reproduced here. She describes how at dawn she was conducted across the glade in front of the hotel by the white hunter, armed with a gun, to make her drawing. While she was working, elephants and rhinoceroses were wading in the pool, the rhinos snorting and grunting suspiciously. Up above, on the balcony, baboons had climbed over the balustrade and were rushing playfully around while other guests were busy

photographing the animals below. She also describes how an artificial moon, seen on the balcony in her drawing, enables visitors to watch the animals right through the night, and how in the darkness hundreds of eyes would be seen shining in the forest, as the beasts approached the pool. Because Treetops is built so high, the animals are undisturbed by the scent of humans and their conversation. At night the ladders are drawn up as a precaution.

Drawn for "The Illustrated London News" by Juliet Pannett, S.G.A.

Chapter eight

Portraits, Yes, Please

*My friends often made fun of me because every time another sitter would
ask for a portrait, I would enthuse, "Yes, please!"*

Father T. Radcliffe

With a few exceptions such as Lady Baden-Powell (see page 43), I find the male sex less troublesome as sitters. Men are much easier to paint because they're not so self-conscious. They never ask me not to put in their double chin or to leave out their wrinkles, which some women do. I remember when I did Dame Myra Hess for the *Radio Times*, she looked at the portrait and said "Oh, don't put that in — my friends wouldn't like it." I don't think I should be asked to flatter but people sometimes do.

I never do preliminary sketches — even for oil portraits. All I try to do is put people at ease. I ask which is their best side — people always know. If you do that, and if you try to get their best expression, that should be enough. I like to get them just as they are about to smile or looking slightly twinkly, which is why I get them talking when I'm doing the eyes and mouth. I also take an eager interest in all the people I paint — to me, nobody is dull.

CHURCHMEN

CARDINAL HUME

Head of the Roman Catholic Church in Great Britain

This is an example of how a sitting unfolds. Usually it is commissioned by somebody else. One of my previous sitters, Father Patrick Barry, headmaster of Ampleforth, a Catholic public school near York, asked me to draw the Cardinal for the college.

The Cardinal's Chaplain offered me an appointment, at 8.45 in the morning. I stayed the night before with friends in London and walked to the Cardinal's residence adjoining Westminster Cathedral. The Chaplain took me up a wide staircase to a room overlooking the Cathedral yard.

The Revd Dr Simon Tugwell, OP

Cardinal Hume

As I was getting my things ready to work I saw this very very tall thin ascetic looking man walking towards me along the passage. I asked if he minded sitting in a certain position behind his table because the light from the window would come on to him very nicely.

I started the charcoal drawing with a little touch of red chalk, and white chalk on the highlights.

He said, "I'm afraid I will have to have my secretary with me because I have several things to discuss with her." She came in, sat down at the table and. he began dictating. I was drawing happily and after half an hour he said "We will have a little pause now and I will tell you about the sittings I have had before." He said he had been painted three times and he didn't like any of them. "Would you like to see them? They are in the next room." I said "Yes please", so he got up and said "I will leave you for a while and I will be back in five minutes." So I went into the next room, which was obviously his bedroom. His bed, I think, was about 8 ft long.

On a large table were laid out six pairs of scarlet socks; I found that rather amusing. Three portraits were stacked in the corner and I must say I didn't like any of them either.

I sat in my place again, and had about one hour and a half with him altogether, but sadly, try as I might, my portrait of him wasn't my best. I didn't dare ask for another sitting; I knew he was too busy.

FRIAR GARETH MOORE (died at 37 of cancer in Nov. 2002)

He was 27 in 1993 when I drew him in charcoal, at Blackfriars in Oxford, where I stayed because I was painting Father Simon Tugwell (see previous page) – whose mother, a life-long friend, helped me with this book. I painted an oil of Simon, not very interesting. When I saw this young man I knew I wanted to sketch him. Looks like a medieval saint. Then I ran into him again and asked if he would sit for me; he said "I have about 25 minutes." So he sat for that amount of time, posing for me. I really concentrated and it came out well. I like to work under pressure. It suits me.

FATHER PATRICK BARRY

Abbott of Ampleforth, succeeding Cardinal Hume

I stayed in The Grange, which is the guesthouse of Ampleforth College, a Roman Catholic public school. We had our meals in the guestroom, where my oil portrait of Father Patrick was eventually to hang. The next day I had a sitting with Father Patrick in his study and it was arranged that he should come to me for the sittings of the oil portrait. He was an excellent sitter, and as he enjoyed listening to music. I didn't have to talk all the time, which enabled me to concentrate on my work. He told me they had recently invited some Borstal boys to stay, and they were horrified at the discomfort and the old basin on pedestals — "Do the parents PAY for this?" Afterwards all the hi-fi equipment was stolen, but they got it back in a few hours.

Friar Gareth Moore

Schoolboys from all over England came to stay for a cricket week, most put up in the guesthouse, but some had to be put in the college and Ampleforth chose the public schoolboys for this as they were used to the discomfort. (They were there for selectors to see them play).

Father Patrick Barry

CUTHBERT BARDSLEY, BISHOP OF COVENTRY (*portrait in Coventry Cathedral Catalogue*)

For this appointment I left home at 6.45 a.m., but it was a foggy day and the train arrived late at London Bridge. I queued for a taxi, but soon abandoned that idea as hopeless and hurried to the underground, which got me to Euston with three minutes to spare. Two friendly young men took me in hand; one grasped my suitcase and the other my sketching bag, and we all ran to find the right platform, where we were just in time to see the train pull out. I rang up the Coventry Cathedral Festival office, which said they would contact the bishop for me. When I rang again in half an hour's time, a sitting had been arranged for four o'clock in the afternoon. I arrived with prolific apologies, but the bishop, who had formerly been Bishop of Croydon, soon put me at my ease.

"As a matter of fact this time really suits me much better," he said. "I feel more relaxed now than I should have done this morning with my day's work before me."

He sat for me for an hour and a half, and as he was himself an artist, we had no lack of conversational interests. After the sitting he showed me some of his palette-knife paintings.

Portrait Techniques: Charcoal

Leonardo once said "First of all copy drawings by a good master."

DRAWING IS THE MOST PERSONAL of all methods of artistic expression – a process of exploration and discovery. The language of drawing is relatively simple and there are no rules. Each artist works differently – different tools, methods, outlook, and always different results, so that one can usually tell who is the artist by the personal style – the individual 'handwriting' – in the drawing.

A portraitist has many special problems to overcome. The portrait must be like the sitter, but if a likeness is the chief aim, a camera is just as good. The portrait artist first looks for character and personality, which are found by keeping the sitter occupied and amused, and by watching him closely – the carriage of the head, the mannerisms, the way he looks, speaks and moves, the bone structure and, most important of all, the expression in the eyes and mouth. We get in contact with our fellows largely through what we can read in their facial expressions, and the expression I aim for in my drawings is when the model is about to smile. The way to capture expression is to observe your model critically and draw what you see. The character and personality will then emerge automatically.

Good draughtsmanship is as important as a likeness, and your penstroke must be as clear and economical as possible. Portraitists suffer from the vanity of their sitters, which sometimes has an unnerving effect. John Singer Sargent once said "I shall scream if another duchess enters my studio!" Only one woman – a well-known composer – has ever said to me "make me as ugly as you like." One can only draw the sitter as he is made, but, without flattery, it is important to bring out the sitter's best points.

Lighting should be kept simple; a narrow and single source of light is best.

Paper. There are many papers suitable for charcoal drawing, my favourite medium for portraits. Fabriano, Ingres, Michalet, Canson – any paper with a good grain – but not cartridge paper or hot press paper which is too smooth, and not coarse watercolour paper which is too rough and unyielding; it is impossible to achieve a decisive line on it.

White and Red Chalk. Grey, beige or pink paper can be used with white chalk to get the effect of highlights. Surprisingly lovely effects can be produced with these touches of white. My portrait of young

Mary Quant

Timothy Lawson was drawn on buff Ingres paper, and touched up with white and red chalk. This technique was used by Rubens and Titian. I love Ruben's sketch of his son, which I think is charcoal or pencil, with sanguine. **Charcoal**. For charcoal I prefer Rowney's Willow in thin sticks; some artists prefer a thick charcoal which covers the paper more quickly with broad shadows. There is an uncommon richness in the velvety black of charcoal, while the opaque tones can be worked in with a stump or by rubbing with the finger-tip. Don't let your soft sticks of charcoal rub against each other in their box; that friction reduces the warm black and the stick is harder to use and less sympathetic. Flora Lewis, a distinguished graphic artist, buys toothbrushes in little plastic cases specially to keep her charcoal sticks in!

Rubber. Winsor & Newton's plastic, or putty, rubber is essential; it can be squeezed into points to pick out highlights in eyes, nose and hair. But take care not to get the putty rubber tacky or it will make dirty smears on the paper. And when it's cold, knead it a bit before using it.

It is essential that the *model be at ease* in a relaxed atmosphere, so I never make my sitters sit still, but give them a point to look at – preferably something cheerful; and as long as they go back to this point I let them move as much as they like. No one is self-conscious after the first five minutes, however shy, and I always encourage them to talk even if it is so interesting as to be rather distracting! The exciting adventures of Col. W.F. Sterling, Lawrence of Arabia's Chief of Staff, almost stopped me working.

I like to draw really busy people while they are absorbed in their work. Lady Reading interviewed people throughout my portrait session.

Conductors and musicians are wonderful to draw in action, rapt attention in their faces, lost in their music.

Men are easier to draw than women, and the older the better. I enjoy doing legal faces most of all: the firm jaw, well-cut humorous mouth, keen eye and general air of interest and alertness. People like these are a gift to the portrait artist. Incidentally, I have noticed that many great men have large noses. Among women, ballet dancers sit best – they have the knack of arranging their bones comfortably and always have poise and generally beauty — even in old age.

The Drawing. I always start the drawing round about the nearest eye, which I place in the centre of the width of the paper; this ensures a little more space in front of the head than behind. If my model is tall I put it nearer the top, if short or a child, lower down leaving plenty of space above. If the sitter wears spectacles, I only suggest them very delicately after the head is completely drawn. I always ask the sitter to take them off while I draw the eyes, as the glass distorts them. From the nearest eye I work outwards, and always try to finish each detail as I mean to leave it finally. This helps me check shapes of shadows and distances as I go along; it doesn't suit my style to sketch in the whole head first. And I try to work from left to right so I don't run the risk of smudging the charcoal with my hand.

A bow tie is good in drawings of men, it seems to finish off the head neatly.

My little *mirror* is a great help: placed close to my eye I observe both model and drawing in it every three minutes, comparing sitter and portrait to catch the faults and the likeness. This is like looking at the sketch with a fresh eye, and two short sittings are better than one long one. Coming back to a portrait later makes one's mistakes apparent immediately, as does putting the portrait next to the sitter, standing well back to view the two from a distance.

An incredible number of tones can be made with charcoal. Light as a feather, it can produce strong intense darks – right up the scale to the airiest, fairiest hint of a tone. *Use the charcoal* sideways and broad sweeps of shadows can be put in instantaneously. It can be used right down to the stump, and doesn't need sharpening – if a thin accent is needed, just break a piece off the end. Drawings in charcoal can be made very quickly. I rarely take more than an hour to finish the portrait, often far less If my sitter is blonde, or white haired, I often make my background dark to emphasise this.

Nahari

The art of drawing is a heritage of which we may well be proud. Turner, Cotman, Constable and Cox, and many others, filled sketch books with fleeting impressions, figure studies and landscape. It is impossible to do too much sketching and it is a good idea always to carry a sketchbook, *and* use it as much as possible.

Most newspapers and magazines preferred pen and ink drawings to charcoal or pencil work, largely owing to technical difficulties of reproducing subtly nuanced work in half-tones. My drawings of one of our greatest young ballerinas were so badly reproduced in her biography that she seemed to have a moustache! And it's the artist that gets the blame for a sloppy line-block reproduction.

My maxim was always to get as much work published as possible, and topical drawings delivered to newspapers or magazines in good time often had an excellent chance of getting published. These in turn led to many commissions, and these works I would show at the annual exhibition of the Society of Graphic Artists. Keep your name in front of the public, and you will get work.

At first sight, *the portrait is often a shock to the sitter*, who is used to seeing his face in the mirror – the opposite way round to the artist's view. Therefore I do not let him see the drawing too soon, and I really prefer someone else to see it first to give a true and unbiased criticism. Frequently the model sees likenesses to their relations:"I didn't realize I had Father's nose!" or "Exactly like the portrait of my Grandmother."

Finally the portrait has to be sprayed to "fix" it so it can't be rubbed or spoiled. Any *good fixative* such as Winsor & Newton's can be used. Stand about two feet away from the drawing (pinned upright), while spraying evenly from top left to bottom right. One sitter helped me spray his portrait; but he blew too enthusiastically and too near, and a little runny beard appeared from the chin!

The artist hopes for much. A good portrait, a good drawing, a good composition, and in addition a good likeness. Even if he gets all these he will only get one facet of the sitter's personality, and his portrait will not please everybody. Drawing a portrait is a voyage of discovery for truth, and although there are bound to be disappointments, it is always interesting, and when a portrait "comes off", very rewarding too.

When I had to finish a portrait quickly, either because it was for a daily newspaper or a commission when the sitter had an hour or less, I worked in sanguine (red chalk) or charcoal. Sometimes I drew with charcoal and then put in a little sanguine where needed. Occasionally I used pastels for children as that produces a very pretty pretty portrait

In a landscape watercolour I never use blotting paper. Whilst using "1/4 Imperial" sheets of thin watercolour paper, I put the paper under cold water, hold it up by one corner for a minute to drip off excess water, put it on a flat surface and very carefully roll it up, then put it on one of my two stretchers, unrolling it carefully to keep it flat. It must stay flat on the stretcher to dry and when the paper is fully dry, it is stretched and ready to use. I like to use Arches paper, which is very expensive (5 yrs ago it was £4 a sheet.) but so thick it doesn't require stretching.

Chapter nine

"The Valiant Years"
War leaders

I n the 50's there was a film being made, *The Valiant Years*, interviewing the war leaders, and I was invited to go to the recordings — unfortunately the invitation came after the first interview with Churchill, which I missed.

Sketching these heroes during the production was very, very exciting, and later I saw the film which was really marvellous.

LORD MOUNTBATTEN

A friend of mine at the BBC told me in confidence that Lord Louis Mountbatten would be at the Ministry of Defence the next day at 12 o'clock. If I wanted to go, I could sit and sketch while they were interviewing him. So of course I said "yes please" — it was wonderful! He would have been much too busy to give me a private sitting ever. Not that I tried.

I should think I had about 20 minutes to half an hour to do a quick sketch. Luckily, it just came off straight away and I consider it one of my best. They don't always come off.

Lord Louis was in very good form and told the story of how he went to see Churchill at the height of the war, taking with him some blocks of different substances to be tried out for Mulberry Harbour – where the British landed in Normandy on D-Day. He was informed that Churchill was in his bath.

"Just where I wanted him to be," said Lord Louis. "I went up, banged on the door and was allowed in. Churchill loves toys, so I gave him the blocks to play with in his bath."

On another occasion Churchill asked him if he liked the idea of going to tidy things up in Burma. Mountbatten thought this meant just a staff job, and said:

Juliet with Lord Mountbatten

"Wouldn't one of your Chiefs of Staff be better for that, sir?"

Churchill corrected him. "I don't think you understand what I am offering you. I mean you to take complete control and reorganise everything. What do you think of it?"

"Well sir, I have a disconcerting habit of thinking I can tackle anything, so I'd like to do it."

When he stopped, I went over to him with the drawing. He hadn't seen me there because I was rather hiding. There were a lot of people and cameras and all sorts of things going on. I said would you be kind enough to sign this for me and he said "Oh yes, certainly — oh that's very good! Much better than a photograph!" He liked it and he put it in front of me and got out a very grand, real fountain pen with a nib and he signed it. One of the photographers took a lovely photograph of me with him, which I have in my studio.

FIELD-MARSHAL VISCOUNT MONTGOMERY OF ALAMEIN – AND HIS DOUBLE

Though I was disappointed not to visit Field Marshal Viscount Montgomery of Alamein at his Hampshire house with the BBC team, I had the next best thing, a live sitting with "Monty's Double." He was so exactly like the Field Marshal in appearance as to make no difference. In his book *I was Monty's Double* he told the thrilling story of his impersonation, and how the enemy were hoodwinked into believing Monty to be in the Middle East, when he was, in fact, very much occupied elsewhere.

Juliet with "Monty's Double"

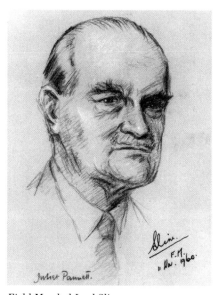

Field Marshal Lord Slim

FIELD MARSHAL LORD SLIM
Hero of the Burma Campaign

He began by apologising for his face. "I look a bit fierce, but people expect generals to look fierce. Once when I was Governor General in Australia I was with a group of journalists and photographers, and one young chap said 'Would you smile please, sir?' I said, "I *am* smiling. I really thought I was. I can't help it, I look like that."

When the drawing was done, he leaned over my chair and said approvingly:

"What a pity I didn't have you with me in the war; I could have dropped this sketch and shown the Japs what was coming to them. That would have shaken them."

GENERAL SIR MARTIN FARNDALE *The Master Gunner* (See next page)

A great soldier and a delightful man. He didn't talk much except about Saddam Hussein. One time when Sir Martin was in Iraq quite a few years ago, he heard the story of a person who didn't agree with Hussein. Saddam said, "Step out here," and shot him through the head. "Most awful man," said Sir Martin.

FIELD MARSHAL SIR CLAUDE AUCHINLECK
Supreme Commander in India and Pakistan

Our meeting was in a small private bank in Queen Street, Central London. The Field Marshal rushed upstairs ahead of me two steps at a time (he was eighty years old). Seeing that his room was full of people he said "We can do the portrait in Lord Aldington's room — the Director of the Bank — he won't mind." We were getting on very happily with me drawing the Field Marshal when suddenly the door opened and Lord Aldington walked in, carrying a pile of books. Seeing us, he dropped them. It was really very embarrassing but the Field Marshal said "Oh it's all right, I know him very well, he won't mind." Lord Aldington went away, saying "It's all right — I suppose!"

I had a lovely afternoon doing the Field Marshal. He even invited me to Suffolk, where he lived in a windmill. He was keen on painting and said "Come and do some paintings there." I wish I had now and wish I'd taken my son Denis who loved windmills. Anyway, I didn't. I didn't take half the opportunities I was offered.

Field Marshal Sir Claude Auchinleck

Gordon Armstrong, High Sheriff of Northumberland

Sir Martin Farndale, General

LIEUTENANT-GENERAL SIR BRIAN HORROCKS *Black Rod*

On the evening of November 7th I was to draw him at the Women's Press Club, where he was lecturing. But fate decreed otherwise. Rick and I set out to catch our train to town, and at East Croydon station I had a bad fall and sprained both my wrists. We proceeded to the club, but I was in great pain. Rick had to feed me at dinner, my wrists being so swollen that I couldn't hold a knife and fork. It was clearly out of the question for me to try to draw. Before the evening was over, Rick insisted on taking me to Charing Cross Hospital. I was glad to get to bed that night, after a hectic day, which included:

Field Marshall Viscount Alanbrooke

10.30 A portrait sitting.
11.30 Shell Mex House re magazine drawings.
12.30 A session at Rutland Gate for work on portrait of Walter de la Mare.
2.30 Appointment with business manager at *ILN*
4.30 Appointment with impresario Gorlinsky re use of drawings for programme.
On the way back to Croydon with Phoebe, a slight car smash on Blackfriars Bridge. Nobody hurt.
Change in Croydon and take the train back to London, falling on platform, spraining wrists.
Dinner Party at the Press Club.
Charing Cross Hospital.
Train back to Croydon.

Sir John Glubb (Glubb Pasha)

Colonel Digby Thompson, Inns of Court and City Yeomanry   *Major General T.A. Boam*

My sprained wrists needed constant treatment and kept me out of action for a long time. Phoebe massaged them every day, but for more than six weeks I couldn't grip anything. At last I made a tentative start again with charcoal, which I found the easiest thing to hold.

Sir Brian Horrocks was sympathetic and promised to give me a sitting at some other time.

When my wrists became supple enough for me to use my hands, I got in touch with him, and a sitting was arranged in his Black Rod's office at the House of Lords, which I then visited to do the first of my two Black Rods.

In spite of his friendly co-operation, I found him difficult to draw because he never kept still for a moment. While sitting for me, he was correcting notes, talking to messengers, dictating letters, both business and personal, signing a pile of copies of his autobiography, and dealing with queries from a BBC secretary who was typing his forthcoming talk on Oliver Cromwell. He was full of enthusiasm and interested in everybody and everything; there seemed to be nothing that he didn't know. Dictating a letter to his goddaughter, who had written to say that she was going to buy a new overcoat, he said:

"I strongly advise you to go to C&A, their winter coats are excellent." Turning to me, he added: "Did you hear that? Their coats really are first-class, you know."

Bill Elliot, Queen's Company of Archers

Squadron Leader Barbara Wilbeforce

SIR BASIL LIDDELL-HART *Military Historian*

When I wrote asking if he would give me a sitting at his home, he said "Yes, of course, delighted … come. Bring your husband and stay for lunch with us." Of course, Rick enjoyed it immensely because they talked about the war and had a lot of things in common. It was interesting. This is in the National Portrait Gallery.

MAJOR GENERAL G. N. WOOD *First Colonel of the amalgamated Devonshire and Dorset Regiment (Rick's Regiment)*

"I am absolutely delighted with your really wonderful portrait, which will be a tremendous asset to the Mess," wrote the Commanding Officer of the 1st Battalion, "and for those of us who know General Wood well, it will remind us of his kindly, wise and strong personality which you have portrayed very well."

COL. WALTER F. STIRLING *Lawrence of Arabia's Chief of Staff*

Captain John Taw, who has been a friend for many years, invited me to go to stay in Morocco with Col. Stirling. It was a most wonderful experience because we stayed one night in the Rock Hotel, Gibraltar, which was lovely. Then we took the boat over to Tangier the next morning and I stayed there for two weeks and did lots of drawings of Col. Stirling and really enjoyed staying there with his charming American wife.

Major General GN Wood

Captain John Wilsey

Captain Roger Gerard Pearse

Colonel "H" Jones, V.C.

The Three Charmers

Chapter ten

Qantas trip

Completely out of the blue, Julia Bradbury, Qantas Airlines' Public Relations Officer, telephoned offering me a seat on the inaugural Boeing 707 flight from London to Sydney if the ILN was prepared to publish my drawings. The trip would take three weeks, returning via Qantas' Kangaroo Route — Singapore, Bangkok, Calcutta, Karachi, Cairo, Athens and Rome.

Knowing that I would be drawing at every stop, Sir Bruce said the ILN would definitely publish some of my pictures and I could "go and get my kangaroo!"

We left London Airport in September 1959, roaring off the tarmac at 185 m.p.h. like a great beast suddenly unleashed. Once up, jet planes being new in those days, I was astonished to find there was no sensation of flying, and none of that deafening noise one hears when a jet passes overhead.

There were 110 passengers. The press party was eight men and me, the only artist. I had given careful thought to my materials, rejecting the idea of oil paints as too heavy and slow drying. The final choice: one sketchbook with thick paper - which turned out to be a good idea - and three with banknote paper - which turned out to be a very bad idea because the pictures on this paper were too flimsy to frame. I also took forty sheets of half imperial Whatman paper, twenty-five Whatman boards and thirty sheets of my favourite Ingres Fabriano paper for drawing, my box of watercolours, some tubes of brilliant gouache, charcoal, two Flo-master pens, twelve carbon pencils and some process white.

We flew up the West Coast of England at 525m.p.h. and forty minutes after leaving London Airport, we were over the Hebrides, the world looking like a well illustrated map eight miles below. We refueled at Keflavik, Iceland, where I sketched American airmen and an Icelandic airhostess.

Then we flew over some enormous icebergs looking like pale green cones far below, with a light green perimeter — the reflection of the ice under the water. Big waves were dashing against them, making a white rim round the central cone.

On over Newfoundland, Nova Scotia and Boston to New York, whose silhouette in the afternoon sunshine looked exactly as I'd expected — Empire State Building, Statue of Liberty and all. We had to sit in the aircraft until a doctor had made his rounds to look for suspicious spots; even after we got a clean bill of health no one was allowed to leave Idlewild, so I had to be content with a few sketches at the airport.

Continuing west, we flew for hours into a superb sunset, speed keeping pace with time, with fine views of the Great Lakes. Then we landed in San Francisco and saw the floodlit splendour of the Golden Gate Bridge. A car whisked me away to do a few sketches.

The night flight took us on to Honolulu, warm and scented, where I was garlanded with mauve orchids, white ginger flowers, and frangipani. At dawn we went to see some Hawaiian girls making garlands. We took off for Fiji, trying to beat the record at all times because that was the point of the inaugural flight. The soft, still, pearly-grey water below turned gradually to jade green as we passed two volcanoes rising out of the water.

Landing on a tropical island in Fiji, I visited a small village and sketched a family. They had beautiful manners and looked very clean. I drew a policeman in Fijian uniform: a smart drill jacket and white gauntlets, with a white cotton skirt. He was barefoot, with hair combed up in a big fuzz.

Crossing the International Date Line, we went straight from 11th September to 13th — and never made up that lost

Juliet in Australia

I spent time on the flight deck with the captain and crew, and was fascinated with the hundreds of controls and the beautifully planned interior, with six seats for the crew dovetailed into a tiny cabin. The pilot said he made 66 pre-flight checks when he prepared to take off.

Australia. The journey drew to its close with Sydney's Harbour Bridge shimmering in the afternoon sun. We had left a London autumn and arrived in the Australian spring. It had taken thirty-one and a half flying hours — twenty less than the previous standard — a total of forty two hours including stops. We had set a new world record.

I had had only four hours' sleep since leaving London, and long before that first evening in Sydney was over, I fell asleep at the welcome dinner. The others woke me up and took me back to the hotel.

At every stop Qantas arranged for the journalists to have a car and driver take us to picturesque sights. At the Sydney zoo to my delight a friendly koala bear climbed up and put its paws round my neck and its furry little cheek against mine. It was one of the pleasantest experiences imaginable. Tom Hustler of the *Tatler* took a most delightful photograph. The *Wollongong Mercury* showed me holding a large blue-tongued lizard. Mother and I loved reptiles.

Australian hospitality is well known. At one lunch, half an hour after I mentioned that I found their oysters particularly good, we were each served with a surprise plate of a dozen oysters. They were not on the menu, but had been ordered at a moment's notice.

I had to step carefully in the midst of this Australian lavishness as my drawing eye can be put out by a couple of drinks, and I had to be ready to work at any given moment.

I drew the champion boomerang thrower, Joe Timberley, at the Aboriginal Settlement at La Peruse. His boomerangs travelled in a two hundred yard arc and returned to his hand every time – or almost.

On the tour to the Snowy Mountain Hydroelectric Project bringing water to the parched plains of the west, Tom Hustler and I had a chance encounter with Lord and Lady De La Warr. "Oh dear," exclaimed Lady De La Warr after Tom had taken her picture "I'm sure your readers have never seen me looking as untidy as this before." She was not the least surprised at meeting a *Tatler* photographer on a remote Australian mountaintop.

At Prime Minister Bob Menzies' reception for us in the House of Representatives at Canberra I did two drawings. On seeing the portraits he said "You're the artist I've looked for all my life — you make me younger than I am!"

I loved Australia, the warm, friendly people, the koala bears, and especially the bleached bones of the dead gum trees, white against the grey-green bush. The last place we visited was Brisbane, where I sketched the amazing houses built on stilts over the lake. The *Brisbane Courier* reported "A whirlwind one-day Brisbane visit by famous press artist Mrs Juliet Pannett could make our quaint old houses on stilts famous overseas."

Singapore. I shall never forget the terrific impact of the Far East, as I encountered it on our "Kangaroo Route" home. The bustle and colour in the streets. Red Chinese characters on the banners. Teeming crowds of people eating day and night. Footsteps on the pavement in the dark. People talking around the clock. Singapore never sleeps. There are no seasons. Every day is a heat wave, but people are healthy, in spite of the very smelly canal. I sketched a Chinese child with an interesting hairstyle. The little topknot, tied with red ribbon, is for pulling the child up to Heaven.

A Hindu temple caught my attention, and I settled down to sketch the painted figures of gods, humans and beasts. I particularly liked a blue man with four hands and a mustachioed figure with wings.

I was attracted away from the temple to watch some fishermen, who said Malays actually hear fish. The expert dives and listens, to decide where to set the net. They said that a skilled listener can even tell what kind of fish he is hearing.

By lucky chance, the naval husband of a friend was in Singapore, and I dined aboard his ship. The next evening we went to dinner with Lok Wan To, a Chinese millionaire, who showed us his collection of Ming china and jade.

A tailor's shop in Singapore had the delightful sign "Ladies Given Fits Upstairs."

One night Julia and I were driven down Sago Lane to see the Death Houses. Traditionally it is bad luck for the Chinese to die in their own homes, which are tremendously overcrowded, sleeping 15 or more to a room. A community project called *Kongsi*, hundreds of years old, deals with the aged and dying. When their time comes to pass to the next world, they go to these Death Houses, where they wait to die, in two-tiered bunks. Coffins are made on the spot, and a death is announced by the beating of a gong. Professional, paid mourners stand in the doorway, and the relatives and friends of the dying sit at tables in the street, smoking, drinking tea, and receiving financial contributions, duly acknowledged in black ink on red strips of paper. There is a strange contrast between the quiet of these Death Houses and the lavish and noisy Chinese funerals, with their gongs, and shoutings to keep the devil away. The funeral is often paid for by the gold in the teeth of the deceased — the final insurance.

Singapore - The Death Houses

Thailand. I flew on alone to Bangkok — a magical city of startling beauty and my favourite of all. I drew the entire household staff of Australian Press Attaché Norman Bartlett, from the ancient head gardener to the youngest baby, not forgetting the Siamese cat. I noticed to my astonishment that the old gardener had beautifully kept hands and nails. An elderly servant begged me to draw her kneeling, paying homage to her master and mistress. They showed me the Spirit House, which shelters the all-important household gods. It stood by a lake in the garden, and there I sketched the servants bringing offerings of cakes, joss sticks, garlands and little effigies to placate evil spirits and thank good ones for favours shown.

The Bartletts introduced me to a Thai journalist called Manas, who spent the next three days showing me round Bangkok, the Venice of the East. Everything happens on the klongs (this was before the Thais filled in so many klongs-canals). At dawn, floating on a sampan, we ate pancakes of coconut milk, flour and sugar (very nasty!), and I saw the wonderful floating markets and shops on stilts. There are no rules on the water. The Siamese are so naturally polite that they always give way to the other boat, and it seems to work! Washing is done from the boats or banks. I saw Siamese bathing inside loose garments. Dishes are washed in the klongs, and I also saw people brushing their teeth in the same grey/green water. These people must be immune to typhoid!

The boat women wear enormous hats, like lampshades on a wicker frame, which keeps the head cool. I did a great many sketches on the klongs which were, at the time, the principal arteries carrying eighty per cent of all transportation.

The sampan brings pale pink and green lotus blossoms (which the Thais put in soup), melons, star fruit, red chilis, dried and fresh fish, charcoal, and a thousand other commodities, to sell to the little waterside shops. There were big rice boats, smaller ones selling coffee, and among them, the canoes, with the Buddhist monks in saffron and gold, begging from the boats and banks. The Buddhist monks leave the wats (temples) at dawn. When there is enough light to read the lines in the palms of their hands, they know it is time to take their little teak bowls to beg for food. These, they have to fill before they go home. There is no begging, as we understand it, as the gift of food is due to the followers of Buddha. Therefore no thanks are given by the monks. They walk, or canoe, with eyes cast down as they are not supposed to look more than three yards ahead. Devout Buddhists put spoons full of rice or little parcels of fried bananas or other food wrapped in banana leaves into the bowls. They usually put a lotus flower into the hands of the monk too.

*Monks begging on the Klongs
of Thailand*

I did quick watercolours, which sold very well at my exhibition back home. I went on painting them from memory for quite a long time because they were such an attractive subject. The streets were wet and the reflections of the monks carrying black paper umbrellas were wonderful.

Every Thai boy becomes a monk for three months of his life, as part of his training in humility. It is the only time in his life that his parents will kneel to him. His studies consist of scriptural reading, writing and casting horoscopes.

Thais possess charm and friendliness to a degree. My three days in Thailand were an unforgettable experience. As it was the monsoon season, it rained all the time, making Bangkok especially beautiful. There was a marvellous melancholy about all those wet tiles and the temples dripping with rain.

Manas took me with some Thai dancers to see silk spinning and weaving. Richly costumed in turquoise, purple, cerise and yellow, the dancers were a feast for the eye. Also, he obtained permission for me to enter a Buddhist temple barefoot, to paint the monks at prayer. Though I was told that I was the first woman ever to be granted such a privilege, my disbelief was later confirmed when I discovered that a woman friend had also been "the first woman" admitted to do a painting!

It was an unforgettable sight. The great dark temple, the little Buddha high up in the dim interior, glints of pure gold, crimson carpets and the monks in their flaming habits, chanting and intoning. Buddhism seems a free and easy and happy way of life. As soon as the service was over, the monks relaxed in the temple, lit cigarettes, and one even produced a bottle of Coca-Cola from his robes!

On my last evening, Manas had a Buddhist priest friend, Akaria Samang, cast my horoscope in the Temple of the Angelic Daughter. When he took Chester Wilmott, the Australian journalist, the priest had warned him not to travel the next day. Chester was killed the following afternoon in the Comet crash at Rome.

Manas never takes any important step without consulting Akaria Samang. We visited the monastery at night, wandering along mysterious corridors, peering into darkened cells until we reached the little square temple with Chinese lanterns, Buddhas, and two very fierce small dogs who bared their teeth at me. Obviously not used to women in the monastery! With Manas translating, the priest asked a lot of questions and promised to send me my horoscope.

I saw the Palace of the King of Siam, where Princess Alexandra was staying while I was there. It was a riot of colour: gold everywhere. Wonderful wall paintings. Enamelled and jewelled decorations. Thai silk hangings and hundreds of Buddhas. We saw the Emerald Buddha, and the immense reclining Buddha, a hundred yards long lying on his side with feet three times the height of a man. There was even a lottery Buddha! When the people want a number to back, they spin two wheels in front of the Buddha. They back the numbers which come up on the wheels, and if they win, they stick a little square of pure gold the size of a postage stamp onto the Buddha to thank him. This Buddha was covered in gold from head to foot, so he must have been an excellent tipster!

One Buddha which was moved from one temple to another in Bangkok during the Buddhist jubilee year of 1956, proved too heavy for a five-ton crane. They discovered that it was not of plated brick, as supposed, but of solid gold.

I loved all I saw in Bangkok, but apparently I didn't see the bad side. Rabies is prevalent, pricipally because according to Buddhism, no living creature may be killed. There are 50,000 lepers in the country and of course, there is terrific opium traffic and much prostitution.

The description "Lotus Eaters" is often applied to the Siamese, and is not disparaging. The people of Siam do eat lotus seeds. You can buy them in markets and at railway stops throughout the country. They have a clean, musky, stimulating taste that lingers on the palate and in the mind — like Siam itself.

India. Then on to this great sub-continent, over the gigantic, brown meandering Ganges, flowing between islands of olive green. At Calcutta, I sketched a family of snake charmers. Their apprenticeship begins at the age of three. While children in the West play with toys, the Indian toddler destined to be a snake charmer is learning how to handle the snakes, let them coil round his body and share his milk. Small girls are taught to care for the snakes. The young snake charmer learns to play the eerie reed music, which lures the snakes from their wicker baskets. I was reminded of the snake I brought home from school which mother and I presented to the London Zoo, where we often visited it.

Greece. From Calcutta we went on, via Karachi and Cairo, to Athens — so serene and beautiful. Such a vivid blue sky behind the Acropolis! At Sounion, site of the temple of Neptune, peasants harvesting grapes gave us large fragrant bunches. The Greek stories of my childhood came flooding back as I sketched the remains of the temple. Then to Mount Hymettos, to smell the heather from which the bees make their famous honey. I did a watercolour of the panorama spread before me, the Parthenon rising white and clear from the plain, and all Athens spread out below.

A strange figure appeared in an Athens street — a sponge seller. I pointed to one in the middle and he snipped the string with scissors, took off the sponge, tied the string together again and went on his way.

Italy. Coming in to land in Rome we saw St Peter's, the Vatican, the Forum and the Tiber with its beautiful bridges, winding through the rose and sand-coloured city. Here, I drew a group of priests and nuns — black and severe.

Then on, over the Alps. Lake Geneva lit up like a diamond necklace, and home to London — just three weeks after I had left — laden with a boomerang from Australia, slippers from Calcutta, grapes from Greece, and enough memories to last a lifetime!

Home. Then it was down to earth again, back to the hardship of Sydenham Road, with the money problem ever present. Among all the souvenirs, my most precious were three hundred pictures and sketches. This drew a report in a newspaper noting all the work involved in producing so many pictures in what must have been an exhausting three weeks. In fact it was hard work, but as I always want to draw or paint everything I see, it makes no difference whether I call it work or play: I love it.

I worked on some of the sketches after my return, developing them into oil paintings and full-scale watercolours.

At the *ILN*, Sir Bruce laid out my work on his enormous table. In no time he had made up four pages which appeared on the news-stands two weeks later.

Soon, after a day painting musicians at the BBC Studios, I received a letter from Manas, the Thai journalist, enclosing my horoscope.

"My Very Dear Friend," Manas wrote, "I want to thank you for your most enjoyable company. Your drawing of me is being greatly admired and is having a special place in my drawing room. I am dying to see those pictures you have painted. When the *ILN* arrives it will be a day for me to be proud of."

The horoscope, among other things, said: "Great fortune will be yours when you grow older, and you will be lucky with an unexpected windfall...Your life will be complete in all ways. Your finance, your standing, your work and your happiness will be at the highest level beyond expectation. Greater ambition should be encouraged, for international fame is in store for you."

Results of the trip. An Exhibition of ninety-five of my paintings and drawings, together with photographs by Tom Hustler, at Qantas House in Piccadilly was opened on December 11th 1959 by the Australian High Commissioner, Sir Eric Harrison. There was so much demand for my vivid picture of Buddhist monks in Bangkok caught in the rain that I had to recreate it several times back in England, with each one being a little different. This is something I don't usually like to do, for one thing because I don't work well from imagination. But I can when the subject really excites me, as this did.

My portrait of Mr Menzies was presented to him in Canberra by four English schoolchildren who had won an essay competition. In late November, now quite busy as a lecturer, I spoke at the Croydon Arts Club about my trip round the world, illustrating it with quick sketches.

Sir Robert Menzies

Chapter eleven
Public Figures

Investiture of Baroness Swanborough

LADY READING *Head of the Women's Voluntary Service*

I went to WVS headquarters, where I drew Lady Reading interviewing people. I found it absorbing to hear her methods of dealing with another's problems, and I was very impressed by her quick assessment of the facts. She seized at once upon the salient points as each case came before her.

It wasn't long before I was to see Lady Reading again, on a more important occasion. On October 21st 1958, the first life peeresses were introduced into the House of Lords.

Three days beforehand I had a telephone call from the *Illustrated London News* to say that they had got permission for me to be present in the press gallery. I only had those three days in which to produce a double-page spread and I wasn't allowed to take my drawing board in with me on the day. There was nothing for it but to cancel my other engagements and work in the House of Lords to complete the background. At the actual presentation of the peeresses I did small drawings in a reporter's notebook of the most important participants in the ceremony, and transferred them afterwards to the full size drawing. The first peeress to take the oath was Lady Reading, now Baroness Swanborough. The picture shows her taking the oath, standing between her sponsors Lord Chorley and Lord Burnham; Sir George Bellew, Garter King of Arms, is in the centre, and beside him are the Earl Marshal (the Duke of Norfolk) and Black Rod (Lieutenant-General Sir Brian Horrocks).

"It was such a lovely surprise, opening the *Illustrated London News* and seeing your wonderful drawing with myself as the centrepiece," Lady Reading later wrote to me. "I cannot begin to imagine how you managed to put so much detail on paper... my sincere congratulations on a beautiful piece of work."

LADY BADEN-POWELL *Founder of the Girl Guide movement*

I stayed with her twice at her Grace & Favour apartment at Hampton Court Palace, and in all, did five portraits, one for the Girl Guides Association. She was utterly charming to me.

"Have you got a husband?'

"Yes."

"Good."

Her son, the present Lord B-P, joined us and talked about his farm, where he bred and raced American Quarter horses.

SIR DOUGLAS BADER *Aviator who lost both legs in a flying accident in 1931, and went on to be a World War II Ace*

When I arrived he slapped me on the back — frightfully hearty — and said " Sit down. Are you all right there?" It was very amusing.

"Are you interested in music?" I asked. "I'm afraid not [apologetically] — I'm really a very dull chap."

And so I did two drawings of him, one he liked, but the other —he said — "looked like a chap who was had up for living on the immoral earnings of a woman or a night club band leader."

LEONARD ROBINSON *Swanmaster of the Dyers' Company*

He sat for an oil portrait in his livery as one of the Queen's Watermen. I had to obtain permission from the Lord Chamberlain, since Mr. Robinson was a servant of Her Majesty, and the uniform had to be insured for £200 before it was allowed to leave the tailor's. There were eight sittings altogether. I had the uniform all the time in my studio which was in its usual state of chaos and I was terrified that someone would spill a cup of tea over it. But it was all right; the livery didn't come to any harm.

The painting was hung in the City of London Art Exhibition in February 1958. It was the first public showing of this portrait, in which Mr. Robinson looks a little anxious; perhaps he was thinking of the £200 insurance for his livery! He attended the exhibition wearing a sombre grey overcoat, a contrast to the magnificent scarlet, gold and silver of the picture.

"The swans are increasing every year," he said. "I'm constantly called out to help them, as they are always getting into trouble. They land in the streets, they get snared by fish-hooks or covered in oil, they get hit by motor launches and squashed by barges."

SIR STEPHEN TALLENTS *Medallist of the Order of St John of Malta*

He sat for me in the 13th Century chapel that he used as a study at his home "St John's Jerusalem", in Dartford. "It is in an even greater muddle than my own." I said, "and that's saying something." When I arrived, he dived into a tangle of fishing tackle, books, magazines and gardening implements, to extract an enormous Scandinavian sweater, which he wanted to wear for the portrait. In the letterpress, which accompanied it, he was accidentally referred to as St Stephen.

Public Figures

H.R.H.
Princess Alexandra

Norfolk

Juliet Pannett
1970

His Grace
the Duke
of Norfolk

C.J. Harman,
Lord Mayor of London

Juliet Pannett.
1970.

Mary Fitzalan Howard

Lady Mary Fitzalan Howard

Earl Spencer,
Princess Diana's uncle

Sir Isaac Wolfson

Juliet Pannett

Lord Morris of Borth-y-Gest

H.R.H. Princess Marina,
Duchess of Kent

Lord Marks

Sir Edward Howard,
Lord Mayor of London

Admiral Gordon Lennox

Princess Soraya

1970.

DAME BARBARA SALT
Foreign Office Official

I was lucky enough to have been able to do a portrait of Dame Barbara Salt, a woman of outstanding courage and distinction. She surely would have been Britain's first woman ambassador, if illness had not made it impossible for her to take up her appointment in Israel. After having both legs amputated, she was determined to walk again and carry on with her work. "It is not an easy life," she told me, "but no one could be bored by it, which is more than could be said of most professions. One of the disadvantages for a woman is that she is single-handed; most men have wives to help them, and can work as a team."

She spoke with humour and without embarrassment of her disability, saying that she had had nice legs, and insisted that the artificial ones should be equally shapely.

"It was a terrible blow, just when the most interesting of all jobs had been assigned to me. But life doesn't come to an end like that; one door closes and another one opens."

SIR THOMAS LERNEY
LORD LYON, KING OF ARMS (one of the oldest British titles)

As Chief Herald of Scotland, he sat for me in all the splendour of his highly embroidered tabard.

During the sitting, the fire got very low and he knelt down at the hearth to make it up; I was on tenterhooks as his velvet hat fell further and further over his eyes, but just as it was about to fall into the fire, Lord Lyon got up and resumed his pose.

Twenty years later he bought the portrait. Another twenty years on, his son, in the meantime Lord Lyon, asked me to do his portrait.

Lord Delfont

*Malcom Innes
Lord Lyon*

Chapter twelve

Academics

| William Stewart, | Jean Morrison, | Dr David Newsome, |
| Master of Haileybury School | Headmistress, Christ's Hospital | Master of Wellington College |

SIR ERIC ASHBY *Master of Clare College, Oxford*

He had invited me to come at three and stay to tea. He wrote afterwards: "We did enjoy your visit yesterday, and this is to confirm (since dons have a reputation for being forgetful) that we would like to buy the drawing."

PROFESSOR A. J. AYER *Wykeham Professor of Logic at Oxford*

Two sittings in 13 Conway Street, W.1. Did three drawings, two while reading. All the time he reads he twiddles a little silver chain in his right hand, sometimes biting it. Very difficult to draw, as he isn't an easy sitter, getting fidgety and bored, and when he reads he becomes quite absorbed and head sinks lower and lower, and goes from right to left according to which page he is reading — and he sometimes leans his head on his hand which obscures features.

His wife had a baby one and half weeks ago, and he took drawings to show her when finished.

Pink, brown and primrose yellow padded Victorian chairs and a French wine taster for an ashtray, in which I deposited small pieces of charcoal as I broke them off to make sharp edges with which to draw.

Drawn about 1963 and published by the *Illustrated London News*. Signed.

SIR JOHN COCKROFT *First Master of Churchill College, Cambridge*

This chalk drawing was commissioned by the *ILN* for publication when Sir Winston Churchill laid the foundation stone of the central buildings of the college. He was the quietest sitter I ever had, as he didn't speak a single word while I worked. I mentioned this during a talk a little later, and a member of the audience said afterwards:

"I know Sir John Cockroft well, and one of his favourite sayings is 'Only fools open their mouths'."

JOHN GRIFFITH *Public Orator, Oxford University*

I drove to Oxford and went to the senior common room at Jesus College for tea at 4.15 to met an old friend, Dr John Walsh, who has arranged all the three portraits I have done of Fellows (Dr Walsh, Paul Pager and John Griffith).

After a rest I went down to the bursary opposite the Common room and was met by John Griffith, who greeted me with an enthusiastic kiss and introduced me to the ten Fellows — old friends and former students who had commissioned the portrait which was sitting on a window sill wrapped in brown paper. Champagne was served, and then John tore off the paper with a flourish and put the portrait on view. It was greeted with great enthusiasm, although John Smith (second master at St Paul's School and an old Pauline himself) said that he had rarely seen John Griffith with his mouth shut (he is a tremendous talker!) but that I had got his twinkle and humour.

LORD JAMES OF RUSHOLME *Vice Chancellor of York University*

This was quite fun, because I went up to York by train with one of the writers from *The Times*. We got to York about 12.30, and I asked if I might start a sketch at once while we were talking because he was being interviewed at the time by the man who was with me. He said, "No no, not now. We can't do anything until after lunch in the way of work." I couldn't argue of course but it was very disappointing because in that half hour I could have got well started. I looked out of the window instead, and was amazed by the thousand-year-old yew trees which had finally grown so large they were touching. Eventually we had lunch and I did a not very good drawing of him leaning back in an armchair and smoking his pipe. It was very disappointing because I could have done a very good one of him, full of life and very interesting.

DAME KATHLEEN LONSDALE *Professor of Chemistry, London University*

Sir Henry Dale told me that Dame Kathleen was on old friend of his. At the beginning of the war, as soon as he heard that she was to be arrested for refusing to register for war duties, he said:

"That's all right, I'll come and bail you out."

But she wanted to go to prison and answered passionately:

"If you do any such thing, I shall never speak to you again."

SIR NEVILL MOTT *Master of Gonville and Caius College, Cambridge*

Arrived at Sir Nevill Mott's (the Master's House, Gonville and Caius) at 11.00 am. Did a good portrait, stayed to lunch and was shown his collection of pictures. Saw the Reynolds portrait and many others. At lunch were Sir Nevill's father — 88 and very charming; a woman professor of fine art; Lady Mott's mother. Sir Nevill wrote me a list of suggested names.

I remember the frivolous rhyme told to me by someone at his luncheon party:

"I'm God," said Todd.

"You're not," said Mott.

LORD TODD *Professor of Organic Chemistry and then Master Elect of Christ's College, Cambridge*

I also did his portrait and found he didn't like the above rhyme.

Dr Margaret Murray
anthropologist

Arnold Toynbee

G M TREVELYAN *Master of Trinity College, Cambridge*

The doyen of English historians. One of my most interesting sitters. Delicate featured old man — white moustache and hair, long elegant hands, which he tucked under his pullover for warmth.

I drew him in his large book-lined study after instruction from his housekeeper that on no account was I to stay more than an hour for fear of tiring him. I worked fast, and after three-quarters of an hour I was in the middle of my second drawing when he asked suddenly:

"Could you stay on and do another one for the National Portrait Gallery?"

G.M. Trevelyan

Then he leaned back and resumed his friendly talk about his undergraduate days with Vaughan Williams, and asked me who else I had drawn lately. "Lord Samuel," I told him.

"I'm no grand old man like Lord Samuel, " he said modestly. "I'm not at all interesting to draw I'm afraid."

I had only spent an hour and a half there by the time the third drawing was completed. Dr. Trevelyan bought the one he liked best for presentation to the National Portrait Gallery, of which he was a trustee. I made out a cheque for myself and he signed it right off.

A grateful letter from his housekeeper told me:

"You did not tire him, but gave him something to think and talk about out of the usual channels."

Hugh Trevor Roper

HUGH TREVOR ROPER (LORD DACRE)

Regius Professor of Modern History, Oxford.

I arrived at his home in Oxford at the appointed time and was met by his wife who said she was terribly sorry but he had flu. However she volunteered to ask him if he would still sit for me and he said yes. He sat up in bed in his pyjamas and flu didn't stop him from being extremely witty.

He talked about the Bay of Pigs (it was at that time) and was hilariously funny though I can no longer remember the details.

Sir Fred Hoyle

Techniques: Watercolours

THE TRADITION OF WATERCOLOUR PAINTING in England is strong, and some of the best exponents are Cotman, Cox, Constable, Turner and Girtin, whose works can be studied at the Victoria and Albert Museum, the National Gallery and the British Museum.

For watercolour painting there are no strict rules; each artist must develop his own style, but a few hints may be of use.

Method. I like to work out of doors, seated on a low stool, or on the ground. I never use an easel, as it adds weight to what I carry, and colour washes can run on its upright stand, and can leave marks. I sit with a board on my knees and my favourite paper – Whatman. I prefer old mellow paper, which adds atmosphere to the work. Greens Pastless Board is very good. Tinted papers sometimes flatter a sketch and make it look better. However start painting on white paper, as the colour can be correctly observed, and one can have more control. To stretch paper soak it in cold water for half a minute, then roll up right side inside. Hold it vertically for the surplus water to run off, then roll it flat on to the board, allowing no air bubbles to be caught under it, finally sticking the edges with scotch tape. Stand the board on its side till dry. A thick paper, such as a 200lb Whatman or Green's Pasteless Board need not be stretched at all. Half imperial is an ideal size, smaller is too limiting.

Paints. A japanned box is best, with three deep palettes for colour washes and space for sixteen large pans of Winsor and Newton's, or Daler-Rowney's colours. I buy viridian, cobalt blue, oxide of chromium, and rose madder in tubes as they harden somewhat when exposed to the air. I use a restricted palette which is easier to handle, and this economy of colour helps pull a painting together, give it unity. I never use all these colours together but find my preferences besides the four above are: vermilion or Winsor red, light red, French ultramarine, cerulean blue, yellow ochre, raw sienna, burnt sienna, raw umber, burnt umber, cadmium, chrome or Winsor yellow, lamp black. I use three times as much French ultramarine as any other colour in the box.

Brushes. Sable brushes are expensive, but it's essential to get the best, both for the work, and the brushes' lasting quality. Over 30 years ago I was given a Winsor and Newton sable brush size 12. I used it until I couldn't paint any more, and although its a little blunter now, it is still perfect. Only three brushes are

The Tool Shad

The Bothy-Ben Damph

of the changing light; therefore I mix up a good strong dollop of French ultramarine and light red in one of the deep pans with plenty of water, and wash it in quickly over every part of the drawing which is in shadow, varying it slightly by picking up a little burnt sienna, or raw sienna or perhaps yellow ochre – the latter especially where there is reflected light on the buildings. Then, whilst this is still rather wet, add the darkest darks, inside doorways, windows, etc. using French ultramarine and burnt umber which make an excellent warm black. When painting into wet paint, always use a thicker mixture of colour than the original wash. This method calls for speed, but adds vitality. In this type of sketch, tone is much more important than colour, but a few touches can be added now. I like to have a small dash of red somewhere – a curtain in a window, a child's cap or jersey. This gives contrast and extra interest. In one painting I moved a letter box to where a touch of red was necessary – artist's licence!

Brushwork. Watercolour is dependent on good brushwork. Paint broadly and try to avoid retouching. Don't worry if little white spaces are left by the brush traveling quickly over the paper. This adds sparkle to the sketch. For old stonework, several combinations of colour can be tried. Cobalt and raw umber, or thin lamp black and yellow ochre, perhaps a touch of burnt sienna. For flesh tints use rose madder and yellow ochre as a base, with some burnt sienna and cobalt blue in the shadows. The sky should always look transparent. I paint it last, and try to vary it to give it more interest. I often use cerulean blue and cobalt for patches of sky blue, and a light mix of raw umber and French ultramarine for undersides of clouds, perhaps with a touch of burnt sienna. Occasionally a dark sky behind buildings in brilliant light is effective, as in a coming storm. I did a picture of Jerusalem this way.

Useful tips. Wet the paints before using them, especially if there is a hot sun. Six-panned enamelled palettes (like cake tins) are useful for extra washes and mixing paint.

Although alterations should be avoided, putting on glycerine with a hog's hair brush will soften and loosen the paint. To keep the paper wet in a windy or hot climate add about 12 drops of glycerine to the water. If on the contrary you want your painting to dry quickly, add some drops of whisky, gin or spirits of wine to the water, and drying will be accelerated.

Finally don't be discouraged if you don't succeed immediately. You'll improve with practice. A retired parson friend of eighty-seven who has been painting for only a year, is now producing some delightful work.

necessary to start with: sizes 12, 6, and 3, and all sable. Look after them carefully, and when traveling strap them with two elastic bands to a longer piece of cardboard or wood. Every few weeks I gently soap them, working them into points to dry until the next painting session. Add a thin willow charcoal for drawing and a putty rubber, and you're ready.

First make a rough rectangle with your fingers and thumbs at arm's length to enclose the view you are considering, and look through it with one eye. This will help you to choose your subject to the best advantage.

Starting the work. .Sketch your subject carefully with charcoal. Do not fix it as its smudges will give tone to the background when watercolour is applied. Extra little details, such as people or animals, give life to a sketch, so put in an old man, or a child with a dog, for a livelier picture. Do not put too much detail into buildings, but practise the "art of leaving out" as Cotman put it. Create an impression by drawing only the essentials: if there are many windows of the same shape draw one carefully to tell the tale, and leave the others a little soft. Interested spectators, such as small boys, will point out telegraph posts, drainpipes and chimney pots to put in. Ignore their advice! Check the perspective when the drawing is finished and you're ready to paint.

Painting.. Some painters wash pale yellow ochre over the whole drawing before they start. This softens the white and helps make the paper more receptive and the colour run freely. This wash requires much practice. Mix up a full well of colour and, tilting the board slightly, fill your largest brush and draw it across the paper from left to right, starting at the top. Fill the brush again and make another stroke slightly overlapping the first one, repeating the process till the bottom of the paper. If surplus paint collects at the foot of the paper soak it up with a dry brush immediately, and on no account disturb the wash by going over it a second time.

I prefer to establish the shadows as quickly as possible because

Chapter thirteen

New York & Canada

In the Summer of 1960 I flew to New York for another exhibition of my Qantas pictures.
David's daughter Vanessa, who was working as a model in New York, and her fiancé, Neil McConnell, helped me get ready for the opening. I was now delighted to spend three days on some typical New York scenes to add local interest to the exhibition — hot dog stalls, ice cream counters, a funeral home, people sleeping rough on the pavements of Harlem. Many of my pictures showed the fire escapes and hydrants, which are such a prominent feature in New York.
Quickly, I sketched my way through Chinatown, Washington Square, Greenwich Village, Wall Street, Broadway. It was only ten o'clock in the morning when we got to The Bowery, but there were a lot of men lying about in the streets. Vanessa and I couldn't tell whether they were drunk or drugged, but later on somebody told us that they were probably drunk on cheap red wine.

The heat was tremendous, and after the exhibition opened I decided to visit my younger sister Leonore, another painting Somers, in Vancouver. I approached Trans-Canada Air Lines with some drawings, and they offered to fly me there and back in exchange for a portrait of their Managing Director, plus a few drawings of their newest aeroplane. At Calgary I almost missed the 'plane because I was absorbed in drawing the first real cowboys I had ever seen. Leonore drove me around Vancouver, sightseeing and sketching every day. It was then that I made up my mind to learn to drive. If Leo could do it, I could.

A woman on the ferry to Victoria persuaded us to visit the Cowichan Indian Reserve and we spent all our time there. I found the Indians extraordinarily interesting, and drew them making canoes and carving totem poles. I sketched the first unmarried woman to be elected Chief of the Cowichan, the largest tribe of Indians in British Columbia.

Back in New York, I did a radio broadcast about my trip round the world. It was good publicity for the exhibition which had been crowded every day. Later on, the whole Exhibition — "as fascinating a portrayal as you'll see in a long, long time," said one american paper — was moved from New York to Cleveland.

Immediately on my return to London, I was invited to make a recording for "In Town Tonight." My talk was, by request, almost entirely concerned with the funeral home, something sufficiently alien to the English way of life to be of interest.

I described being taken to the showroom of caskets — a euphemism for coffins. The most expensive, for use in a mausoleum, was the equivalent of £6500 (1960 prices). Description: "A 100% air tight solid bronze sarcophagus, lined with a seamless solid copper deposit casket, taking eight men to lift the lid." The interiors of the caskets were lined with ruched velvet, foam rubber, feathers or wood shavings, according to price.

"What made you take up this work?" I asked the attendant who was obviously gratified by my interest. "Well ma'am," he said, "even in times of depression people have to die, so it was the safest job I could think of." Giving the bronze sarcophagus an affectionate slap, he added: "Some like one kind of casket and some another, but this one's *a real* item."

Next he showed me the preparation room, where the bodies were made ready to receive their friends for the last time. When someone dies in the States, it is the done thing to "call on the body" and perhaps leave a visiting card; sometimes there are even cocktails and refreshments provided.

All the bodies are fully dressed and made up to look life-like. You can wear your old clothes if you like, but a lot of women choose special dresses beforehand, from a selection of clothes made by "The Divine Garment Company." The shoes kept in stock are all size six with sling backs, which makes them adaptable; in any case, unless the doctors make some frightful mistake, nobody is ever likely to walk in them.

Finally, the attendant took me to see some occupied caskets. One contained a war veteran, with the stars and stripes draped over it; another was a young woman who had been killed in a road accident, arranged so that her damaged parts were concealed; a third was a girl who had been a keen tennis player, sitting up cross-legged and holding a racquet. I did sketches of them all.

Chapter fourteen

Stage, Film and Television

MAX ADRIAN *Actor*

He told me he had been learning how to relax properly, which I felt should not be too difficult in his peaceful blue and gold room.

"You lie on your back, lift one leg at a time, and let it drop suddenly," he explained. "Do the same with your arms. Then unhook your jaw — like this." He demonstrated his point. "Now I'll tell you again, to make sure you've got it right."

I probably did have more need of relaxation than most people, but I doubted that I would find time to stop and unhook my jaw, let alone do things with my arms and legs. I was very good at getting myself completely relaxed though, even if only for a few minutes. For example, when I had to wait in the car between sittings, I lay down as flat as possible on the back seat and closed my eyes. If there was time, I might have a short nap. I could go to sleep anywhere at any time; as apparently Napoleon could too.

BERNARD BRADEN *TV personality*

I visited Bernard Braden and his wife Barbara Kelly to do a drawing of their three children. Their home at Shepperton was the house where *Martin Chuzzlewit* was written. The room in which I worked had a wonderful Dickensian atmosphere, and the children were delightful — beautifully brought up and quite unspoilt.

The Bradens were so pleased with the picture that they asked for drawings of themselves as well. Three weeks later I was spending a quiet evening at home watching TV, when my portrait of Bernard Braden was suddenly flashed on the screen to announce his forthcoming show "Bathnight with Braden."

BRIGITTE BARDOT

I was invited to a press conference at the Westbury Hotel, and was told to be there punctually at half-past seven. It turned out that Brigitte Bardot's plane was late, and she would not arrive until 8.15. When she did finally come, she

spent a long while in her room, by which time the press had been waiting for more than two hours. On her entry she was booed by some and cheered by others, but one and all descended on her in a swarm, three of the hotel chairs getting broken in the scrum. She escaped into another room, to which reporters and photographers were admitted a few at a time. A great many of them left, angry and frustrated, without having spoken to her, and when the original room was not quite so crowded, Brigitte Bardot returned to it. I could get nowhere near, so I took off my shoes and stood on one of the unbroken chairs, and from this vantage point did two quick sketches. By the time I had finished, my shoes had disappeared.

NANCY PRICE *actress and author*

Nancy Price answered my request for a sitting with her characteristic courage:

"It is difficult to say when I could keep still for an hour! I think I should have to be occupied…The only possibility is that of my friend doing some book work to keep me quiet and interested enough to forget my wretched body." Her pet parrot sat on her shoulder throughout.

The drawing appeared in the *Daily Telegraph* on the publication of her twenty-fifth book, at the age of eighty.

HARRY SECOMBE *comedian*

Harry Secombe drove his enormous Rolls to my modest home in Sydenham Road and put sixpence in the meter. When my part-time help, Mrs Codling, brought in coffee, she whispered that two people were waiting in his car. I had to insist that "his folks", as he called his mother and father, should join us.

An hour passed, and Mrs. Codling showed her head round the door to say, "I've put another sixpence in the meter for you." When Harry Secombe left. he said "I owe you sixpence," producing half a crown.

"Toss you double or quits," Mrs Codling replied promptly. She lost and refused to take anything from him.

GINGER ROGERS

I had met her at Eileen Joyce's house. At her request, I drew her in her rented flat in Rutland Gate, London, when she was starring in *Mame*. She spent the whole time giving herself a manicure, soaking her hands in soapy water, filing and trimming her nails.

DAME PEGGY ASHCROFT *Actress*

She entertained me first to tea at her Hampstead home, so that I had a chance to study her face and her movements. Tea over, Peggy Ashcroft curled up on the sofa in a restful position, and within an hour the portrait was finished.

For this portrait I won a Gold Medal in 1995 for the best work at the Painters Stainers Company Exhibition.

Dame Peggy Ashcroft

Ginger Rogers

JEAN COCTEAU

At a rehearsal of *Oedipus Rex* at the BBC Studios, I had an opportunity to do portraits of both Stravinsky and Jean Cocteau. The great Frenchman was pleased with my four sketches:

"How quick you have been, and such delightful drawings."

Jean Cocteau

Chapter fifteen
Medicine

During a sitting of Mr Victor Riddell the top consultant at St George's Hospital, he asked if I wanted to sketch or paint an operating theatre. When he assured me it could be arranged easily, I replied, "Yes, please." When I went to the hospital I was put in the charge of one of Mr Riddell's assistants because he had to reserve his energy before an operation by relaxing and resting. I put on a gown, a mask and a cap. First, there was an appendectomy, during which I began to feel funny. But the theatre sister said Mr Riddel wondered if I would like to look closer, and after looking inside the wound I got over my queasiness and never minded anything again. I often went to see Mr Riddell and some of the other surgeons during their operations. He was a thyroid specialist and during one operation he pointed out a cord, saying "If I cut that by mistake, this patient will never be able to talk again." I chose watercolour for my medical paintings because the scene was so colourful: the green and blue of the gowns and caps, the white masks and the red of the blood, with the bright light spotlighting the central area. The resulting paintings, though difficult to sell, were an incredible discipline to paint, and sometimes the surgeons themselves did buy them.

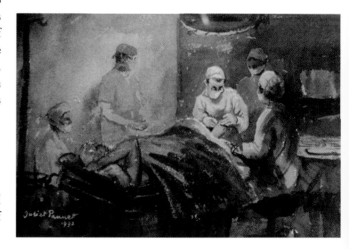

SIR ZACHARY COPE *Eminent surgeon*

"Though I don't think much of myself as a subject, I have a much better opinion of your picture as a work of art, and would like to possess it."

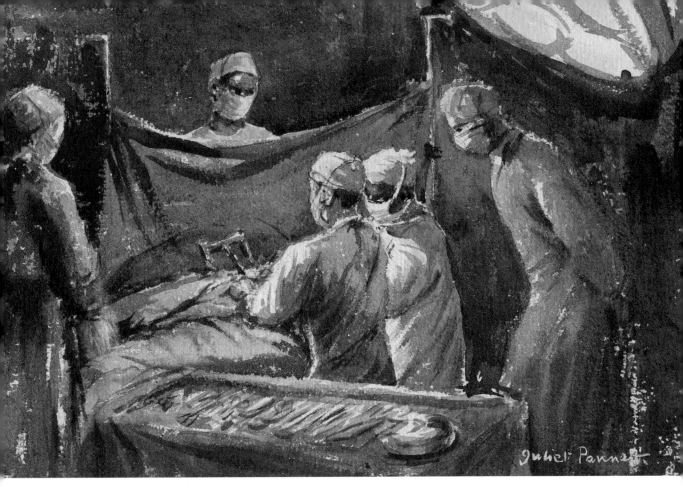

During sittings, he talked about famous doctors and scientists. Living as I did in Sydenham Road, I was naturally interested in the 17th century Doctor Sydenham, after whom the road was called. One of the things he recommended was that, in cases of intestinal trouble "a live kitten be kept continually lying on the naked belly." Sir Zachary and I became great friends and he invited me to go and see him whenever I had an opportunity to do so. For his part, he never missed an exhibition in which I had even one picture on show.

SIR ARTHUR KEITH *President of the Royal College of Surgeons, anthropologist,and former anatomist at the London Hospital*

I much enjoyed meeting this wonderful old man who sat for me at 85 wearing a square crofter's cap of brown velvet. He showed me a bit of jaw of Piltdown man, a famous fake.

ARTHUR DIXON WRIGHT *Another surgeon sitter*
Perils of a portrait painter

This father of the well known TV cook, Clarissa Dixon Wright looked very morose, and I tried in vain to make him smile.

"I *have* made you look severe," I said, glancing up at him hopefully. He was not amused.

"I always do," he replied.

No glimmer of good humour was forthcoming until the very end, when I showed him the drawing and he liked it. Then he smiled.

Ballet Dancers

*You can do pen quicker
than charcoal, so pen is for ballet*

My second favorite subject: such lovely bones, which they arrange comfortably and relaxingly. I first got interested in ballet in the days when I could only afford a 2 shillings seat in the top gallery of the Royal Opera House, Covent Garden. I was so enchanted, that years later I managed to get permission to work at the Royal School of Ballet during rehearsals. I also sketched different ballet companies, like the Kirov and Bolshoi. I watched them and did quick pen sketches. Pen is quicker than charcoal so pen is for ballet. I have always had to do all my work on the spot, and can't work things up afterwards at home Considering that they are continuously in motion, you have to watch closely and wait until they get back into the same position. And they do, they repeat certain movements, and you just have to try to catch those positions. It's not really difficult. I use pens chiefly, good drawing pens. Charcoal is too thick and you can't get the details quickly. With ballet you have to be very very quick, and it's wonderful to try to catch the fleeting moment. If it works, you're very lucky, and if it doesn't, you just tear it out and start another. I saw some of the greatest ballet dancers of the day in the rehearsal rooms. I did several portraits of ballerinas, but never the men, I don't know why.

Chapter sixteen

SVETLANA BERIOSOVA *ballerina*
She talked very little as I drew her on a low chair sewing, quietly absorbed in the dress she was making for a tour on the continent. She was very very beautiful

ANTON DOLIN *choreographer*
Anton Dolin had no time to talk. As I drew him in his dressing room at the Festival Hall after a rehearsal, he was besieged with so many other visitors that his attention was kept fully occupied. He was either being interviewed by reporters, or discussing the engaging of dancers from abroad for the Festival ballet. I sat unobtrusively in a corner, and finished my drawing without saying a word.

KARSAVINA

Karsavina, was once Nijinski's partner in the Diaghilev Ballet. She opened the door herself, wearing a black sweater and skirt, with black slippers on her tiny feet: at the back of her head a cerise ribbon was wound into her white hair. She sat on a small Victorian sofa, and her exquisite bones and natural poise made her one of the best models I had ever had the good fortune to draw. The portrait was commissioned by the *Dancing Times*.

NADIA NERINA

I did Nadia Nerina, in the bedroom of her little mews house. There was no mistaking the fact that it was a ballet dancer's room; even the electric lights were covered in tutus.

MADAME RAMBERT

Another pioneer of the ballet was Madame Rambert. I wrote and asked if I might draw her, and was invited to her steep little house in Camden Hill Gardens. She was still giving classes every morning in spite of her age - she was seventy - and told me that she had turned cartwheels in many a London street. Her head resting on a cushion, Madame Rambert looks the epitome of dignified serenity, but the sparkle in her eye shows the liveliness of the conversation. She talked all the time, reminiscing about her experiences as a dancer, her travels (she had been all over the world, including the Far East), and her personal habits.

"I have never gone in for make-up, or even a night cream," she said. "The only thing I ever use is a little lipstick, and I get that at Woolworth's".

CLOVER ROOPE

"The head and shoulders portrait in oils of a pupil at the Royal School of Ballet, Clover Roope - a pert, cool, brown-haired girl in a green dress - is, as a character study, an absolute knockout" wrote one reporter. "For me, it simply stole the entire show". Her father was Mr. Hughes' partner at Rose Hill when Rick was on the staff. I also did an oil of her untying the ribbon of her ballet shoes, as well as a charcoal drawing.

PHYLLIS BEDELLS

I did a portrait in 1956 of the ex-ballerina Phyllis Bedells, who had taught Dame Margot Fonteyn and Moira Shearer. It was presented to her at a party given by three hundred of her past and present pupils, to celebrate the fiftieth anniversary of her first appearance on the stage at the age of thirteen.

Chapter seventeen

THE OXFORD AND CAMBRIDGE UNIVERSITY CREWS I

Sports

In my teens I was mad about sportsmen and drew many in action

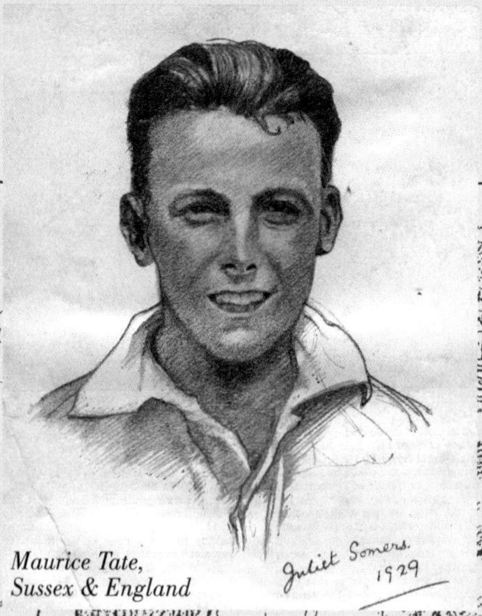
Juliet Somers.
1929

Maurice Tate, Sussex & England

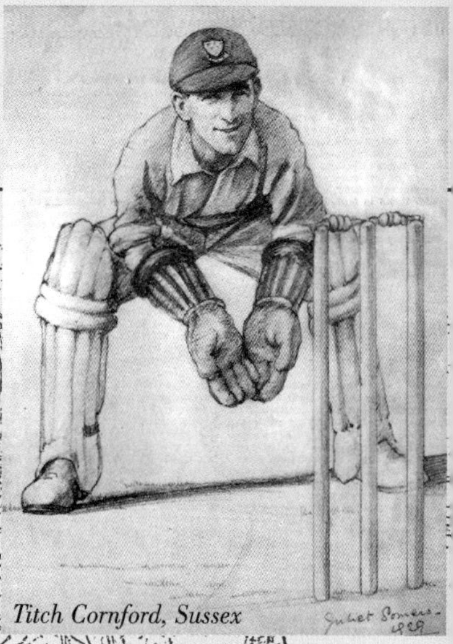
Juliet Somers
1929

Titch Cornford, Sussex

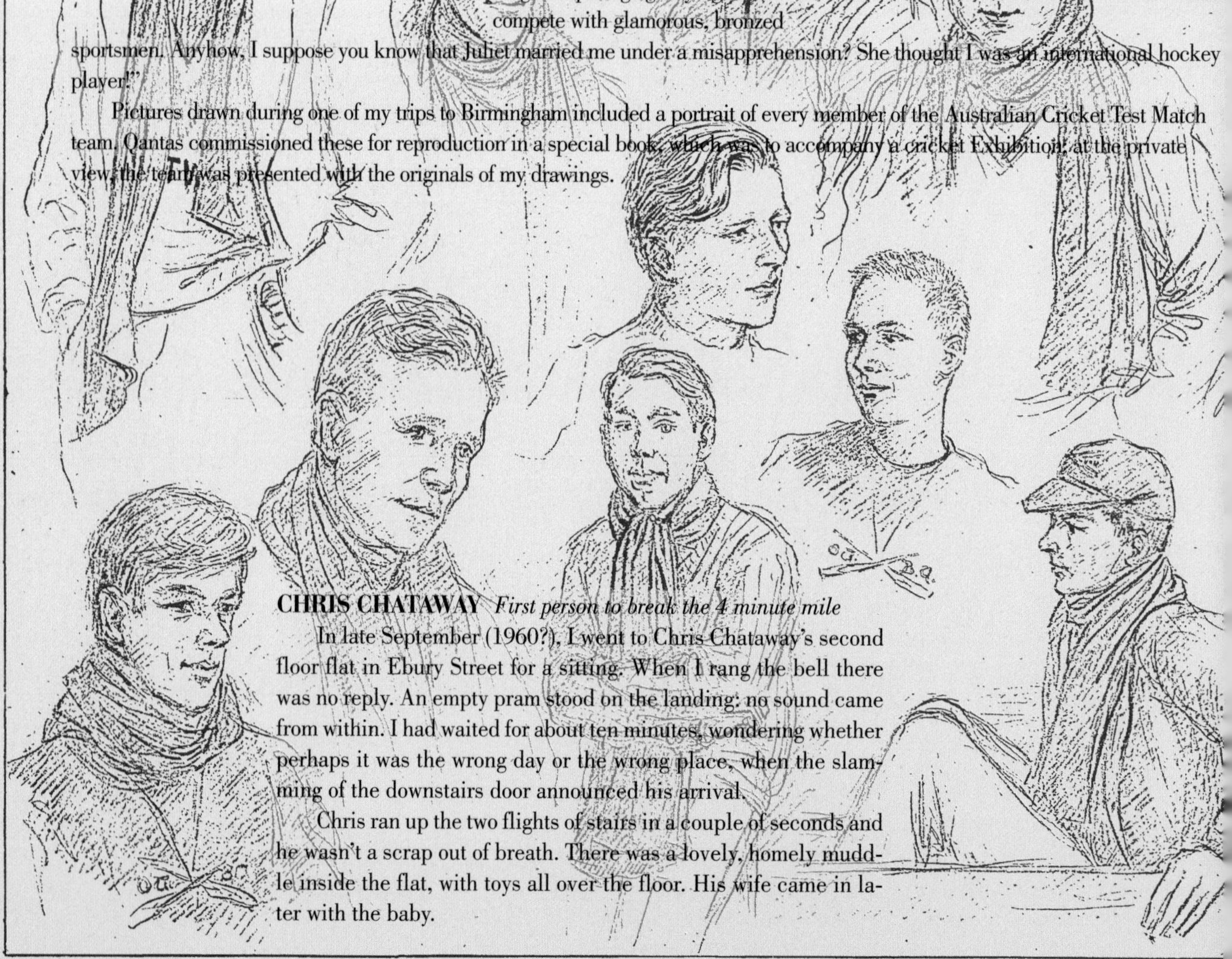

AUSTRALIAN CRICKET TEST MATCH TEAM

"Weren't you jealous of all those handsome cricketers?" Rick was once asked:

He laughed and said: "I gave up long ago trying to compete with glamorous, bronzed sportsmen. Anyhow, I suppose you know that Juliet married me under a misapprehension? She thought I was an international hockey player!"

Pictures drawn during one of my trips to Birmingham included a portrait of every member of the Australian Cricket Test Match team. Qantas commissioned these for reproduction in a special book, which was to accompany a cricket Exhibition; at the private view, the team was presented with the originals of my drawings.

CHRIS CHATAWAY *First person to break the 4 minute mile*

In late September (1960?), I went to Chris Chataway's second floor flat in Ebury Street for a sitting. When I rang the bell there was no reply. An empty pram stood on the landing: no sound came from within. I had waited for about ten minutes, wondering whether perhaps it was the wrong day or the wrong place, when the slamming of the downstairs door announced his arrival.

Chris ran up the two flights of stairs in a couple of seconds and he wasn't a scrap out of breath. There was a lovely, homely muddle inside the flat, with toys all over the floor. His wife came in later with the baby.

THE OXFORD CREW. *TOP ROW, LEFT TO RIGHT:* T. W. TENNANT (PRESIDENT), ETON AND NEW COLLEGE; P. A. V. ROFF, MELBOURNE UNIV. AND NEW COLLEGE; R. A. MORTO BRYANSTON AND KEBLE; D. D. S. SKAILES, ETON AND KEBLE. *CENTRE ROW:* M. Q. MORLAND, RADLEY AND LINCOLN; S. R. MORRIS, RADLEY AND ST. EDMUND HALL. *BOTTOM ROW:* R ETON AND KEBLE; D. C. SPENCER, YALE UNIVERSITY AND CHRIST CHURCH; N. V. BEVAN, SHREWSBURY AND BALLIOL; C. M. STRONG, SHREWSBURY AND KEBLE.

(Drawings b

...tsman Col. Rodney King

WRESTLERS

I particularly enjoyed drawing some wrestlers at a match in Croydon.

Arthur Gilligan, Sussex & England Captain

GOLF: J H TAYLOR

The Times sent me down to Devon to do a portrait of J.H. Taylor, the "Grand Old Man of Golf", just before his ninetieth birthday. Five times he had won the Open Golf Championship, the first time being at Sandwich in 1894, and I listened eagerly to his account of how he rose to the heights from being a caddy at sixpence a round. He showed me a silver salver covered with signatures, which he had just received from the Royal and Ancient.

"My outlook over the links is the finest view in Christendom," he told me proudly. "You will notice that I never use the word "course", I dislike it intensely."

...SEX COUNTY CRICKETERS

...six cricketers for the Sussex County ...azine, including Maurice Tate when he ...young man (in 1929), Pat Cornford the ...t-keeper, Duleep Sinhji the Indian ...eter (an interesting face), and E H Bowley ...Warner, President of the M.C.C. - a ...fully important cricketer who edited The ...keter. commissioned a ...s of portraits, including ...Hammond. ...s paid about £2 each ...y fares.

TENNIS

After weeks of musicians, I visited a pre-Wimbledon tournament to collect a page of tennis personalities. Along with the celebrities, including Christine Truman and Fred Perry, I did a sketch labelled "The Youngest Spectator" - the charming back view of a baby girl in a sundress.

Juliet Pannett
March - 19...

...annett, S.G.A.)

Chapter eighteen

Pound House, Angmering

Lectures, two cities and Rick's sad death

I gave over 100 lectures and quite a few demonstrations in my time. Subjects varied between my trips (Round the World with a Sketch Book, Africa, Israel, and Portraits and Personalities). I did a step-by-step television film showing how I paint, and have written "How To" articles for a number of art magazines. In my most successful lectures I demonstrated my techniques in front of the audience. I wasn't frightened because I had to concentrate so hard.

At the Women's Press Club I met the head of the P&O Line who invited me to give lessons on their cruise ships. It was marvelous as Rick came with me and this made our holidays for twelve successive years. On one cruise I had a student called Van Gogh. When I asked him if he was related to Vincent, he replied, "My uncle." He looked rather like the famous artist and it was amusing doing his portrait. We remained friends and he sent me his book "Vincent Van Gogh in England."

In 1965 Rick retired from teaching French and Geography at Coombe Hill House, where his salary was still £300 per year. Now I decided to secretly take driving lessons, though Rick had never learnt to drive (having had a batman in the Army), and had counselled me against driving as I was "too scatty and would have an accident". Driving meant I would be able to get on with my work. I passed the test first time around to my surprise. Rick was equally surprised but he didn't mind. I bought a second-hand car, and then we bought, with a little windfall inheritance, Pound House in Angmering Village, West Sussex, near Hove where I was born. While the garden had been kept in perfect shape, the XVII Century farmhouse needed a lot of work, including a new floor in what would become my studio. Rick adored working in the garden and we grew ecological vegetables to supply our table. Daughter Lizzie was at nearby Brighton Art School as I had been, and son Denis was working at De Beers.

My sister Phoebe, quite late in life, started giving classes in landscape painting of rural Sussex. She soon had too many students and asked Denis and me to join her. So began 20 years of teaching. Phoebe, Denis and I met some very interesting people who became life-long friends.

Though I don't often paint landscapes, when I do one I use viridian green mixed with a touch with raw umber to cool it down, or occasionally oxide of chromium, another green that is good for trees.

By the mid-sixties, two cities had adopted me: Coventry where I did commissioned drawings from the new cathedral to the youth club, and Birmingham where I did a similar series. Thus began my long association, cultural, architectural and commercial with the two cities.

At 80 years old I was painting better than ever before - I learned to rest after lunch and go to bed early and eat sensibly. Painting provides not only physical exercise but also a unique blending of mind, body and heart on the same wavelength. After a heart attack

My sister Phoebe

in 1987 I was told that I must choose between my work and my social life - I chose my work, and even refused a dinner invitation to meet a High Court Judge, because I was painting an important portrait at the time, although legal portraits are my preferred subjects.

In 1930, when I was 19, I painted a man of 98 who had fought in the Crimean war — he had his medals pinned to his night shirt to prove it, and medals became one of my specialties over the subsequent half century of work. When I painted General Sir John Wilsey in 1997-98 my eyesight was so bad that I asked Denis to help me with the medals. After that I never did another oil portrait.

Dr. Vincent Van Gogh

In 1980 Rick died after a bout with lung cancer. He had been a heavy smoker and suffered terribly. After his death I didn't take any more cruise holidays, so I remained at Pound House. It was a horrid time; I was so sad that the only way I could grapple with it was to plunge into my work.

A few years later Denis, Lizzie and I were asked to do a show in Japan. We also visited China, but travelled so much we didn't really have time to paint. As a threesome we also visited Egypt, and later Morocco where we stayed with my niece Vanessa and her husband Freck (later the American Ambassador to Morocco), and it was there that I lost my travel sketch books.

I believe artists live longer because of this continued interest in painting and the fact that they do not retire. Artists are very lucky. Their work is their hobby, and it goes on for life.

Factories

I LOVED DOING WATERCOLOURS OF FACTORIES, particularly the machinery with people working. At the Eagle Iron Works on the Oxford Canal I drew the illustrations for their Centenary Book. This reminds me of the Bingo Hall I sketched for the ILN. It was a good picture but I was particularly struck by the obvious absence of class boundaries, which delighted me. As an artist I have been at ease in all *milieus*.

Chapter nineteen

Israel

"Why don't you see if one of your papers would like some drawings of our concerts in Israel, and get them to send you along too?" a member of the London Symphony Orchestra asked me, during the coffee break at a rehearsal. *The Times* said maybe, but yes to drawings of the acting troupe, the Habimah Players of Tel Aviv. The *Daily Telegraph* and the *ILN* were also interested, so I visited El Al Airlines. Their Public Relations Officer did not hesitate to offer me a return ticket, an exhibition in Bond Street, and — after a 20 minute telephone conversation in Hebrew — he announced: "You will be a guest of the Government, with car and driver for two weeks, so you can see something of our country."

In January 1961, after an eight-hour flight, re-fuelling at Paris and Rome, I landed at Lod airport. Jacob Levy, my Government guide, drove me through the Judaean Hills to Jerusalem, and the King David Hotel. I awoke at 5 a.m. to the sound of bells, and watched the blue and gold of early dawn gradually change to pure gold above the cypress trees and domed, biblical buildings.

The reply was negative when the Tourist Corporation rang up the Prime Minister's office. Mr Ben-Gurion was too busy. This was disappointing since he was my first request, but I set to work immediately in the picturesque orthodox Jewish district of Mea Shearim. There were old men with side curls and long black coats. Boys in black stockings and round hats over their long hair, and women with heads covered by a scarf or a wig; no one is allowed to see an orthodox Jewish woman's hair except her husband.

Then Jacob Levy, my charming guide, took me to the Hebrew University, where I saw the Dead Sea Scrolls housed in the Shrine of the Book. My charcoal portrait of Professor Yigael Yadin, soldier and archaeologist, now hangs in the Yadin Institute of Archaeology, thanks to my son-in-law, Anthony Fagin, who worked at Masada under Yadin. Jacob drove me to King Herod's family tomb, which was closed by a huge rolling stone. It brought to mind the words of St Mark's gospel about another tomb: "And they said among themselves, who shall roll us away the stone from the door of the sepulchre? And when they looked, they saw that the stone was rolled away: for it was very great."

I did some drawings of the tomb, the walls of the old city and the Tower of David. In the afternoon on the Jordanian border, I sketched Bethlehem and the Garden of Gethsemane in the distance. I did another of armed soldiers on a rooftop just beyond the barbed wire. After dinner Jacob took me to a nightclub; he was not only a first-class driver and interpreter, but a good dancer.

The barking of dogs disturbed my sleep that night, so I breakfasted in bed, doing a sketch of the Mount of Olives through my window. I was almost late for my first appointment of the day, a sitting with Foreign Minister Golda Meir.

After visiting John the Baptist's birthplace I met a couple who talked of nothing but their son Razi, killed two years previously, at age eighteen. They showed me "his" room, where the clothes and books were all neatly arranged and the bed turned down, as if he were expected back at any time. His mother told me her husband even wrote a letter to Razi every day. Very sad.

Walls of the old City, Jerusalem.

Prof. Yigael Yadin

The road to Tel Aviv ran through a rocky gorge called the Road of Courage, littered with wrecks of armoured vehicles destroyed by Arab gunfire from the craggy hills on either side of the road. In Beersheba I sketched Bedouin workers in the fields, I immediately felt back in the days of the Old Testament. Much of Israel was still stone and dust, and it was on this unpromising landscape that the Jews were imposing their own distinctive pattern of life. In other countries money is of great importance to the Jews, but in Israel I did not notice this preoccupation. In 1961 the Israelis had their security and their land, and felt relaxed.

In Sodom, the lowest inhabited place in the world — 1290 feet below sea level — I sketched the rock formation known as "Lot's Wife" and some views of the weird-looking Mountains of the Moon. Bathing in the Dead Sea was quite an experience: full of mineral salts so that no fish can live in it. I was warned not to try to swim, for fear of splashing the too potent water into my eyes. It was so buoyant that it was almost syrupy, and one couldn't sink. I just sat on the water as if I was in an armchair, and paddled gently with my hands. After a while I began to tingle all over, so I came out and got into a hot sulphur spring, after which I felt wonderful. I passed the kibbutz of which Ben-Gurion was a member, and this renewed my disappointment at not being able to draw him. The farmers of the kibbutzim collective farms enjoy a kind of ideal communism where all is shared for the good of the whole. Nobody owns property or receives pay other than pocket money, but everyone has free food and clothing. Children are cared for, and profits are ploughed back into the farms.

At 7 a.m. I was at the camel market in Beersheba, and saw the files of camels slowly approaching across the desert, as they must have done for hundreds of years. I revelled in the colourful sight, and did some quick sketches of the traders at their heated bargaining. Jacob translated snatches of conversation for me. "How much do you ask for that camel?"

"£100."

"£100! For such a small one?"

"Ah, but it will grow."

After breakfast we left for the Nabatean city of Avdat, a long drive through desert and scrub and prickly pears. I sketched the two thousand-year-old ruins at Avdat. From the Red Sea port of Eilat, a new town of up-to-date houses, all with air-conditioning and refrigerators, we drove to King Solomon's copper mines, where I painted an uncanny landscape of pink, turquoise, purple and yellow mountains.

Back in Tel Aviv, Jacob took me to a Bohemian café to draw the artists and poets who congregated there. We also went to the museum to see the "Mona Lisa of glass," a blue Phoenician vase thought to be the finest piece of craftsmanship in the world. Its last owner had been an elderly Jew in America, whose sons constantly urged him to sell the masterpiece for a large sum of money. At last the sons prevailed upon their father to part with his cherished possession, and the vase changed hands. The next day the old man, unable to live without his treasure, threw himself out of the window. After carrying out my commission for *The Times* by drawing the Habimah Players, I went to Caesarea, and Haifa. From my hotel on Mount Carmel I had a beautiful night view of the illuminated town. For lunch in Acre, Jacob took me to a restaurant full of handsome Arabs, and I was so busy drawing them that I could hardly eat.

The next day's drive took us through isolated villages, in which time seemed to stand still, to Nazareth, where I did one of my best

watercolours. It was far less spoilt than I expected. In fact it seemed much the same as Jesus must have known it in his youth. In Israel, every corner contains a ghost from the past. In Tiberias, 206 metres below sea level, I stayed at the Galei Kinnereth hotel, where I learned that Ben-Gurion was also staying: his first holiday in six years. Mrs Ben-Gurion came down for dinner, and from her I got permission to draw the Prime Minister the next morning, while he was having breakfast.

Delighted by this unexpected fulfilment of my hopes, I went off with Jacob to a nightclub to see Danny Kaye. He said the Archbishop of Canterbury had resigned and the Archbishop of York was to take his place. I didn't believe him. "How long have you been away then?" Danny Kaye asked. "It's absolutely true. And if the Archbishop of York doesn't accept, they're going to choose a rabbi as Archbishop of Canterbury, and *then* we'll get into Sunningdale." He grinned at me and asked my name. "Juliet? Oh, I can't possibly talk to you like this then, I ought to be up here." He jumped on to a chair. "No, that's wrong. It's you who ought to be up on the balcony, and me down below." Later in more serious mood he told me he spent all his holidays in Israel when possible and very much admired the spirit there. "I want you to tell people in England about it," he said. " I want you to say you met me here in a remote little town, and we talked about two thousand years of history, when a great deal of blood was shed, and about the wonderful spirit of the new Israel." We talked for a long time, and then Danny Kaye affectionately kissed me goodnight and disappeared. Needless to say, I hadn't missed the opportunity of doing a portrait of him, but in the flickering candlelight I couldn't make it a very good likeness.

I was down early the next morning, had my breakfast quickly and prepared my materials. Shortly afterwards Ben-Gurion came in and sat down with his wife at their table. I set to work. The Prime Minister had been told beforehand that I was going to do a portrait of him, but he had obviously forgotten about it. Suddenly he looked up and saw me busy drawing at the next table; with a smile he laid down his knife and fork, took a comb from his pocket and ran it through his magnificent white hair. The drawing turned out to be one of my biggest successes. When Ben-Gurion had finished his breakfast, I was presented to him. I had just completed a second drawing, and he signed them both. For my last outing, Jacob took me to paint the Italian Church of the Beatitudes, said to be on the exact spot where Jesus preached the Sermon on the Mount. We had lunch in the quiet peace of a convent.

As soon as I got back to London, I began taking my pictures to editors. The *ILN*, *The Times* and the *Daily Telegraph* published a great many of them and the editor of *Housewife* accepted a drawing of a girl from the Israeli Air Force. This girl had thumbed a lift on the road to Beersheba, little thinking that the ride would ultimately bring her to London; for when El Al saw the portrait in *Housewife*, they flew her over especially for my Israel Exhibition. There were many appreciative notices after the Israel trip, but the one that pleased me most was that of the *Jerusalem Post*. In his final summing up, the reporter wrote: "Although Juliet Pannett is not Jewish, the feel of the country is very obvious in her work. The Bible helped a good deal here, and for the rest, she is a sensitive artist with skill and flair."

Chapter twenty

House of Commons, House of Lords

SIR WINSTON CHURCHILL

Whilst working for the *Illustrated London News* I had several chances to sketch him from my seat in the Press Gallery (number 42) of the House of Commons.

On his last day in parliament, I watched from my Press Gallery seat and it was very moving. As he got up to go, walking very slowly on a cane, I was able to do a quick sketch. I was proud of it, because I think I caught him with a very few strokes at this emotional moment.

I subsequently got permission, along with two or three other artists, to portray his lying in state in Westminster Hall. I sat all day at a corner of the stairs to draw in charcoal. The Hall is marvellous with its thousand year old beams and sunlight filtering through the high windows.

Four military officers stood at attention with their heads bowed and their hands on their swords night and day,

Lying in State of Sir Winston Churchill. Drawn in Westminster Hall 29th January 1965.

From "The Last Diaries - In and Out of the Wilderness" by Alan Clark
Tuesday 20 October 1998
"Shaun showed me two little pencil sketches, done by a woman, of Winston on his very last day (in the Commons). The last one of him making his way out of the Chamber with his stick, achingly moving."

68

Four Suffragettes

Dame K. Courtney

A. M. Pierotti

Lilian Lenton

Grace Rose

SIR ALEC DOUGLAS-HOME *Prime Minister*

On 1st March 1964 I rang the bell of No. 10 Downing Street. The door was opened immediately by two footmen, and I was shown into a small sitting room. There, the Prime Minister's private secretary met me and conducted me to the Boudoir. It had gold cornices, old gold brocade on the sofas, armchairs and window seats, and a beautiful pink and gold carpet. I was still admiring the carpet when, punctually at half past nine, Sir Alec came in and shook hands.

"What do you want me to do?" he asked.

"Will you have to work?"

"No, I'll do anything you like until ten o'clock."

"How lovely. It's much more difficult to do a portrait while people are reading, as it means they're looking down, and I can't get the eyes properly." I looked round the room, and added: "Could we have this curtain drawn, please? I like to have a single source of light if possible, and the north light from the other window would be best."

"Certainly." He drew the curtain. "Where shall I look? Straight at you?"

"*Yes, please.*"

We settled down, and I began to draw. While I was working on the portrait, we chatted about my recent visit to Scotland.

"You must have enjoyed drawing Compton Mackenzie," Sir Alec said. "And Lord Lyon too. By the way, I suppose I shouldn't tell you at this late stage, but I've got the biggest head in London. I can hardly ever get a hat to fit me."

At ten o'clock, two secretaries came to fetch him for a Cabinet meeting. Before leaving the room, he took a look at the portrait and said to them:

" I think it's very good, don't you?" They both agreed.

A week later I had a second sitting. This time Sir Alec had a pile of letters to sign while he sat for me.

"My name used to be one of the shortest and now it's one of the longest," he remarked. "I get quite tired of writing it."

In half an hour the portrait was finished, and he went to ask Lady Home and his son to come and see it. Lady Home gave her approval and said she would like to have a photograph of it. Sir Alec asked when the drawing would be published in the *Illustrated London News*.

"I'm afraid I can't tell you exactly," I said, "but it will be just before the election."

He laughed. At that time he was the only person who knew for certain when that would be.

My visits to No. 10 were two of the most enjoyable sittings I ever had. The Prime Minister had great personal charm, and an air of integrity about him. Everything he did he obviously tried to do to the best of his ability — even sitting for me.

Labour Party

LORD ATTLEE *Prime Minister*

I had two sittings with Clement Attlee in his Temple flat. At the first sitting he was chatty, but by the second he was evidently not well. A gentle, quiet man.

HAROLD WILSON *Prime Minister*

I had sent him a drawing I made during one of his television appearances and asked for a sitting. He replied to the effect that he was quite willing to sit for me, but was very pressed for time. At last, after much telephoning and arranging and re-arranging of dates, a time was fixed for the sitting; Mr Wilson said he could give me just a quarter of an hour to finish the drawing.

"This is Mrs Pannett of the *Illustrated London News*," he introduced me to another MP. "She did such a flattering drawing of me from T.V. that it seems a pity to let her spoil it by coming to see the original."

He sent me to get some coffee in the canteen before I had finished while he had a private talk, and then gave me a further three-quarters of an hour while he talked to Mr Wedgwood Benn.

Lord Carrington

Lord Atlee

Harold Wilson

Liberal Party

JO GRIMOND *Leader of the Liberal Party*

While I was still in the throes of drawing eminent Jews, the *ILN* arranged this sitting. I was given precisely half an hour, from 9.30 to 10.00 a.m., in his room at the House of Commons, during which he dictated letters, interviewed people and had several telephone calls. On the first stroke of ten o'clock he stood up and indicated that the sitting was at an end. This appeared in the 10th October 1964 *ILN* with his view "This would be a dull election indeed if left to Conservatives and Labour. Both shy away from new ideas like frightened deer, fearful of anything that might cost them one marginal vote."

Jeremy Thorpe

Jo Grimmond

Conservative Party

Reginald Maudling

REGINALD MAUDLING *Chancellor of the Exchequer*
I renewed my Budget acquaintance with Mr Maudling, when he gave me a private sitting in his office at the Treasury to begin a portrait. The appointment was for four o'clock, and Mrs Codling, my househelp, worked herself into quite a state for fear that I might arrive late.
"Have you got everything?" she asked anxiously.
All was in order, and the Chancellor of the Exchequer was not kept waiting.

EDWARD HEATH *Prime Minister*
Lizzie and I went to tea with him at the Foreign Office. I was so hoarse that I could scarcely utter a word. I was supposed to have a sitting with him but fortunately he was tired too and it was postponed. For some unexplained reason, we had taken Phoebe's pet mouse Beatrix with us. It was such a hot day that we didn't like to leave Beatrix to stew in the car, so we took her in with us. At the door we met Sir Alec Douglas-Home, and Lizzie tried in confusion to conceal Beatrix behind her back!

RT. Hon. R. A. Butler

The long-postponed sitting with Mr. Heath took place on September 18th.
"Do you mind if I read?" he asked when I arrived.
I couldn't very well say that I did mind, although reading meant looking down all the time — people have a more animated expression if they talk. He only gave me half an hour for the first sitting, and I had to ask him several times to raise his head so that I could do his eyes. Considering that he was perusing official papers all through the sitting, his comment at the end was not surprising:
"It's very like me, but I look a bit stuffy, don't I?"

Michael Heseltine

LADY THATCHER
Prime Minister
Portrait carried out while Margaret Thatcher talked to members of the Women's Press Club after a dinner given in her honour. This was done before she was Prime Minster, before she had her teeth fixed, and before anybody realized what a powerful force she would become.

Chapter twentyone

Literary Figures & Explorers

SIR WILFRED THESIGER *Explorer and writer*
29 May 1996

"Where do you want me?" "In the green wing chair, please." Making sure he was comfortable, and that the light was right for me to draw, I started work under his portrait by Anthony Devas; done when Thesiger was 35; it is on the cover of his autobiography *The Life of My Choice*. The other portrait was a pencil drawing done at Maralal by Laputa, a member of his extended Kenya "family." How his face had changed: how full of character now! I had been hoping to do his portrait for a long time. The light was harsh for me, and Sir Wildred offered me his tweed cap. I thought as I drew, perhaps this cap had accompanied him on some of his difficult and famous travels. My charcoal scratched away, and below the wind moaned. "You always hear the wind up here," he mused, and one couldn't help thinking of real winds – of desert, marsh and mountain - that he must have heard during his travels.

He brightened talking about an imminent visit to Ethiopia – his first since Hailie Selassie's death. His eighty-sixth birthday would be celebrated in the country of the noblest man he had

ever met. I told him of my chance meeting with the Emperor.

I also spoke of Sir John Glubb –

Glubb Pasha – and Lord Auchinlech, whose portraits I had done, and whom he had known well..

All around us in neat piles were stacks of papers and books. He negotiated these effortlessly, though he could hardly see. There was a picture of a beautiful woman; also an ornate ceremonial sword in a gold jewel-encrusted scabbard, and amber beads. "I had two Tiepolos which I sold to finance houses in Maralal for my family." Sir Wilfred stopped silent, then said "They're all dead now." He talked of his Danakil Dairies and the economy of style he evolved to write them. His most favourite book was Arabian Sands because his happiest days had been spent among the Bedu in the Empty Quarter. He railed against the internal combustion engine – the motorcar – which was killing the traditional way of life of tribal societies everywhere.

He wanted to use my portrait for his new official biography and suggested it should hang in Magdalen College."

WALTER DE LA MARE
Author and poet

This portrait was a strange commission. He had died a month or two previously, and his son Colin wanted me to do a portrait from a death mask. It was a difficult proposition, with nothing to work on but the death mask and a few photographs, but Colin pronounced it an excellent likeness of his father.

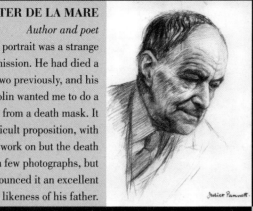

Evelyn Waugh, Author

G.B. Stern, Author

Jeremy Rundall, Author

W.H. Auden, Poet

Carolyn Oxton, Explorer

Bertrand Russell, Philosopher

J. Robertson Scott, Publisher

Lady Naomi Mitchison, Novelist-Poet

Compton Mackenzie, Novelist

Sir Charles Petrie

Dame Edith Sitwell, Author

Lord Shakleton, Explorer

CHRISTOPHER FRY
Playwright

He has such an intelligent face — a joy to draw.

He is a neighbour and became a good friend. I did three portraits of him.

Sir Laurens van der Post

SIR LAURENS VAN DER POST *Explorer and writer*
30th May 1996

The very next day I drew another famous explorer. As I waited to be let in, a confused old lady waited too with a female carer. Her blue eyes were rimmed with pink and she was quite terrified and then absurdly happy. Lady van der Post came up in the lift with me.

On the landing Sir Laurens' first words were: "Oh, my little girl, my sweet darling, you're back from your walk. Go with Mina and have some tea, I'll go upstairs with our visitors and see you soon."

Having thus satisfied himself on his wife's well-being, he welcomed us with great courtesy and led the way up a spiral staircase to a glass-walled room at the top of the flat. I posed him away from the glare of the afternoon sun. "Now this is to be a colour portrait" he asked, "because I can easily take this sweater off?" I told him to keep it on as I could change the colour if necessary. "Now my dear, please don't feel any time pressure at all. I have nothing else to do this afternoon."

He said he tended to reserve the mornings for writing. When I asked what he was writing now he said:"I've no idea, none at all. You see I never really know, but particularly with this book. This is what my publishers think it's going to be about." He handed us a paper about his war experiences in Java, with a philosophical and spiritual dimension.

Did he follow a strict writing regime? "Oh, yes, if you're self-employed, as I've been all my life – and as I assume you are, my dear - it's the only way."

"That's my favourite campsite," he indicated a photograph by David Coulson of a baobab tree in infinite space. We discovered later he had taken the Prince of Wales there, and given him the same photograph which is now in the study at Highgrove.

In his book *The Lost World of the Kalahari* he spoke of the bushmen explaining to him how the stars crackle. He spoke of his "long dialogue," when out in the desert, with the Japanese Comet. And his being the first white man he believed, to cross the Okavango Swamp in Botswana in a dug-out canoe. "Now it is a tourist playground with lodges, power boats, aircraft landing strips. If we're serious about conservation we have to control the greatest predator of all." Us.

When I asked him if he'd like to see my portrait of him he seemed genuinely disinterested. "I'm sure its very good, my dear. I know that you're a famous artist. And you seem to have done it so quickly. But I wouldn't know what I look like." I proferred him my mirror to look at my drawing in reverse, but he couldn't get the hang of it. He signed both my portrait, and one of his books. "Let's hope that the next time we meet, I shall be on a maximum of only one of these sticks."

S.P.B. Mais *Author. 1971.*

Unfortunately he was in one of his gruff moods and said " Sit there, damn you, and have a drink. I can't spare you more than five minutes." However, he spent an hour and a half with us and commissioned me to draw him, his wife and daughter.

S.P.B. Mais

I always loved music, although I had not been to many concerts. I decided I would try to paint the musicians during rehearsals at the BBC Studios in Maida Vale. It was particularly interesting seeing the artists getting ready to play. I became known for my portraits of musicians in action, and they were my most favourite subjects. I've been lucky enough to portray such famous people as Benjamin Britten, Stravinsky and Shostakovich. Also Duke Ellington and Louis Armstrong...

Chapter twentytwo

SIR ADRIAN BOULT CONDUCTING A REHEARSAL OF THE LONDON PHILHARMONIC ORCHESTRA AT THE ROYAL FESTIVAL HALL.

MUSICIANS The four Knights of the Baton

SIR JOHN BARBIROLLI *Conductor*

My first portrait of Sir John was when I sat in a lighting box while he was conducting at the Civic Hall in Croydon. I did many portraits of this wonderful man, and one of them I consider my best. He had the most beautiful hands, with thumbs that went right back – a sign of generosity they say.

My friend in the Hallé orchestra told me that Sir John had only one meal a day, and preferred to cook it himself. When the orchestra was in Rhodesia, he had a beautiful room at the best hotel in Salisbury, but said he wanted one with a cooker. They could produce no such room, so he had to move to a smaller hotel.

Another time Barbirolli was conducting the London Philharmonic Orchestra in Rossini's *Siege of Corinth*, and one of the second fiddles was not quite up to standard. Sir John remarked on it afterwards to Sir Adrian Boult, who replied:

"Oh, So-and-So, he's an awfully good chap. His father's a cricket Blue, and his uncle's a rowing Blue. Oh, a very good chap indeed."

"Well," said Sir John, "he isn't a Rossini Blue."

During one of his sittings he talked about his mother's 90th birthday party, when she cooked for the whole family and then turfed them all out at one o'clock, after a last drink.

AT THE B.B.C. MAIDA VALE STUDIOS: SIR THOMAS BEECHAM REHEARSING THE B.B.C. SYMPHONY ORCHESTRA FOR THE OPENING OF THIS SEASON
KNIGHTS OF THE BATON: AN ARTIST'S IMPRESSIONS OF FAMOUS CONDUCTORS AT REHEARSAL IN LONDON.

SIR THOMAS BEECHAM *Conductor*

I drew Sir Thomas at rehearsal in the Festival Hall, and although I had previously obtained his permission, he had forgotten about it. Half way through the rehearsal he turned to his manager and shouted:

"WHO is this lady?"

"An artist. You said she could do a drawing of you," his manager reminded him.

"A drawing of my back?" Then, turning to me and striking a pose with his baton: "And does the lady require a special POSTURE?"

He continued with the rehearsal until he flung down his baton, remarking in disgust to the orchestra:

"This is supposed to be a minuet, not rock and roll."

SIR MALCOLM SARGENT
Conductor

I showed my portrait of Rick in the Exhibition of the Royal Society of Portrait Painters, and at the *soirée* I met Sir Malcolm Sargent. He gave me permission to draw him at rehearsals, and again I made friends with some of the orchestra who told me this story. A lunch party was given by Sir Malcolm in the private room of a London Club, famous for its Zoffany portraits. Suddenly an American, who was showing some friends round the club, threw open the door, announcing:

"And these are the Zoffanies."

Sir Malcolm rose at once, bowed and said:

"Malcolm Zoffany," and his guests rose one by one and said "John Zoffany," "James Zoffany" etc.

ONE OF THE LEADING CONDUCTORS OF TO-DAY: SIR MALCOLM SARGENT—A RECENT PORTRAIT SKETCH.
Sir Malcolm Sargent, who is perhaps the best-known of English orchestral conductors, was born in 1895 and

REHEARSING THE B.B.C. SYMPHONY ORCHESTRA : SIR MALCOLM SARGENT, WHO CONTINUES AS THEIR CHIEF CONDUCTOR UNTIL NEXT AUTUMN.

SIR ADRIAN BOULT *Conductor*

I found Sir Adrian very easy and friendly, and a man of simple tastes. Once I met him riding in the tube, and on another occasion saw him enjoying an ice cream cone. At rehearsals he always had coffee with the rest of the orchestra.

BASIL CAMERON *Conductor*

At the very beginning of my portrait career I boldly asked Basil Cameron if he would sit for me because I was eager to do a portrait of a conductor. He said "Yes, but my flat is too small for a sitting." I replied, "I'm afraid I live in Croydon" but he said "Oh that's all right I can get the train down there." I asked, "Would you be kind enough to stay to lunch?" to which he replied, "Are you a good cook?" So I said I'd do my best and he came, and was absolutely charming. A cutting from the *Daily Telegraph*, in which the portrait was published, said: "In this drawing Juliet Pannett has caught with singular fidelity the fey Celtic side of Basil Cameron's temperament."

CLIFFORD CURZON
Pianist

My favourite pianist. I did him several times at various concert rehearsals. Once I did a big watercolour of him in action, which took two days.

The first day I concentrated on getting the head right. Luckily, he was playing Mozart, so he had a lovely, sweet expression on his face — very gentle, loving.

The next day, he was playing the Rachmaninoff No. 2 and looking very grim. The muscles on his neck were standing out, his hands were going up and down the piano, and he was playing very loudly. Despite this, I concentrated on the hands, because that's important if you're doing a pianist.

JULIUS HARRISON *Conductor*

"It gave my daughter and me much pleasure, meeting you by chance in front of your splendid drawings of my old composer friends and colleagues," he wrote after we had met at Festival Hall at a show of original manuscripts by 20th century British composers (to which I sent some portraits). "And it will give me equal pleasure to sit for you…I would have liked to have looked at your drawings longer, they impress me so much for their faithfulness and that faculty of seeing under the skin."

At my first visit, Julius Harrison played a recording of his Mass in C, written for his other daughter who had recently died, and at the second sitting I asked him to play it again. This was partly because I had found it very moving, and partly because I wanted to get the same expression on the composer's face. His gentle and very blue eyes had a nostalgic, far-away look that I wanted to capture.

There was something ethereal about the dear old man's face. I somehow felt that he wouldn't live long. He died, in fact, not long after.

YEHUDI MENUHIN *Violinist*

One of my most successful drawings is of Yehudi Menuhin, in which I tried to catch the rapt, almost spiritual expression of the great violinist. He was so sweet-tempered and kind to everybody, and his finely chiselled features were wonderful to draw. His wife said it was the best portrait of him she had ever seen, and invited me to come to his rehearsals any time I liked. I have made many studies of him since then.

MSITISLAV ROSTROPOVICH *Cellist*

This portrait was exhibited at the Royal Festival Hall and bought by Victor Hochhauser, Rostropovich's manager.

OTTO KLEMPERER *Conductor*

Made me most nervous. Another artist had recently attempted a portrait of him, and he strode up to look at it, scowled, and said: "Am I so ugly?"

PHYLLIS SELLICK AND CYRIL SMITH

pianists, husband and wife

After I drew Phyllis Sellick, she invited me to her home to do a charcoal drawing of her and her huband playing together at either end of their two pianos.

BENJAMIN BRITTEN *Composer*

I did three good drawings of him at rehearsal on his 50th birthday, conducting his own compositions and these he signed for me.

ROBINSON CLEAVER *Conductor*

He told me the story of his earliest success. He applied for the post of organist at the parish church of his home near Sheffield. He and the three other applicants, all men, were told to play without the church selection committee knowing which was which, and they selected him for the post.

PABLO CASALS *World Class Cellist*

I went to Hammersmith Town Hall, where Pablo Casals was conducting — not playing his cello. He was over eighty but his new wife, an ex-cello pupil in her twenties, took great

care that he did not get too tired. She was fussing round him and being so sweet to him, making him rest and giving him little drinks. I did three drawings of him — a head and two with the arms as well. He said he liked them very much and would I be kind enough to send photographs of them to his home in South America. He sent me a letter of thanks with a signed photograph, which I have in my studio.

The American Page

LEONARD BERNSTEIN
Conductor of the New York Philarmonic.

I greatly enjoyed drawing this beautiful man, who was kind and considerate with the musicians and even with me when he agreed to sign the portraits. Though extremely good looking he was not at all vain. At Festival Hall. I did two portraits during rehearsals as guest conductor of the BBC orchestra, and they both sold.

DUKE ELLINGTON *Jazz Composer and conductor*

When he played at the Fairfields Halls, Croydon, I knocked at his dressing room door. He answered and I asked if I could sketch him during the concert. He said, "Certainly. I'll put you in the band" He was as good as his word and sat me between two of his players during the public concert. He was playing the piano and I got some good chalk sketches of him, three quarter views. He was wonderful, great fun.

I stayed for both shows, during which he waved to me and winked every now and then to show that he had not forgotten me. I went to his dressing room afterwards to ask him to sign my three drawings.

"Come in, darling," he called brightly, seized me in his arms and executed a few waltz steps. "Sign them? Yes of course I will."

He took out a pen and signed with a flourish. "There, how's that?" he asked, handing me a drawing on which he had written "All my love, Duke."

He kissed my hand and said a fond goodbye, adding: "Thank you for making the platform look so priddy."

LOUIS ARMSTRONG *Jazz Trumpeter*

I did a good drawing of him when he had his band in Fairfield Halls, Croydon. I knocked at his dressing room door and he asked me in. We were joined by Beryl Bryden, the music hall singer, who started doing his nails. He didn't talk much. Two or three times during the evening he left us, went out on stage, performed for 20 minutes or so and then came back and I went on drawing and Beryl went on manicuring. I think I was faster at drawing him than she was at a doing his nails.

I later went with my niece Vanessa to draw him at a vaudeville theater where he was appearing in North London, but he was not well.

Juliet Pannett. Fairfield Halls Croydon. 25.1.63.

Juliet Pannett.

ARTHUR RUBENSTEIN *Pianist*

I went to several rehearsals in different halls where Rubenstein was playing. After seeing me there several times, he said one day "You here again!" and he made some joke but I've forgotten what it was. He was a lovely little man and he used to play so beautifully.

THE DOLMETSCH FAMILY *Musical Performers*

I used to go to the Dolmetsch Festival at Haslemere every year for some years. Once I went, and the old mother was there, with every member of the family down to the youngest, each playing a different musical instrument. *The Times* took a photograph of them all together. I tried very hard to be frightfully quick and I did all the twelve or fifteen people in about a quarter of an hour. But I was so stupid, I gave them the original picture!

Carl Dolmetsch told me how his father, Arnold, came to start the famous workshops for musical instruments.

"We were at Waterloo station," he said, "and Father told me to look after his antique recorder. I was only seven at the time. After the train had started, it was discovered that I had left the recorder behind on the platform. Father was terribly upset, but it was the loss of this recorder that gave him the idea of making another. That was the beginning of the Dolmetsch workshops."

The original recorder turned up two years later in a second-hand shop, but by then the workshops were firmly established. All the family were active musicians, and Carl Dolmetsch said that he not only made his own instruments, from old models, but those of his relations as well.

DAVID AND IGOR OISTRAKH
Father and son violinists

After I had drawn each of them separately, I did another drawing of father and son together along with Yehudi Menuhin, all three playing their violins in concert. The moment the rehearsal was over, a stranger who had been watching me leaped over the barrier and asked if he could buy the drawing there and then. I said that I must get it photographed first, so he wrote down my address and turned up at my studio the next day and bought the portrait. This admirer has since became a friend, and acquired many more of my pictures.

David Oistrakh wrote afterwards from Paris: "Both my son and I would like to thank you for your courtesy and kindness, and for the excellent drawing which we greatly value. We look forward to using it on programmes."

David and Igor Oistrakh

THE GOOSSENS FAMILY

Leon Goossens played the oboe (charcoal); brother Eugene conducted the BBC Orchestra (big watercolour); sister Sidonie played the harp (several red chalk drawings) .

Eugene Goossens invited me to his home in Chiswick: "Can you come next weekend, when the whole family will be there, including my father, and we're going to have a concert because we've got so many musicians in the family." Unfortunately I couldn't; it would have fascinated me.

DR FRANCIS JACKSON *Organist at York Minster*

He brought his family down from York to a small rented house, where I arranged to draw him. The sun was too strong in some of the rooms, while others were too dark. Finally we chose the bathroom with Dr Jackson perched on the bath, while I sat outside in the passage. The background of taps was not included in the drawing! After a while I heard the "daily" knock on the

sitting room door downstairs and ask if we would like coffee.

"We're in the bathroom", Dr Jackson called. "Will you please bring up two coffees."

JAN SMETERLIN *Pianist*

The drawing of Smeterlin was done at a rehearsal, and he liked it so much that he spontaneously wrote "How good; and all the other subjects could say the same." He also commissioned a second portrait.

"This artist, whose gift for portraiture is distinguished," said the *Daily Mail*, "shows us the great ones, many of them working hard, shirt-sleeved or linen-jacketed, at rehearsal."

RALPH VAUGHAN WILLIAMS *Composer*

A notoriously unwilling sitter. By great good luck I happened to find myself near him and his wife while I was sketching Piatigorsky rehearsing the Walton cello concerto. I managed to draw Vaughan Williams as well as Piatigorsky and Mrs Williams was pleased with the portrait. So later I was allowed to draw him openly listening to a rehearsal of his ninth symphony. When I asked him to sign my two drawings he said: "Hmm, I don't look as if I'm enjoying my own music much, do I?" and signed them.

Both these portraits are now in the National Portrait Gallery.

Ralph Vaughan Williams

JOHN IRELAND *Composer*

I did several drawings (one of which was published in *The Times*) at his windmill near Washington, in Sussex. Dr Ireland was immensely interesting to talk to, but somehow he always seemed sad. I regretted not being able to do an oil portrait, but his eyes were bad and he couldn't sit facing the light. A third drawing I gave to his devoted housekeeper and companion who had a nervous breakdown after his death and whom I visited several times in the nursing home.

After John Ireland died, his Rock Mill was for sale for £12,000. I was keen to buy it because we had to move and I rather wanted to go back to Sussex. But my brother David, a chartered surveyor, said, "On no account — a terrible fire risk — you certainly can't move there." So he wouldn't allow it. A lovely romantic place to live.

John Ireland

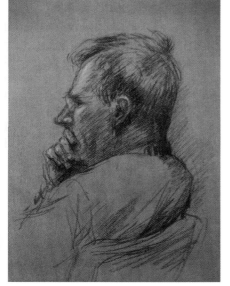

Dmitri Shostakovich

DMITRI SHOSTAKOVICH *Composer*

At the Royal Festival Hall, Shostakovich was sitting a few seats away from me listening to the rehearsal of some of his music. I did two very quick drawings of him, which he happily signed.

IGOR STRAVINSKY *Composer*

At a rehearsal of *Oedipus Rex* at the BBC Studios in Maida Vale, I had an opportunity to do portraits of both Stravinsky and Jean Cocteau. It was the second time that I had drawn Stravinsky. He was small and frail looking, but full of a dynamic driving power. He used up so much energy during the rehearsal that he almost fainted when it was over, so I couldn't ask him to sign my picture.

BENNO MOISEIWITSCH *Pianist*

One of the few musicians who preferred me not to draw during a performance, in case a movement should distract his attention. Instead he gave me a sitting on the stage before the recital, while he was practising. When he had finished, he got up, bowed and shook hands before returning to his dressing room.

"I will not charge you for sitting for you" he said, "but I shall certainly charge you for listening."

Two years later I did another portrait of him, and as soon as he saw me he exclaimed, "Haven't you finished that drawing *yet*?"

Igor Stravinsky

The Ladies

ADELINA DE LARA *Pianist*

I also drew Adelina de Lara, who was not quite ninety years old. She sent me a letter in her own, still excellent, handwriting, inviting me to lunch, and giving me clear instructions for finding my way.

"You will see on your right a pillar box, and there is my path, called Cinder Path. Some years ago the Council renamed it Adelina's Path and some jealous people nearby objected, so after a week the name had to be altered back to Cinder Path. The people have now left. I presume because I own neither a car nor T.V. (even if I *have* been honoured by Her Majesty) I was not thought good enough to have the path named after me!"

Adelina de Lara was a very happy person, and talked about her life with vivacity and humour.

"My husband proposed to me in a hansom," she told me. "All he said was 'Will you come to America with me?' 'What as?' I asked cautiously. 'My wife, you fool.' That was all. He didn't even kiss me."

Then she jumped up to show me the gold sovereign that Dvořák had given her for playing his music so well. She had just been photographed by Mr Antony Armstrong-Jones for her ninetieth birthday in January 1962, and my picture of her was to accompany an article in *The Times*. Adelina de Lara was very excited about this event, and looked forward to it with childlike eagerness. It was sad that she did not, after all, live to see her birthday.

ANNIE FISCHER *Pianist*

This beautiful pianist with an enormous bun of hair had a number on her wrist because she had been a prisoner of the Nazis.

I got to know her when she practised in London, at a mutual friend's flat. She impressed me tremendously — partly because of her great beauty (good bone structure, wide, Slavonic eyes, lots of hair, and a most disarming smile) and partly because, although small and slender, very shy and gentle, she possessed great power and strength of character.

The first time we met, we made coffee and sandwiches, which we ate sitting on our hostess's bed.

"What little hands you've got," I

said to her, to which she replied:

"They are enough big."

Annie Fischer then posed for two and a half hours while I did three red chalk drawings of her hands, two on the piano keys and one resting on a music score. We met twice more, and I was greatly touched and pleased when we parted after the fourth meeting. Annie Fischer took both of my hands and said that normally she hated to be photographed or drawn, but this time she had really enjoyed the sittings.

DAME MYRA HESS *Pianist*

When she was rehearsing at the Albert Hall I did a drawing, which turned out very well. Afterwards, when I asked her to sign it for me she said, " Oh, but you mustn't put this in (pointing to her double chin) — my friends wouldn't like it." So I said "Oh all right," and actually I took off just a very little bit but not very much, because I don't think it would have been her without her chin. I thought how strange it was because I'd always thought of her as such a strong, wonderful woman — grand, like Beethoven. I never thought she'd bother about a little thing like a chin, but she did.

ELIZABETH LUTYENS *Composer*

Elizabeth Lutyens sat for me at her home. She was the only woman who said, "Make me as ugly as you like!" Actually though strange looking, with rather a long nose, she wasn't ugly at all, and was interesting to do.

JOAN SUTHERLAND *Soprano*

I drew her in her tiny dressing room at Covent Garden, commissioned by *The Times*. She talked about her work, and was modest and friendly. While I was working Margot Fonteyn came in and asked if she could get something out of the dressing table drawer.

AMARYLLIS FLEMING *Cellist*

I enjoyed painting this beautiful red-haired, illegitimate daughter of Augustus John.

Amaryllis Fleming

EILEEN JOYCE *Pianist*

Eileen Joyce commissioned eight watercolours of herself playing with different orchestras and conductors which hang in the music room of Chartwell Farm, her house in Kent next to Chartwell where Churchill lived. She became a good friend and I enjoyed going there, as well as to her London house. Besides the watercolours, I did many sketches and drawings, including one of the hands alone.

She also wanted me to do portraits of Crotchet and Quaver, her two dreadful little miniature poodles — not my favourite dog — but they were so woolly.

They had no faces and it was frightfully difficult, so I couldn't do it.

Since I had no car in those days she used to come over to Croydon from Westerham to fetch me in her lovely little sports car.

Once she took me with her to the Albert Hall where she was playing. I was surprised that such a well-known pianist should be so nervous before the performance. So I helped her into one of her glamorous Norman Hartnell, evening dresses very low-necked, elegant and costing a fortune.

Sir MICHAEL TIPPETT *Composer*

One of the musicians I most enjoyed painting was Michael Tippett, who became a friend. We talked of music, art and philosophy, and I found his conversation so interesting I could hardly concentrate on my work. When the oil portrait (which was purchased by the Royal College of Music) was displayed at the Festival Hall Exhibition he told me he overheard the following snatch of conversation in front of the picture.

"Can you believe that a man with a face like that could write music?"

"My dear, didn't you *know*? Someone writes all his music for him."

Sir John Barbirolli

The Legal Profession

Lord Denning

Lord Thomas

I think my favourite faces — if I had to choose a group — would be legal faces. They've always got a keen eye, a good chin usually and a good big nose.

Chapter twentythree

THE LAW LORDS in the House of Lords

LORD PARKER OF WADDINGTON He was the Lord Chief Justice when I wrote for permission to draw him.

Soon a letter arrived, bearing the seal of the Lord Chief Justice of England. Perhaps it was only a refusal from some secretary, I thought, trying not to feel too excited as I tore open the envelope. I looked at the signature — Parker of Waddington. It was a hand-written letter (like most important people wrote), saying he would be perfectly agreeable to a sitting.

The day before the appointment, Lady Parker rang up to make some helpful suggestions as to the best angle and expression to aim for. She also invited me to go in for a drink in the evening and take the portrait to show her.

In the morning I parked in the judges' car park and punctually at 9.30 was shown into Lord Parker's room for an hour's sitting, plenty of time to get the portrait finished. I went for a drink to the Vine House in Romney Street where Lord Parker himself opened the door to me. Sipping sherry from a beautifully engraved Venetian glass, and admiring the 17th century embroidery on the cushions, I waited in some trepidation for the verdict. At last judgement was pronounced, and I was not condemned; apart from one slight alteration to the mouth, Lady Parker declared herself satisfied. Both she and Lord Parker helped me put my things into the car in the pouring rain, and saw me off with a promise to come to Croydon one day to see my other work.

The evening almost ended in disaster when I moved a marble top table and it fell on the floor. It was awful, and I had a very cross letter from Lady Parker afterwards saying, "You know, you broke my table, it was very careless of you." She was an American and very peculiar.

Lord Parker

Lord Davies

LORD DENNING *President of the Law Society 1980 (p. 87)*

A few days after I did Lord Parker of Waddington, I had a sitting with Lord Denning, Master of the Rolls, at his Cuckfield, Sussex, home.

I was commissioned to do a red chalk drawing of him for the cover of *Law Guardian*. (I did the President of the Law Society every year and he happened to be President that year).

"I should be delighted for you to draw a picture of me," he had written previously, "though I am afraid I am a very bad subject."

He turned out to be just the reverse. I arrived three quarters of an hour early, left my car in a nearby lane and went for a country walk. During the walk I met what I thought might be Lord and Lady Denning with a little dog. As we did not then know each other, only a polite "good morning" was exchanged on both sides.

"We wondered if it might be you!" they said, when I presented myself at the house a little later.

I had a two-hour sitting, and was invited to stay for lunch, cooked by Lady Denning. During lunch he told me of his visit to Exeter, where a custom dating from the Bloody Assizes of Judge Jeffreys demands that all troops be confined to barracks on the visit of a judge, until he asks permission for them to be let loose. There were notoriously few soldiers in Exeter at the time of his visit, but the formalities had to be observed.

"Are all troops loyal?" he enquired, according to the prescribed formula.

"Yes sir, all three of them," was the reply.

It was really great fun. He was absolutely charming and put on his lovely black robe with gold all over it.

Lord Denning agreed with his wife that the portrait was the best that had ever been done of him, and they suggested I should also do an oil in full robes. For this he sat on four consecutive Saturdays, and lent me his robes and wig to take home, so that someone else could pose for that part of the painting.

Buckingham University bought his portrait in 1980, for the Denning Law School.

He said to his wife Joan, "I think John the gardener would like to see me in my working clothes because he has never seen me in the Courts?" She agreed. When the gardener came in he didn't say anything for some time: then, "I thought they was red. Very disappointing."

They were both absolutely natural and friendly.

Earlier, when I was doing Lord Parker I told him I was going to draw Lord Denning the following week. He said "Do tell him to get some new teeth." They were indeed very bad!

Lord Harman

LORD HARMAN *High Court Judge*

He asked me if I would do a portrait in the same style as the portrait on the wall of his room in the Law Courts . A pencil drawing with a little touch of watercolour afterwards in a very Victorian way. The portrait took a long time — at least two mornings — and sometimes he went off to preside over a court and left me on my own to work.

When he took my portrait back to his native Ireland, he also sent some carpets from the Middle East and told me he was annoyed because he had to pay duty on them.

When I finished, he said, "I suppose you wouldn't like to come and clean the wall for me one day?" I didn't really want to, but said "Yes, with pleasure." Though I felt he was treating me like a servant I duly toiled up to London from Croydon — went to the Law Courts with my sponges and things, and I washed all the glasses and dusted them all and took them down. He was quite grateful, but never offered to do anything for me in return! It was very peculiar.

He told amusing stories and reminisced about his childhood:

"When our nanny took us down to see our mother in the drawing-room after tea, I had to put on a purple velvet suit with a white lace collar, just like Little Lord Fauntleroy. I hated it...I remember seeing Queen Victoria's diamond Jubilee. I was at one end of the pram and my elder brother at the other, and we had Union Jacks on sticks. He poked his in my eye."

LORD GODDARD *Lord Chief Justice*

Lord Goddard had an interesting head. very heavy, strong face – and rather cruel. He was known as the Hanging Judge because he was in favour of hanging. I did him several times and I went to his home. I remember he was the first important sitting for me after I returned from my Israel trip. True to his word, Sir Arthur Bryant had asked permission for me to do a drawing.

"I can't imagine anyone wanting to publish my portrait, at least until it is used to illustrate my obituary!" Lord Goddard wrote to me. "Still, as Bryant has asked me to give you a sitting, I will certainly do so."

I went to his home in Queen Elizabeth House in the Temple. He was rather deaf and did not talk much. Since there was nothing to keep him amused, the drawing turned out to be on the severe side. When he saw it, he said:

"You've made me look as if I'm about to put on the black cap."

I agreed that his expression was too stern, and we arranged a sitting for a second portrait. Lady Bryant was present the next time, and she talked to him and kept him alert and interested, with the result that he looked more lively.

"I think the published drawing quite excellent," Lord Goddard wrote later, when it appeared in the *ILN*.

One of three drawings done of him in about 1962 hangs in the National Portrait Gallery.

Lord Goddard

Rt Hon LORD REID *Senior Judge in the House of Lords*

Drawn in 1968 in his chamber in the House of Lords.

One of my favourites. he had been an important judge in Edinburgh. I needed two sittings so they invited me to lunch to finish the portrait. His lovely wife was a good cook and gave us a delicious lunch. Later, they came to lunch with Rick and myself on a beautiful day; we ate in the garden, which looked particularly colourful.

LORD WILBERFORCE

Someone I enjoyed doing very much. He had a lovely sort of elfin face — really wonderful to do. I went to his home to do it and on the wall was a very blackened portrait of his great-great-great grandfather — the Wilberforce who freed the slaves. He asked me if I could take it away and clean it up in some way but I didn't feel capable of it. I thought you'd need a professional for that because it had gone dark with age and damp. So I didn't do it. He was a charming man. I really enjoyed meeting him.

LORD SHAWCROSS

During a television programme, I did a drawing of another prominent legal personality, Lord Shawcross; I sent it to him and asked if he would be kind enough to sign it, if he thought it a good likeness. He replied:

"I nearly kept this for myself, it is so good. But I sign it gladly."

Later that year, he gave me a sitting to do a portrait from life, and I drew him at his London office while he dictated letters.

A signed portrait of him drawn in his office in Great St Helens about 1963 hangs in the National Portrait Gallery.

SIR DAVID NAPLEY *President of the Law Society*

He became famous as a criminal lawyer defending Jeremy Thorpe during his notorious trial involving homosexuality. Since he was too sick to pose for me the day I went up to London for the second sitting, he wrote a letter of apology asking me to come for lunch and finish the portrait. We had smoked salmon and I don't remember what else.

When the time came to pay for my drawing (he wanted to buy the original) Sir David said, "Oh, by the way, you have received a fee for this drawing from the Law Society, haven't you, for the cover of the Magazine?" I said yes and he said how much was it — and I think I said £20. So he deducted that from my fee! And he was so rich — you can't imagine what a wealthy man he was!

LORD WIDGERY *Lord Chief Justice*

Had been a soldier. He was very nice to do — very good looking, and sat beautifully. He held a book in his hand, and instead of moving his head from side to side as he read the book, he moved the book a little bit to the right or left which was so helpful to me, and so thoughtful. He bought the original. Some time later, I was having an exhibition in London at the Law Society — an exhibition of all my legal portraits (because I'd done a tremendous number by this time). I asked him if I could borrow his portrait to put in the exhibition. He said, "Oh no, I don't think so, it'd leave a gap on my dining room mantelpiece!" So I said that's all right then. Then he said, "If you really want it, I suppose I could bring it there, but it's not easy" I said all right, don't worry, I've got a lot of others.

THOMAS EGGAR *Law Society President 1890*

Later, I was commissioned to do a big, big portrait — the biggest I've ever done I think — of the founder of the firm of Thomas Eggar, solicitors in Chichester. This had to be done from photographs because the late Thomas Eggar had been President of the Law Society back in the 1890s. This is hanging on the stairs in the Law Society in Chancery Lane — or it was when I was there last.

Lord Widgery

Juliet Pannet painting Sir John Willis

SYBIL CAMPBELL *First Stipendiary Magistrate at Tower of London Courts.*

I was commissioned by the Sybil Campbell Library (in Chelsea) to paint a portrait of her for their Hall.

We became great friends and she invited Lizzie and me to stay with her in a village by Loch Fyne in Scotland. The stone house was two or three hundred years old. She was the Metropolitan Magistrate, Tower Bridge, and the first woman to be made a magistrate.

I did her portrait three times, the third for Girton College, Cambridge. When I was in Cambridge a few years later I went to see it.

Around this time, I started to do all the Presidents of the Law Society every year. As soon as the election was due, I had a letter from the Law Society saying could I do various people.

LORD SCARMAN

He was absolutely delightful. He asked me if I would get the portrait framed and let him buy it, and he would keep it secretly until his wife's birthday. After photographing it, I brought back the portrait duly framed and it was put in a cupboard in his office. When it was reproduced a few months later in Peterborough's column of the *Daily Telegraph* Lord Scarman wrote to me saying, "Oh, we love the drawing you did of me, would you allow me to buy it for my wife?" Of course he had bought it already and forgotten all about it!

Lord Scarman

Sir George Coldstream

Lord Leslie Stemp

Lord G.A. Peacock

David Karmel

Lord Justice Russell

SIR MILNER HOLLAND *Queen's Counsel*

Knowing that his wife Eileen would like me to do his portrait, I suggested that if Milner were willing, I would do a portrait, which could be given to Eileen as a surprise present. My only "condition" was that I might first be allowed to show it in the City of London Exhibition, to all of which Milner agreed.

"Well, our clandestine affair is now over," Milner said, as he helped me on with my coat after the drawing was finished "I've enjoyed sitting for you very much."

Eileen still knew nothing about the portrait, but it didn't remain a secret for long since I was lucky enough to win the top award in the exhibition, and my work was shown on television. The prize-winning picture was actually not his portrait, but an oil painting called "Refugees". The award gave me the Freedom of the Worshipful Company of Painter-Stainers, which also entitled me to become a Freeman of the City of London.

Dennis Smith

Sir
John Will..

LORD

GARDINER
Lord High Chancellor of England.
When I drew him in his office in the House of Lords, the radiator kept on making a
funny noise, so he got up and without a word, gave it a kick and it stopped.

Techniques: Oil Painting

Palette. I always used an oval palette, an old one given to me by an artist who had owned it since she went to art school in about 1860. Old palettes are much nicer to work with — not because they were better made in the first place, but because they acquire a patina over years of use, rather as furniture is improved by years of polishing.

Brushes. I used good-quality hog hair brushes, with flat ends, not round, ranging in size from small to very large (about one inch). I had about 30 — you need plenty so that you can take a new one whenever you need a new colour. I also had a few very small sable brushes (with foot-long handles so that they could be used at a distance from the canvas). I never put on paint with a palette knife.

Paints. I kept to only a few colours, always arranged round the edge of the palette in the same order (with the centre kept free for mixing). Titanium white (or flake white) would be in the middle of the row, with much more of it (up to ten times as much or more) than of any other colour. For flesh tones I also had light red (vermilion), yellow ochre or raw sienna, rose madder (good but always *very* expensive), raw umber, viridian green and cobalt blue (these last two are useful where flesh is in shadow). Other colours I normally used were ivory black and French ultramarine. (Paint unused at the end of a session will keep for a week or so under water.)

Sitters. As I've said in my Charcoal Techniques (page 30), it's best to have a single source of light. If possible, I would arrange sitters with the head at a slightly different angle from the body and not show the side with the cauliflower ear!. It is important that they should be comfortable, then they're more likely to sit well. Also, I tried to keep them amused, either listening to the wireless or simply talking — a sitter needs to be happy, as smiling gives life to a portrait I didn't flatter, but made the best of what I'd got. It's possible to make a good portrait of anyone — though it was obviously easier to give of my best when I had a handsome sitter in gorgeous clothes! Men are much easier to paint than women — they're not so vain. Women often think they ought to look more beautiful. It's difficult to get good results with very fat people. Older people are easier to do — their faces are more interesting because of the 'lines of character'

Painting a portrait. Starting with a white canvas, I liked to cover it with a light brick-red thinned with turps, to 'kill' the white. I would then sketch out the whole design onto the canvas, using paint thinned with turps. Depending on size, an oil portrait would normally take about four sittings of an hour and a half or so — long enough for both sitter and artist. (For comparison, a charcoal took about an hour in all -and sometimes only 10 minutes - a pastel perhaps two sittings.) I'd obviously put in many hours' work in between sittings. Uniforms etc. can mostly be worked on without the sitter. Hands are very important, and could take up to two sittings. I'd usually work on one section of the face (e.g. forehead, mouth) at a time, but always worked on both eyes together to be sure they matched. Background is quite important; sometimes it would be plain, but often I'd use a building or landscape associated with the sitter; this could be done from photos.

Edwin Osorio, Master, Worshipful Company of Painter Stainers

R. Large, Master, Worshipful Company of Painter Stainers

Artists

I von Hitchens was quiet and didn't want to sit very much, but grudgingly said "Oh, alright".
He was so inspiring it turned out to be one of my best portraits.

I don't go in much for abstract art, but I admired his work and bought 2 of his paintings.

George Bruce, President,

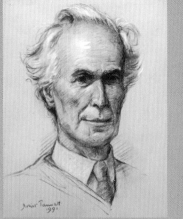

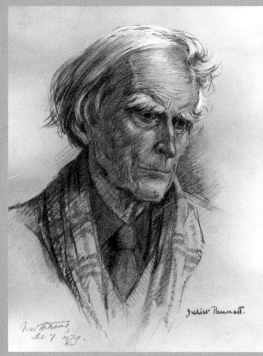

Royal Society of Portrait Painters

Ivon Hitchens, famous abstract artist and his studio

Cecil Beaton, drawn from TV

My first summons to Buckingham Palace was in 1974. The Painter-Stainers' Company had asked the Queen whether she would accept a portrait of her second son, Prince Andrew. She agreed and they then invited their members (Freemen), luckily including myself, to send in samples of their work. About fifty portraits were submitted, which were gradually reduced to five to be forwarded to the Queen at Windsor. I could hardly believe the news, when I received a letter saying I was the Queen's personal choice.

Chapter twentyfive
Buckingham Palace

The sittings were fixed well in advance for July 16th and 17th, with a third sitting to be arranged if necessary. I went to the Palace on the afternoon of the day before, to see about the lighting, and leave my materials. Miss Reid, secretary to William Heseltine, the Queen's Private Secretary, met me, and, with the help of a page, they took my materials up to the first floor. I didn't get time to stop and look at the portraits that lined the long, red-carpeted corridor, but I guessed I'd have an opportunity to do so later. At the end of this corridor was the Yellow Drawing Room, where I was to do my portrait. It was a beautiful room, overlooking the courtyard at the southwest corner of the Palace. The wallpaper was Chinese, and also the lamps, lacquer cabinets and embroidered sofas. Some of the chairs were rose pink damask and gilt, others of inlaid ivory. The room is kept for portrait painting and on a two foot high dais is a model of the Queen; the face is blank but the manikin has her hairstyle and you can hang clothes on it. I was relieved to find a drugget over the carpet, as pastel can be difficult to clean off. The room contained a screen, a throne and an easel. I asked Miss Reid whether I ought to wear a hat. "No, we are very informal here," she said. "And by the way, you don't curtsey to the young princes, only to Prince Charles and Princess Anne, if you happen to meet them."

The first sitting was at ten o'clock the next morning. I arrived early, and was shown to the Yellow Drawing Room. Presently. Heseltine came in, followed by Prince Andrew and his nurse, Miss Mabel Anderson. "It has been suggested that he should wear his Gordonstoun School shirt, open at the neck," Miss Anderson said.

"I don't want to wear it, I like my pale blue," protested the fourteen-year-old prince.

"Well, fetch the Gordonstoun shirt anyway," she replied.

When he had left the room, Miss Anderson turned to me. "the Queen wants him to wear it."

"I'd like him to wear it too," I said "but don't let's make an issue of it. I want him to be happy. How about letting him wear the pale blue shirt today, and see what happens to-morrow?"

However, Prince Andrew gave in with good grace to his mother.

While the sitting was in progress, he had a good laugh listening to Terry Wogan on his transistor. Then he played pop, switching it off occasionally to chat with me. One of the Queen's corgi dogs came in and was taken away by Miss Anderson, and that prompted the prince to talk about his own dog, a small black Labrador which was kept at Sandringham. Miss Anderson came back at the end of the sitting and asked Prince Andrew what he would like to do that afternoon.

"The Churchill Exhibition is still on, or we could go to the Science Museum," she suggested.

"I don't know. I'll think about it."

I wondered if perhaps I had kept him too long; I had already been there almost an hour and a half, and that was the first time he had sat for a portrait. I asked him if he was tired.

"Not really. I don't mind sitting for you, if that's what you mean. I could sit like this for hours."

After the sitting, we watched the Changing of the Guard from the window, and in the course of conversation, Miss Anderson drew my attention to the gold curtains.

"Aren't they beautiful?" she said.

"Yes, they must be very old."

"Everything here is old," remarked Prince Andrew.

I saw myself out, and got my chance to study the pictures along the corridor. They were portraits of kings and queens, and included a Landseer of Queen Victoria and two Sargent oils of the Duke and Duchess of Connaught with lovely little highlights on the Duke's decoration — beautiful! The collection of Winterhalters included one of Queen Victoria's family. The next morn-

H.R.H. Prince Andrew

ing I presented myself at the Palace again, and William Heseltine told me that Prince Andrew liked the portrait.

"My mother has an investiture this morning," the prince told me. "I can see the people collecting in the courtyard."

It was not long after the attempt to kidnap Princess Anne, and I asked: "Are the policemen who helped your sister to escape being decorated today?"

"No. I did look at the list, but the only name I can remember is Bernard Delfont."

"Oh, how interesting. He's our next door neighbour in Sussex."

"Is he? What's his house like?"

"New, but built with old materials, in the Georgian style. We sometimes go for a swim in his pool, and he has a small private cinema in the summerhouse."

The portrait was finished at that sitting, and left for the Queen to look at it when the investiture was over.

Prince Andrew was very charming, lively, and full of personality, with large blue eyes like his grandfather, George VI. His whole face lit up when he smiled.

I was told that the Queen and the Duke of Edinburgh both gave the portrait their unqualified approval.

Two days later, a request came for me to do a portrait of Prince Edward, as the Royal Household wished to commission a companion portrait of the Queen's youngest son for her birthday.

So, back I went to the Yellow Drawing Room, where I found the ten-year old Prince Edward just as interesting as his older brother although opposite in personality. He had a cassette recorder, and his taste in music was classical; most of the time he listened to Khachaturian and Mendelssohn.

He was very interested in my art materials, especially the putty rubber with which he helped me to clean up the finished portrait.

"I think my mother would like a bit of that," he said politely.

I broke off a piece and gave it to him, for which he thanked me charmingly. After the sitting, Prince Edward helped to put all my pastels in order in their box.

H.R.H. Prince Edward

The portrait of Prince Andrew was formally presented to the Queen on August 8th I was given a ten-minute audience, in the company of the Master of the Worshipful Company of Painter-Stainers, Mr Charles Magnus.

The portrait stood on an easel, and the Queen said she liked it very much, and was delighted that she was going to have one of Prince Edward too.

DRAWING CHILDREN requires a special technique of being able to entertain and amuse the small model – I never try to make children "sit", but rather make them happy and comfortable, and try to attract their attention at the moments I want them to look at me. If I am drawing a full face portrait, I have a toy farm and a zoo, which I put on a rather high table between the little model and myself. I find children are frequently easier to manage when their parents aren't there, but of course, that depends very much on the individual child.

Television is a godsend to the artist with a figetty child model - a child can be completely absorbed and still with a delightful interested expression maintained for the length of the programme. Getting someone to read aloud is helpful, but television to attract the eyes in the right direction is even better.

I prefer to draw children, girls or boys, in a shirt neck; it is more becoming than something fussy, or a round neckline.

My most important commission came quite late in life. One day towards the end of 1986, the phone rang. It was the Secretary General of the Chartered Insurance Institute. He said that HM the Queen, who was Patron to the Institute, had agreed to sit for an official portrait to hang in the Institute's Great Hall, behind Guildhall. "Would you like to do it?" he asked. I couldn't believe it; it was completely out of the blue. I was very excited but not really nervous. I'd met other artists who had painted her and they all said she was very nice and easy. I didn't think I would find her intimidating because I always get quite lost in what I'm doing, but I did think it must be a terrible bore for her.

Her Majesty The Queen

Another reason for my lack of trepidation was that I had had what effectively amounted to two dress rehearsals when I painted Prince Andrew and Prince Edward. I knew it would be done in the Yellow Drawing Room.

The commission was for a very large portrait in official dress. I love doing uniforms and gowns because the materials are so nice to paint; but I needed to get her looking relaxed. I knew she gave four sittings — three would be wonderful for the face and I wanted one sitting for the hands. They are very important because everyone's hands are so different.

As requested I sent some photographs of my portraits up to Robert Fellowes, the Queen's Deputy Private Secretary to show the Queen. He wrote enthusiastically to say the Queen liked my work, and that he would be in touch about dates early in 1989.

On 8th February 1989, I arrived at Buckingham Palace with my son Denis for a 2.30 appointment with Mr Fellowes. He had rung previously to arrange the sitting days, and I had asked if I would be allowed to borrow some photographs from the Press Office as obviously I would not be able to finish a life-size portrait in four sittings of 90 minutes each. He had replied "Oh no, we never do that, but you can take as many photographs as you like." I told him I didn't even possess a camera but that my son was a good photographer and asked if he would be allowed to come with me. I was told that he could, so Denis accompanied me on every occasion at the Palace.

Mr Fellowes took us up to his room to discuss the Queen's clothes. I asked for a tiara and decorations and he said she would comply with anything.

"What should we wear?" I asked. "Any old clothes you like; it doesn't matter. Would you like her to stand or sit?"

Robert Fellowes told Denis he could photograph as much as he liked. Also, he could photograph the portrait at each stage.

He said he would arrange for our car to be parked in the Palace Courtyard during the sittings, and that we could leave it in the Royal Mews at night.

Then he took us up in the lift to the first floor, called the Palace Floor, and we walked down the long red-carpeted corridor.

There were masses and masses of Chinese artefacts — huge pagodas seven feet high — a five-decker Chinese junk carved out of ivory - and big ivory elephant tusks standing at the entrance of the doors, and set into the floor.

When I had drawn the princes there was an old fashioned lavatory close to this room, with a pull-up plug set into the mahogany seat. Sadly, now there was only a cream plastic loo and nothing but a mark on the wall to show where the mahogany seat fitted.

An artist, Howard Morgan (commissioned by Unilever), was at work painting a large portrait of Her Majesty to match one of Queen Beatrix of the Netherlands. His palette was piled high with very bright colours, thick and sticky looking, and enormous round brushes two and a half to three feet long. He squeezed about four ounces of lime green paint on to his palette - a blob about three inches wide - while we watched. The Queen wasn't there but he was working on his portrait between sittings. Peculiar sticky mauves and crimsons. All the windows were curtained, and the floodlights and chandeliers were all on. I would hate to paint in that artificial lighting but I suppose Morgan liked the dramatic effect. He asked if Robert Fellowes could lend him a secretary for half an hour or so to paint the hands in the portrait and the answer was no.

We came back through the Palace another way, overlooking an inner courtyard, and walked along another superb corridor, down the red carpet stairs seen on television when the Queen receives her guests. There were many more Chinese *objets*.

The first sitting was on 17th February 1989. We stayed at the Rubens Hotel on the night of the 16th and arrived at the Palace at 10.00 am on the big day.

Her Majesty The Queen

In a bedroom adjoining the Yellow Drawing Room, I changed into an old but clean overall and Denis put on a navy smock.

We squeezed the paints on to the palette, resting on a big trestle table provided for artists. Denis rubbed in my light red undercoat thinned with turpentine.

There was a small dais about one foot high and five feet square with a charming gilt chair upholstered in rose damask, with gold leaf on the arms and back. We tried to invent compositions by taking turns sitting on the chair and turning our heads in various ways and pulling the dais in different directions — nearer the window, further away from the window etc — until we found the best position.

It was pouring with rain but there was an excellent painting light from three 20 foot high windows.

I sketched in a possible composition very faintly in light red, a technique that has been used for hundreds of years.

At 11.45 am there was a faint scuffle outside the door. It was opened by a footman, who bowed very low to the Queen as she entered.

She looked absolutely dazzling in a white brocade dress with little silver circles like sixpenny pieces woven into it, and puffed sleeves to the elbow. When I admitted I did not fancy wrestling with the circles, the Queen agreed, but admonished me to make the material look silky. She also wore silver shoes, and a blue Garter sash with family decorations and miniatures pinned on to them, Garter star, sapphire tiara, necklace, earrings and bracelet.

I had understood from my earlier conversation with Robert Fellowes that I was not to make a deep curtsey, so I just bobbed, and we touched hands – without the usual gloves. Then he, having followed her into the room, introduced us. "Mrs Pannett you have met before, Madam – and this is Denis Pannett."

The Queen said "Oh good — a chair. Last time I had to stand. It was very tiring, and I had to ask for a support to lean against."

She then sat in the position Denis and I had arranged, and it was right. She looked out of the window and reminisced that the nurseries were at the other end of the Palace, and as a child she had always enjoyed looking out from there.

She asked if we had seen the guard mounting and the band, as she thought it might have been cancelled because of the rain.

She commented that you couldn't hear them marching now because they wore rubber-soled boots. She said some of the soldiers wore boxes on their backs for sniffing explosives. They have had to have them since the Hyde Park massacre. Very sad. She then said how ridiculous it was that they still covered the drums in the rain even though they were now made of nylon. There is a Grenadier Officer who always marches them straight out of the gate, taking it for granted that the traffic will stop for them. Perhaps it would be rather difficult to run over marching guardsmen. "I would be more cautious and go out at an angle," she said.

She told us that recently, two old generals were walking very slowly to the gate — one with a limp which he received as a result of a riding accident, when his horse died on Salisbury Plain, falling on top of him, and pinning him down for 12 hours before a search party found him.

She drew our attention to swans flying by, and told us that the previous week-end she had been walking the dogs alone at Windsor when some swans flew past making a swishing noise which she imitated, waving her arms up and down. They landed near her, and walked towards her, hissing at the dogs, which was quite a frightening experience.

She also said that when they had a fireworks celebration at Windsor Castle by the lake, she had been concerned as to whether a nesting swan would be disturbed, but it had ignored the whole show.

She discussed the October hurricane of 1987 and told us she had been in Canada at the time and was out riding with a Mountie, when she heard the news from him that London's Trees had been flattened. She said now she finds she carefully does a mental measurement of the distance of trees from buildings in case there should be another gale. They had to replant some of the Palace garden. Also, when the Hilton Hotel was built they had to plant more trees to get more privacy.

She hoped St George's Hospital wasn't going to be turned into a hotel, as it would be in a very bad position on a roundabout that doesn't go round. She said the Duke of Westminster wasn't given the offer to buy — it was sold to developers.

The Queen told us that when Prince Edward was a little boy staying at Balmoral he went for a walk alone with his dog. Mist descended, and they lost little Prince Edward and his black Labrador. The police sent out a search party that followed his footsteps, but Philip guessed correctly which side of the mountain he would descend, and met him coming down the track.

She said that the day before in Windsor Great Park, one of her corgis had bitten her policeman quite badly. I asked about

Her Majesty the Queen and Juliet Pannett

Jolly and Socks, the two corgis I remembered from the time they came in with Andrew and Edward. She said they had both died. This weekend she said, she had 11 dogs to look after. She couldn't understand why all the family left their dogs with her, and terriers don't get on with corgis. Charles has a terrier, Andrew a labrador.

She commented on the fire at Carlton House Terrace, saying how beautiful it looked now that it was repainted. She was driving past there with a new driver the other day, when a woman deliberately walked out behind her motor cycle escort and in front of her car. The driver had to brake and swerve violently and she — the Queen — had been thrown forward, nearly going through the glass. The Palace has since received a letter from the woman's husband apologizing for the incident but most unfairly blaming the police for not having stopped her.

She discussed her recent portrait by Howard Morgan, who has the reputation of being disorganised and careless. He had stayed a month in the Dutch Royal Palace, painting Queen Beatrix. The two royal portraits were meant to be a pair but made our Queen look half Queen Beatrix's size – which she is not. "I had to stand with my heavy Garter robes and I got very tired." I said that a large vase in the painting was leaning and looked as if it was about to topple over on to her. She laughed so much that she had to wipe her eyes.

She said how clever the botanists are to adapt plants to our climate and commented on the lovely fuchsia hedges in Scotland and Ireland adding "I must plan my life better so that I can visit the West Coast gardens in June."

We told her that in April we were going to the Scottish island of Gigha, to stay in Achamore House. Her Majesty said she remembered visiting Achamore Gardens in Gigha, and anchoring *Britannia* in Queen's Bay, Gigha.

At 1.00 p.m. she said, "Is this a good moment to stop?" This was the end of the first sitting. At least once at each sitting the Queen raised her hands and butterflied them, saying that Queen Mary taught her to do this to relax them — good for the circulation.

The second sitting was on 2nd March 1989. Denis and I went to the Yellow Drawing Room. The Queen came alone — no footman or Deputy Secretary this time. She came a little late and apologised, saying her maid Bobo, who had been with her since she was three, had fallen and hurt her hip. She had slipped carrying a tray, and refused to go to hospital.

The Queen told us that the previous evening they had had the awards for Industry and Export on the Royal Yacht for the first time. This was in the Pool of London and as there were so many people to entertain, two parties had to be held on consecutive nights. Some people were disappointed that it wasn't at Buckingham Palace but it seems it had been a success and the yacht looked very pretty lighted from stem to stern. Philip she said had only missed speaking to three of the people.

When Sir William Heseltine and Robert Fellowes came in she discussed the previous evening: "I only got one glass of wine and no food at all." The two private secretaries started to tease her — "The smoked salmon was delicious, the Parma ham was very good indeed. Nobody offered you food because you were wearing gloves." "But I always wear gloves," she said. "Well, be sure you see I am looked after tonight." "We will see you are well supplied with everything," they said.

After the first day we were allowed to come and go alone whenever we wished, which gave us a wonderful opportunity to study the paintings and interesting things in the long corridor.

We were brought coffee at 11.00 am in a beautiful silver Queen Anne coffee pot, and at tea time we had tea from King George V's tea service with his insignia on the cups, saucers and plates.

When we went to the Palace between sittings there was a dummy figure dressed in the Queen's gown, on her chair. We rang the Page who brought the tiara, necklace and earrings and put them on the model. The jewellery is never allowed to be left alone, so when our session was finished, we rang the Page again and waited for him to collect them. Robert Fellowes told us

Pastel of Queen Elizabeth, given by Prince Phillip to the President of Malta to celebrate 25 years of independence

that an Australian artist who was painting the Queen accidentally knocked the dummy off the dais, tripped over her cloak, and was found wrestling on the floor with the model. Incidentally the model wasn't in the least like her. It had far too small a head. You would think they would have got the figure right anyway, but they didn't. It was quite horrible.

We went to the Palace 18 times to work on the portrait, staying at the Rubens Hotel, close by, as guests of the Chartered Insurance Institute, who had commissioned the portrait.

One day, the Chartered Insurance Institute's Secretary General, Mr P G Saxton, gave us lunch at the hotel and afterwards came to the Palace to inspect the portrait when it was about half finished.

At the third sitting the Queen suddenly said "Oh there is mummy going by — she must be off to a luncheon. I had an investiture yesterday and while pinning on a decoration the woman fell over backwards. Nobody rushed to pick her up. Also, nobody told me that she had had the shock of her husband's recent death."

I mentioned that a school friend of mine, Thelma Gray (née Evans) had bred the Queen's first corgis. The Queen remembered Thelma well, and still hears from her son in Australia, where she emigrated when she married, and where she bred corgis for the rest of her life.

She asked about my family and I told her of my daughter, son and sister who are all painters, and that there were a number of other artists in the family. "I have heard of a family of musicians," she said, "but not families of artists." I mentioned that my daughter taught in the USA and that we all had completely different styles.

"My grandmother, Queen Mary, dragged my sister and me to all the museums. We loved it — we used to travel by tube. Once the Press saw us at the Tower of London, and followed us all the way back on the Underground. We were easily spotted after that and we couldn't do it anymore. It was good for our backs being with Queen Mary. She was so straight and upright I think the Tower is a good place to take children. We enjoyed going there with Queen Mary. But I have never been to Madam Tussauds."

"The Duke of Edinburgh's Awards are to be presented today. Parents enjoy this event more than the children I think."

The Queen had just been to Barbados since the last sitting. "Did you enjoy the sun, Madam?" "There wasn't much chance for the sun. We were too busy at the evening receptions." She said a man ran towards them from a warehouse in Barbados and a guard arrested him.

"My mother has poetry readings in her home. Once there was a blind poet and I said — are you still writing poetry? And he answered, 'It becomes a habit.' A good answer to a silly question."

"At one of these readings, Lord David Cecil was to lecture on his book *New Views on Reading*. Sir John Betjeman was there. Afterwards, Lord David said to him "I didn't expect to see you here, John," and Betjeman replied, "I didn't expect it either, I thought I was to hear some new views on Reading – the town." Ted Hughes came one night and lots of others.

Looking out of the window — "Good gracious there is a Wallace Arnold coach going round the Victoria Memorial — they haunt me at Balmoral. They discovered which gate I use and I am always being pushed into the ditch by them. And there goes a Harrods electric van. Philip likes it so much he has one himself now."

At 1.00 pm I looked at my watch. "Is it time to stop, Madam?" She said "No, we will go on a little longer as I came late. I

22nd March, 1989.

Dear Mrs Pannett.

The Queen, as you saw, was very touched
by your little portrait of Prince Harry. Her
Majesty, after the sitting, asked me to send
you her warmest thanks and to say how much
she has enjoyed sitting for you over the last
weeks. Apart from enjoying your company and
Dennis's, Her Majesty congratulates you on
what promises to be a highly successful
portrait.

Looking forward to hearing from you when you're
in London.

Yours sincerely

Robert Fellowes

(ROBERT FELLOWES)

Mrs. J. Pannett.

expect they will keep my lunch hot for me." We stopped at about 1.20.

The fourth and last sitting was on 22nd March 1989. Denis asked if he might take a close up photograph of the Queen's hands on her lap. He got into position, leant forward about 18 inches from the hands, clicked the camera and no! — he had run out of film. He had a 12 exposure film and thought he had 24. He felt very embarrassed as he thought she would think it rather stupid. He asked if he might go down Buckingham Palace Road and buy another. The Queen said, "I have got a much better idea. Ring no. 5 on the telephone and ask for my Page Stephen. Ask him to bring you one of mine — that would be much easier." In five minutes Stephen brought in a little rather crushed yellow box, probably from her handbag. I had previously asked Robert Fellowes if I could give the Queen a tiny watercolour of Prince Harry that I had done for her the day before the sitting from a very good small photograph in a magazine. I had put it in a little Florentine carved antique frame made of gilt and gesso. He said, "Yes, certainly, everybody likes a present." So when she came in I asked if she would be kind enough to accept it. She thanked me for it, and wrapped it in the tissue paper again and put it in her bag loosely. I said Harry had a sweet little face and she said he has got a wicked little face. Later in a letter I received from Robert Fellowes I read "The Queen, as you saw, was very touched by your little portrait of Prince Harry."

The very next day, I had a letter of thanks, saying that she had enjoyed the sittings and the conversation with Denis and me, and congratulating me on what promises to be a highly successful portrait. I had shown the painting to her at the third sitting and she said "Oh good, you have made me smiley."

For the first ten minutes of the last sitting the Queen was very subdued and quiet, as she was upset because Ernest Bennett, an old servant in the Royal Household for 50 years, had died the previous night. Robert Fellowes and the Queen discussed who should be written to, and what should be put in *The Times*.

Denis asked her if he might go round the other side to get a different view for photography, and the Queen said go anywhere you like. So he went behind her chair and she said "Oh dear, now you will see I haven't got my tiara on properly!"

Robert Fellowes told us the Queen is incredibly quick at changing her clothes, and only takes one or two minutes to reappear completely changed.

While I was painting, the telephone rang in the Yellow Drawing Room. Denis answered it and a voice said, "May I speak to Eartha Kitt?" The Queen said that sometimes calls get through to her room from total strangers.

"People — house guests — are not in the least surprised to see me in my tiara and evening dress in the middle of the day if I meet them in the corridor on the way back from a sitting. Some people think I wear these things always."

She isn't very keen on the Victoria Memorial. Too much gold, and it blocks the view. "Once upon a time you could see right up the Mall." At almost 1.00 pm Robert Fellowes came and said "The Peruvian golf champion is here to see you, ma'am - he is incidentally the Peruvian Ambassador! You have an appointment with him." The Queen said to me, "You go on for a bit. If I run down the corridor taking off my dress as I go, I shan't be very late."

Several times during our visit to the Palace, Col. Blair Stewart Wilson — Equerry to the Queen — came in to see how the portrait was progressing (not when she was sitting). Also, Mr Timms, Deputy Master of the Queen's Household, said it was one of the best portraits of Her Majesty he had seen. He asked who had commissioned it, and said, "They are very lucky."

The day after it was finished, Robert Fellowes told me that the Queen had said she had enjoyed the sittings. "Wasn't that nice? She certainly doesn't say that about everybody. She said you were jolly nice people." A few days later he said, "The Queen really did say that, you know. The portrait is smashing. I hope you get really good publicity." Sadly, I didn't.

After 18 visits to Buckingham Palace we moved the portrait to the Chartered Insurance Institute, where I added the last finishing touches. It was unveiled at the Annual General Meeting and hangs in the beautiful Insurance Hall in a gilt carved frame topped with a crown.

The Queen has a very sharp humour. She is witty and doesn't miss a trick. Two ladies were having tea in the teashop at Sandringham when a scarved figure came in to buy a chocolate cake. As she turned to leave, one of the ladies said, "You do look like the Queen", and her piping voice said "How very reassuring."

So ended the most fascinating commission of my life.

Her Majesty the Queen decorating Juliet Pannett with the MBE

Denis, Juliet and Elizabeth with her MBE

Epilogue

General Sir John Wilsey

While painting General Wilsey (in 1998 when she was 87) due to her failing sight Denis had to help Juliet with the medals. She never did another portrait. It took her ages to come to terms with her Macular Degeneration, the worst thing that could happen to a painter. In 2004, just before her 93rd birthday, she had a very close call indeed. The heart surgeon, Mr. Forsyth, said she was "running out of petrol"! and proposed a transplant of her aortic valve, giving her a fifty-fifty chance of survival. She said "yes please," and came through the operation with flying colours. Being of a venerable age, she had up days and down days, but she was totally alert in London for the opening of her retrospective show at the National Portrait Gallery in December 2004. The Director, Sandy Nairne, summed it all up in his excellent presentation, when he praised her portraits for that rare virtue in the age of photography: the rigorous discipline of drawing a likeness. The show lasted for 6 monts.

In the Spring of 2005 Juliet said "Each day the world grows darker physically, but I'm very happy with wonderful friends and relations who help me enormously, and I've had the most fascinating life to look back on." She died August 22, 2005.

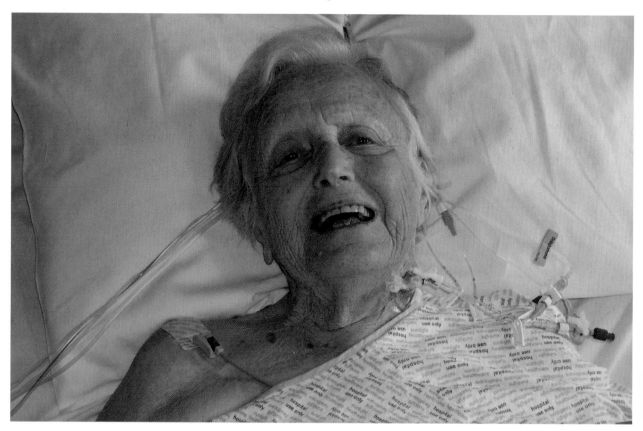

Juliet Pannett in *Who's Who* 2004

PANNETT, Juliet Kathleen, MBE 1993; FRSA; portrait artist; b 15 July 1911; 2nd d of Charles Somers and May (née Brice); m 1938, Major M. R. D. Pannett (d 1980), late the Devonshire Regt; one s one d. Educ: Wistons Sch., Brighton; Brighton College of Art. Special Artist to Illustrated London News, 1957-64. Exhibitions: Royal Festival Hall, 1957, 1958; Qantas Gallery, 1959; New York, 1960; Cleveland, Ohio, 1960; Cooling Gallery, London, 1961; Coventry Cathedral Festival, 1962: Gloucester Three Choirs Festival, 1962; Brighton Corporation Gallery, Rottingdean, 1967; Arun Art Centre, 1967, 1969, 1972; Fine Art Gall., London, 1969; Mignon Gall., Bath, 1970; Brotherton Gall., London, 1980; Pacific and Fringe Clubs, Hong Kong, 1986; Wigmore Hall, 1989, 1991; Royal Northern College of Music, 1989; Stamford Arts Centre, 1995. Exhibitor: Royal Academy; Royal Society of Portrait Painters; Royal Inst. of Painters in Watercolours, etc. Official Artist on several Qantas and Air Canada inaugural jet flights. Freeman: City of London, 1960; Painter Stainers Company, 1960 (Gold Medal, 1995). Work in Permanent Collections: 22 portraits in National Portrait Gall.; Scottish National Portrait Gall.; Bodleian Library; Ashmolean Museum; Oxford and Cambridge colleges; Royal College of Music; Painter Stainers Hall, London; Edinburgh Univ.; D Day painting for Devon and Dorset Regt, 1963; Commemorative Stained Glass Window (St Alban), Garrison Church, Munster, 1967; painting of Duke of Kent presenting new colours to Devon and Dorset Regt, 1982. Portraits, many for official bodies, include: HM the Queen (twice); HRH Princess Alexandra; HRH Prince Andrew, HRH Prince Edward, for HM the Queen; HRH Princess Marina, Duchess of Kent; HM King Hussein of Jordan; Field Marshall Viscount Alanbrooke; Lord Annan; Louis Armstrong; Dame Peggy Ashcroft; Earl Attlee; Lord Auchinleck; W. H. Auden; Prof. A. J. Ayer; Lord Baden-Powell; Lady Baden-Powell; Group Captain Sir Douglas Bader; Sir John Barbirolli; David Ben-Gurion; Leonard Bernstein; Sir Arthur Bliss; Sir Adrian Boult; Sir Maurice Bowra; Sir Benjamin Britten; Sir Arthur Bryant; Lord Butler of Saffron Walden; Lord Callaghan; Lord Carrington; Pablo Casals; Lord David Cecil; Group Captain Leonard Cheshire; Sir Winston Churchill; Jean Cocteau; Lord Dacre; Sir Colin Davis; Walter de la Mare; Lord Delfont; Victoria de los Angeles; Lord Denning; Sir Alec Douglas-Home; Jacqueline du Pré; Duke Ellington; Gracie Fields; Sir Ranulph Fiennes; Christopher Fry; Lord Gardner; Sir John Glubb; Lord Goddard; Lord Goodman; Lord Grimond; Lord Hailsham; Lord Harewood; Michael Heseltine; Ivon Hitchens; Sir Stanley Holloway; Prof. Sir Fred Hoyle; Bishop Huddleston; Cardinal Basil Hume; John Ireland; Augustus John; Colonel H Jones, VC; Carl Jung; Otto Klemperer; C. S. Lewis; Sir Basil Liddell-Hart; Sophia Loren; Humphrey Lyttelton; Sir Compton Mackenzie; Lord Marks; Sir Neville Marriner; Golda Meir; Yehudi Menuhin; Sir Robert Menzies; Naomi Mitchison; Field Marshal Lord Montgomery; Patrick Moore; Lord Morrison of Lambeth; Lord Mountbatten of Burma; Sir David Napley; Lavinia Duchess of Norfolk; Dame Marie Rambert; Ginger Rogers; Mstislav Rostropovich; A. L. Rowse; Edmund Rubbra; Bertrand Russell; Lord Salmon; Sir Malcolm Sargent; Sir Harry Secombe; Lord Shackleton; Lord Shawcross; Dmitri Shostakovich; Dame Edith Sitwell; Field Marshal Viscount Slim; Lord Snow; Gilbert Spencer; Earl Spencer; Igor Stravinsky; A. J. P. Taylor; Lady Thatcher; Sir Wilfred Thesiger; Sir Michael Tippett; Lord Tonypandy; Prof. Arnold Toynbee; G. M. Trevelyan; Sir Laurens van der Post; Sir William Walton; Evelyn Waugh; Sir Ralph Vaughan Williams; Sir Barnes Wallis; Sir Harold Wilson. Has broadcast on art subjects on TV in UK and USA. Publications: cover portraits for books by Sir Thomas Beecham, Charles Causley, Henry Cecil, Canon John Collins; Mary Drewery, Louis Golding, Gerald Pawle and Cyril Scott; drawings reproduced in The Times, Daily Telegraph, Birmingham Mail, Radio Times, The Lancet, Leisure Painter, The Artist, Law Guardian, Guardian Gazette, etc. Recreation: water-colour painting, especially landscapes and old buildings. Address: Pound House, Roundstone Lane, Angmering Village, Sussex BN16 4AL. T: Rustington (01903) 784446.

Juliet of a Thousand Faces

Julius Harrison

Jascha Horenstein

Pierre Monteux

Robert Jacoby

Carlo Maria Giulini

Ernest Ansermet

Benjamin Britten

Denis Matthews

Edmund Rubbra

Leonard Bernstein

Sir John Barbirolli

Rudolf Schwarz

Istvan Kerstesz

Partial List of Portraits

Abel, A. Lawrence
Abicair, Shirley
Ackroyd, Sir Cuthbert Lowell
Adams, John *Pastel*
Adrian, Max
Aggs, Julian Hanbury *Child*
Alanbrooke, Field Marshall Viscount *NPG,*
Aldred, Joel
Alexandra, Princess
Alport, Lady
Alport, Lord
Alsbury, Tom
Alwyn, Kenneth
Alwyn, William
Anderson, Del
Anderson, Rev. Prof. George *Pastel*
Andrew, Mr *Pastel*
Andrew, Roger *Pastel*
Andrews, Eamonn
Annan, Lord (Noel)
Ansermet, Ernest
Archer, Jeremy *Child*
Archer, Simon *Child*
Arieli, Celia
Armstrong, Claire *Child*
Armstrong, Gordon *Oil*
Armstrong, Mrs Gordon (Rosie) *Child*
Armstrong, James *Child*
Armstrong, Louis *Pastel*
Armstrong, Sir Thomas *NPG*
Arnold, Malcolm *NPG*
Arnold, ? *Child*
Arran, Lord
Ashby, Sir Eric
Ashby, Dame Margery Corbett
Ashcroft, Dame Peggy
Ashkenazy, Vladimir
Atcherley, Air Marshall Sir Richard *Pastel*
Atkins, Christopher
Atkins, John
Atkins, Richard
Atkinson, Lady Fenton
Atkinson, Lord Justice Fenton
Atkinson, Margaret Mary
Attlee, Earl *NPG*
Auchinleck, Field Marshall Lord *Pastel*
Auden, W.H. *Pastel NPG*
Ayer, Prof. A.J.

Baden-Powell, Lord
Baden-Powell, Olave Lady (2) *Pastel*
Badenoch, ?
Bader, Group Captain Douglas
Baillie-Grohman, Vice Admiral H.T. *Pastel*

Bain, Victoria *Child*
Baker, Mrs Hollis M. *Oil*
Ball, Miss
Ballantrae, Brigadier Lord
Barbara, Erica + Anthea *Child*
Barbirolli, Sir John *Pastel (2)*
Barclay, Prof. William *Pastel*
Bardsley, Cuthbert, Bishop of Coventry *Pastel*
Barou, Dr Noel
Barry, Father Patrick *Oil*
Bassett, Mrs, RAS Librarian
Baxter, Jane
Beard, Paul
Beaumont, Timothy
Beaumont, Victor
Beecham, Thomas *Pastel NPG*
Beer, Ian *Pastel*
Bell, Major W. *Oil*
Bellasis, Oliver, *Child*
Ben-Gurion, David *Pastel*
Benjamin, ? *Child*
Benjamin family *Child*
Berger, Admiral Peter *Pastel*
Beriosova, Svetlana
Berkeley, Lennox
Bernstein, Leonard
Bevan, Sir Timothy *Pastel*
Bewley, Dr W.F.
Biart, David *Pastel*
Bigham, James *Child*
Bigham, Lucinda *Child*
Bigham, ? *Child*
Bigland, Alexandra *Child*
Bigland, Charlotte *Child*
Bigland, Hermione *Child*
Bigland, Rosamund *Child*
Birkett, Lord
Blacker, Dr C. *NPG*
Blaikley, David *Child*
Blaikley, Gavin
Blaikley, Isobel
Bligh, Sir Edward
Bliss, Arthur
Boam, General T.A. *Oil*
Bolt, Anne
Bonnycastle, A.H.
Boodle, Dr L.A.
Booker, Mrs Gwenda *Oil*
Borradaile, General Hugh *Oil*
Borradaile, Mrs Hugh
Boudard, Lucinda *Child*
Boudard, Simon *Child*
Boult, Sir Adrian *Pastel*
Bowdon, Miss
Bowra, Sir Maurice
Bowyer, Charles Percival
Boyle, Sir Edward
Braddock, Joseph
Britten, Benjamin *Pastel*
Brown, George

Brownie' *Child*
Bruce, George *NPG*
Bryans, Dame Anne
Bryant, Sir Arthur
Buckley, Sir Denys *Oil*
Buckmaster, Maurice
Burton, Dr Maurice

Cadogan, Sir Alexander
Caldecote, Lord *Pastel*
Callaghan, James *NPG*
Callaghan, Lady *NPG*
Cameron, Basil
Campbell, Sybil
Campbell Smith, Dr W. *Pastel*
Carrington, Lord *NPG*
Carson, Willie *Oil*
Casals, Pablo
Caterham School, *Oil*
Cattell, Jeremy *Child*
Cattell, Jonathan *Child*
Cattell, Sally *Child*
Cattell, Simon *Child*
Causley, Charles
Cecil, Lord David *Pastel*
Chain, Prof. E.B.
Chamberlain, Col. F.W.
Chandler, T.R.
Channon, Mick *Oil*
Charbot, Sylvian
Charlesworth, Mr *Pastel*
Charnley, Sir John
Chataway, Christopher
Cheshire, Group Capt. Leonard
Chetwynd, George
Chorley, Richard *Pastel*
Churchill, Winston (4) *NPG*
Clark, G.T. *Pastel*
Clark, Sir William *Oil*
Clarke, Stewart D., F.C.S.
Clive ? *Pastel*
Cockcroft, Sir John
Cocks, Sir Barnett *Pastel*
Cocteau, Jean
Coldstream, Sir George *Oil*
Collett, Lieut. Col. T. Kingsley
Collins, Canon John *Pastel Oil*
Colville, Rhoda *Pastel*
Comyn, James
Cook, Gladys Spearman
Cook, Melville
Cope, Sir Zachary *Pastel*
Copper, Bob *Pastel*
Cork and Orrery, Lord, Admiral of the Fleet
Cottrell, Leonard
Courtney Dame Kathleen *Pastel*
Cowdrey, Colin
Cox, George *Oil*
Coxhead, Elizabeth
Cranmer, Peter
Cranmer, Dr Philip *Oil*
Crossley-Holland, Kevin
Cruden, Harry
Cunningham, Sir Charles *Oil*
Curzon, Clifford
Dale, Sir Henry *NPG*
Dalton, Lord (Hugh)

Danehurst, Harold *Pastel*
Darlington, Susan
Davey, Dr E.M.
Davidson, Neville *Pastel*
Davies, Vice Admiral Bell
Davies, Mrs Bell
Davies, Lord Justice Edmund
Davies, Meredith
Davies, ?
Davis, Colin
Davison, Arthur
Davison, Darrell and Beverley
de Moubray, Crispin *Child*
de Moubray, Jocelyn *Child*
de los Angeles, Victoria
de la Mare, Walter *NPG*
de Manio, Jack
Dean, Sir Patrick *Pastel*
Deed, Basil L.
Delfont, Lord *Oil*
Denby, Sir Richard *Pastel*
Denning, Lord *Oil NPG*
Denniss, Helen *Child*
Deutscher, Isaac
Devlin, Baron, of West Wick
Diplock, T.
Dobson, Christopher
Dodd, Rosie
Dolling, Mr *Pastel*
Donovan, Lord
Dorati, Antal
Douglas, Lord, of Kyrtleside
Douglas, Sholto *Pastel*
Douglas-Home, Sir Alec *NPG*
Down, Maurice *Oil*
du Pré, Jacqueline
Dudley, Prof. H.A.L. *Pastel*
Duncan, Sir Arthur
Duncan ? *Pastel*
Dyson, Edward

Edmonds family *Pastel*
Eggar, Sir Thomas *Oil*
Eldridge, Eric
Ellington, Duke *Pastel*
Elliott, Bill *Oil*
Elwes, Sir Richard
Errol, Earl of *Oil*
Evans, Rev. Fred *Oil*
Evans, Geraint
Evans, Seiriol, Dean of Glouc.
Everall, Mark
Eyston Child *Child*

Fagin, Anthony
Faid, Prof., daughters of
Fanhanel, ?
Farndale, General Martin *Oil*
Farndale, Lady *Oil*
Farndale, Captain Richard *Oil*
Fasano, Renato
Feltham, John
Fennell, Prof. John
Fields, Gracie
Fischer, Annie (2)
Fischer-Dieskau, Dietrich
Fisher, Sylvia
Fistoulari, Anatole

Fitzalan Howard, Lady Mary   *Pastel*
Flanders, Dalma
Fleming, Amaryllis
Fletcher, Dr ?
Florey, Prof. Howard W.
Flynn, Caroline   *Child*
Flynne, Patrick   *Child*
Ford, Dr   *Pastel*
Ford,. Peter and Dr Grace   *Oil*
Foster, Sir Harry Hilton
Fou Tsong
Fowler, Sir Derek   *Pastel*
Fox, Sir Theodore
Foxall, Dennis   *Oil*
Foyle, Miss B.
Foyle, J.
Franks, Arthur
Freeman, John
Friedland, Szi   *Pastel*
Fry, Christopher   *Pastel*
Fulton, Lord (John)
Fulton, Lord, sons of   *Child*
Funge-Smith, Mark   *Pastel*

Gafftom, Polly
Gafftom, Simon
Gafftom, Barney
Gafftom, Phillipa
Gage, Mrs Bette   *Pastel*
Gamba, Pierino
Gammell,. General Sir James,
Gardiner, Lord   *Pastel NPG*
Gareth, Father   *Pastel*
Garling, David   *Pastel*
Genee, Dame Adeline
Geraldine ?   *Pastel*
Gheorghieu, Valentin
Gibbs, Field Marshall Sir
   Roland (2)   *Oil*
Gibson, Alexander
Godber, Geoffrey
Gilbert, Prof. E.W.
Gillett family   *Child*
Gilligan, Arthur E.R.   *Oil*
Giulini, Carlo Maria
Gladstone, Sir Wm.   *Pastel Oil*
Gladstone Sir William and Lady
Glubb, General Sir John   *Pastel*
Gluckstein, Sir Louis
Goddard, Lord
Godrich, John   *Oil*
Golding, Louis
Goldsmith, Samuel
Goldsmith, Tessa
Goodbody, ?   *Child*
Goodman, Lord   *NPG*
Goossens, Sir Eugene
Goossens, Leon
Gordon, John   *Pastel*
Gordon, Mrs A.   *Oil*
Gordon, Aileen
Gordon, Denis
Gordon, John
Gordon-Lennox Alexander
Gough, John Clifford   *Oil*
Grant, Pauline
Gray, Anne
Gray, Charlotte Acherson

Gray, Duncan
Gray, George   *Pastel*
Gray, Giles Acherson
Gray, Henrietta Acherson
Gray, John
Gray, Keith
Gray, Quinton
Gray, Ruth
Gray, Simon Acherson
Green, Mr   *Oil*
Grey, George B. R.
Grieve, T.R.
Griffiths, Dr John   *Pastel*
Grigorieff, Serge
Grimond, Jo   *Pastel NPG*
Grinke, Frederick
Groves, Charles
Guest, Dr Douglas   *Pastel*
Guest, Ivor
Guingand, Major General Sir
   Francis de   *NPG*
Gullick, Rowley
Gumpert, Benjamin
Gunn, Lieut. Ward
Gusterson, Francis (2)   *Pastel*
Guy, Basil, Bishop   *Oil*

Hadfield, Esmé   *Oil*
Hailwood, John
Hall, Donald
Hallowes, Odette   *Pastel*
Hansard, John   *Pastel*
Harden, Giles + Alexander
      Child
Harding, Field Marshall Lord,
   of Petherton
Hardinge, Lady, of Penshurst
Harewood, Lord   *Pastel*
Harley, Sir Stanley
Harman, Lord Justice
Harper, Heather
Harris, Major Campbell
Harrison, Sir Eric
Harrison, Julius   *Oil*
Hart, Sir Basil Liddell
Hart, Catherine
Hart, Louise
Haskell, Dr Arnold   *Pastel*
Heap, Sir Desmond
Heaton, Dr Trevor   *Pastel*
Heaton, Mrs Trevor
Heaton, Dr   *Pastel*
Hemingway, Nicola
Henriques, Col. Robert   *Pastel*
Hepner, Linda
Herbison, Margaret
Herd, T.
Herd, Mrs T.
Heron, Peter
Heron, Wendy
Heseltine, John   *Child*
Heseltine, Lady   *Oil*
Heseltine, Michael   *NPG*
Heseltine, Sophie   *Child*
Hewitt-Jones, Tony
Higgs, ?
Highton, Cecil (deathbed)
Hildred, Alexandra and Pamela
      Pastel Child

Hill, Adrian   *NPG,*
Hill, Lord, of Luton
Hill, R.H.
Hilton, Dr Gwen
Hinshelwood, Prof.   *Pastel*
Hinshelwood, Sir Cyril
Hitchens, Ivon   *NPG*
Hobbs, Charlotte
Hobbs, H.
Hobbs, Mrs H.
Hobbs, Jenny
Hobbs, Sally
Hodge, Mrs Jane   *Oil*
Hodgetts, Sarah   *Child*
Hodson, Lord
Hogg, Quintin
Holdsworth, Judge   *Oil*
Holland, Sir Milner   *Pastel*
Hollingsworth, John
Hollins, Mrs Jane   *Oil*
Holloway, Stanley   *Pastel*
Holmes, Ralph
Holttum, Prof. Richard
Home, Sir Alec Douglas
Hoogewerf, Teddy   *Oil*
Hooton, Florence
Hope, Alexander
Hope, Rev. W.J.
Hore-Belisha, Lord
Horenstein, Jascha
Horn, Prof. Gabriel
Horrocks, Brian   *Pastel*
Horsley, James   *Child*
Horsley, Kate   *Child*
Howard, Sir Edward (2)
      Pastel Oil
Hoyle, Prof. Sir Fred   *NPG*
Huddleston, Trevor, Bishop of
   Stepney   *NPG*
Hudson, Laurence
Hughes, ?   *Child*
Hull, Sir Percy   *Pastel*
Hume, Cardinal Basil   *Pastel*
Humphreys, Sir Olliver, C.B.E.
Hunt, Warren, Bishop of Derby
Hylton-Foster, Sir Harry   *NPG*

Inchyra, Lord
Ingram, Hugh   *Pastel*
Inman, W.
Innes, Malcolm, of Endingight
Innes, Sir Thomas, of Learney
Ireland, John   *NPG*
Isham, Sir Gyles
Ismay, General Baron, of
   Wormington
Isserlis, Julius   *NPG*

Jacob, Dr Gordon   *NPG*
Jacob, Lt General Sir Ian   *NPG*
Jacoby, Robert   *Pastel*
Jacoby, Mrs Robert
Jacques, Dr Reginald
James, Lord (Eric), of
   Rusholme
James, Rev. Eric
Jameson-Green, Ronald (2)   *Oil*
Jarvis, Andrew, F.R.C.S.
Jochum, Eugen

Johnson, Dr Christopher   *Pastel*
Jones, Gen. Sir Charles   *Pastel*
Jones, Lady   *Pastel*
Jones, Colonel H'   *Oil*
Joseph, Mrs Joyce   *Pastel*
Joyce, Eileen (2)
Jung, Prof. Carl

Karmel, Lord Justice David
Karsavina, Tamara   *NPG*
Katin, Peter (2)
Keith, Sir Arthur   *Pastel NPG*
Kendrew, Sir John   *Pastel*
Kent, Princess Marina Duchess
Kentner, Louis
Kenyon, Sir Harold
Kenyon, Dr Kathleen
Kerby, Tessa
Kertez, Istvan
Kilmuir, Lady
King, Mrs Heather   *Pastel*
King, Jack   *NPG*
King, Rodney   *Oil*
Kingsbury, Dr Alan   *Pastel*
Kingsley, Mary   *Pastel*
Klemperer, Otto
Knowles, Prof. M.D.
Kosygin, Alexei
Kremer, Mr   *Oil*
Kremer, Mrs   *Oil*
Kripps, Henry

Laird, Dorothy
Lambert, Henry   *Pastel*
Lambert, Uvedale   *Pastel*
Lambert, Mrs Uvedale   *Pastel*
Lancing College, headmaster
Langhorne, Rosemary   *Pastel*
Lardy, Elizabeth   *Pastel*
Lardy, M. Pierre   *Pastel*
Lardy, M., Senior   *Oil*
Lardy, Mme., Senior   *Oil*
Large, R.   *Oil*
Laski, Neville
Lawley, Sue   *Pastel*
Lawley, Tom   *Child*
Lawson, Sir Henry
Lawson, Timothy
Lawson, ?
Laycock, Major General Sir
   Robert E.
Lee, Desmond
Lennox, Admiral Gordon
Lenton, Lilian   *NPG*
Leon, Henry Cecil
Lepine, David
Leslie, Hubert
Lewis, C.S.   *Pastel*
Lewis, Richard
Liardet, Major General Sir
   Claude F.
Liddell-Hart, Sir Basil   *NPG,*
Limerick, Angela, Countess of
Linfield, Arthur G.
Lister, Moira
Lockwood, Henry   *Pastel*
Lockwood, Sir John
Lohmeyer, Philippa   *Child*
Long, Sir Ronald

Longhurst, Carolyn	
Longhurst, Timothy	
Lonsdale, Miss Constance	
Lonsdale, Dame Kathleen	
Loren, Sophia	*Pastel*
Loss, Joe	
Lovell, Prof. Sir Bernard	*Pastel*
Lovely, Percy Thomas	
Lovett, Sydney	
Lowe, John	
Lund, Paul	
Lushington, Sir John	*Oil*
Lutyens, Elizabeth	
Lynn, Vera	
Lyons, Jack	
Lythgoe, Clive	
Macarthur, Lieut. General Sir William	
Macaulay, Dr	
McCahearty, Ven. R.G.H.	
McClare, Brig. J.R. ,	
Macfarlane, Robert Gwyn	
Macfarlane, Mrs Robert	
McGregor, Captain	*Oil,*
Mackenna, R.M.B.	
Mackenna, Mrs	
McKenna, Christopher	
McKenna, David	
McKenna, ?	
Mackenzie, Chantalina	
Mackenzie, Compton	*Pastel*
Mackintosh, Captain Kenneth	
MacLeod, Baron, of Fuinary	
Manser, Michael	
McMahon, Father Malcolm	*Oil*
McNeill, David	*Pastel*
MacTaggart, Sir William	
Maddison, Mrs ?	
Maddison, Dr ?	
Mais, S.B.	*Pastel*
Malcolm, H.G., VC	*Oil*
Malcuzynski, Witold	
Malko, Nicolai	
Mankowitz, Wolf	
Marks, Lord	
Marlar family	*Pastel*
Marlar, ?	*Child*
Marriner, Neville	
Marshall, Sir James	
Marshall, Lady	*Oil*
Marshall, Katie + Debbie	*Child*
Marshall, Michael, M.	*NPG*
Marshall, Rev. Michael	*Pastel*
Martin, Prof. A.F.	*NPG*
Martin, Mrs Stella	*Oil*
Martin, Toby	
Masire, Dr Quett	*Oil*
Matthews, Denis	*NPG*
Maudling, Reginald	
Mayer, Philippe de Lima	
Mayhew, Christopher	
Meir, Golda	*Pastel*
Meldrum, Peter	
Mellers, Wilfred	
Menges, Herbert (2)	
Menuhin, Yehudi (2)	*Pastel NPG*
Menzies, Sir Robert	*NPG*
Metcalfe, Dr C.R.	
Metcalfe, Mrs C.R.	
Midwood, Bill	*Oil*
Miller, ?	
Miller, Mrs ?	
Millis, L.W.F.	*Pastel*
Mills, Air Chief Marshall Sir George	
Milmo, Sir Helenus	
Milne, Jackie	
Milsom, Prof. Toby	*Pastel*
Miskin, Sir James *Pastel*	*Oil*
Mitchison, Naomi	*Pastel*
Moiseivitch, Benno	
Montagu, Lady, of Beaulieu	
Montagu, Lord, of Beaulieu	
Montagu, Hon. Jonathan, of Beaulieu	*Child*
Montagu, Mary, of Beaulieu	
Montagu, Ralph, of Beaulieu	
Monteux, Pierre	
Montgomery, Field Marshall Viscount, of Alamein	
Moran, Lord	
Morey, ?	*Child*
Morris, Gwyn Rhyse Francis	
Morris, Lord, of Borth-y-Gest	
Morrison, J.J.	
Morrison, Miss Jean	*Oil*
Morrison Lord of Lambeth	*NPG*
Morton, Sally	*Pastel*
Mountbatten, Admiral of the Fleet Earl, of Burma	*NPG*
Muncaster, Claude	
Munsch, Charles	
Murray, Dr Margaret	*Oil*
Murray-Willis, ?	
Mursell, Sir Peter	*Oil*
Mursell, Lady	*Oil*
Myles, Maurice	
Myott family	
Myres, Dr, Bodley's Librarian	
Nahari, ?	
Napley, Sir David	*Pastel*
Nash, Mr	
Navarra, André	
Nerina, Nadia	
Nevill, B.	
Newsome, Dr David	*Oil*
Newsome, S.H.	
Nickalls, G.O.	
Noorduyn, Antie	
Norfolk, the Duke of	*NPG Pastel*
Norfolk, Lavinia, Duchess	*NPG*
Norman, General Charles Wake	
Nunneley, John	*Oil*
Odone, Annabel	*Child*
Odone, Benedict	*Child*
Odone, Sebastian	
Odone, Toby	
Ogdon, John	
Oistrakh, David	
Oistrakh, Igor	*Pastel*
Oliver, Rev. Kenneth	*Oil*
Ormerod, Lord Justice	
Osmond, A.H.	
Osorio, Edwin	*Oil*
Oswald, Rev. William	*Oil*
Oxton, Caroline	*Pastel*
Palmer, Alec	
Palmer, Emma	
Palmer, Michael	
Pannett, Prof. Aubrey	
Pannett, Belinda	*Oil*
Pannett, Denis (3)	*Child*
Pannett, Liz (3)	*Child*
Pantin, Professor .	*Pastel*
Panufnik, Andrej	
Parker Lord, Waddington	*NPG*
Parker-Smith, Mrs	*Oil*
Parker-Smith's grand-daughter	
Parkin, Eric (hands)	
Parkinson, Georgina	
Paterson, Arthur Spence	*Oil*
Patey, Elizabeth Gerard	*Pastel*
Patterson, Dr	*Oil*
Peacock,. Colonel G.A.	*Oil*
Pearce, Lord	
Pears, Peter	
Pearse, Admirsl Roger Gerard	
Pearson, Lord Justice	
Pemberton, Jeremy	*NPG*
Pennock, Emma	*Child*
Pennock, George	*Child*
Peto, Sir Henry	*Oil*
Petrie, Sir Charles	*Pastel*
Phillimore, Hon. Mr Justice	
Phillips, Ailne	
Phillips, Montague	
Piatigorsky, Gregor	
Pictet Child	*Child*
Pierotti, Miss A.M.	
Piggot, Timothy	
Pile, General Sir Frederick A.	
Pole, Prof. Jack,	
Pope, W.J. Macqueen	
Pope John	
Porteous, Prof. Norman	*Oil*
Powell, W.	
Prince Edward	*Child*
Prince Andrew	*Child*
Pritchard, John	
Procter, ?	
Purchas, Lord Justice	*Oil*
H.M. the Queen (2)	
Radcliffe, Nicholas	
Radcliffe, Father Timothy.	*Oil*
Radcliffe, Major Walter	*Oil*
Radcliffe, Mrs	*Oil*
Radzinowicz, Prof. Sir Leon	
Rae, Dr John	*Pastel*
Rambert, Dame Marie	*NPG*
Rawsthorne, Alan	*NPG*
Rayson, Thomas	
Read, Ernest (2)	
Reading, Eva, Marchioness of (Baroness Swanborough)	
Reddaway, Prof. W.B.	*Pastel*
Redmayne, Martin	*NPG*
Redpath, Anne	*Pastel*
Redwood, Hugh	
Reeve, D.A.D.	*Oil*
Reid, Andrew	
Reid, Fiona	
Reid, Irvin	
Reid, Brig. Sir Francis	
Reid, Lord	
Reid, Nicholas	
Renison, Sir Patrick	
Rickards, Jenny	
Reid, Jill	
Riddell, Victor	*Pastel*
Rignold, Hugo	
Roberton, Neil	
Roberts, Edward, Bishop of Ely	
Robertson, J.G.	
Robinson, John, Bishop of Woolwich	
Robinson, L.J.	*Oil*
Robson, Mrs Jan	*Pastel*
Robson, ?	*Child*
Roe, Miss Grace	
Rogers, Ginger	*Pastel*
Roope, Clover	
Rosencraft, ?	
Ross, Rev. C.	
Ross, James McLean	*Oil*
Ross, Sir James Paterson	
Rostropovich, Mstislav	*NPG*
Rothenstein, Sir John	*NPG*
Rothwell, Evelyn	
Rowan School, headmistress	
Rubbra, Edmund (2)	*Oils*
Rubbra, Edmund	
Rubidge, ?	
Rubinstein, Artur	
Rundall, Jeremy	
Rushworth, Dr Geoffrey	*Pastel*
Russell, Audrey	
Russell, Lord (Bertrand)	
Russell, Sir Charles	*Oil*
Russell, Prof. Donald	*Pastel*
Russell, Prof. Gerald	
Russell, Dr Joy	*Pastel*
Russell, Lord Justice	
Rutland, Harold	
Salmon, Lord Justice	*Pastel*
Salt, Dame Barbara	
Samuel, Viscount	*NPG*
Sanders, John	
Sanderson, Dr R.M.	*Pastel*
Sandison, Dr	
Sargant, Henry Edmund	
Sargent, Sir Malcolm	*NPG*
Sautter, Christof	
Scarman, Lord	*Pastel*
Schneur, Zalman	
Schwarz, Rudolf	
Scott, Cyril	
Scott, John Robertson	
Searle, Humphrey	
Segovia	
Seiber, Matyas	
Sellick, Phyllis	
Shackleton, Lord	*Pastel*
Sharp, Dame Evelyn	
Sharp, Molly	
Shaw, Harry	
Shawcross, Lord	

Shearer, George
Shlanski
Shostakovich, Dmitri — NPG
Siemaszko, Doncia
Siemaszko, Marek
Silverman, Sydney
Simon, Sir Jocelyn
Simon, Lucette and Michael — Oil
Simpson, Dr Leonard
Simpson, Mrs Lilian — Oil
Sir David Stephens
Sitwell, Dame Edith
Slade, Sir Benjamin — Oil
Slim, Field Marshal — NPG
Sloman, Dr Albert
Slot, Dr Gerald
Smart, Chrissie + Gregory — Oil
Smith, Anna Parker
Smith, Cyril
Smith, Judge Dennis — Oil
Smith, Dolly
Smith, Hubert
Smith, Parker
Smith, Ronald
Smith, T. Dan
Snow, John — Oil
Snow, Lord (C.)
Solicitors Company, — Pastel
Somers, Claire-Lise — Pastel
Somers, David
Somers, Giles — Pastel
Somers, May
Somers, Natasha — Child
Somers, Richard — Oil
Somers Vreeland, Vanessa — Pastel
Somervell, Austin
Somervell, Matthew
Spence, Elspeth
Spencer, Earl
Spenser, Gilbert — Pastel
Spenser, Wing Commander
  Maurice — Oil
St John of Fawsley, Lord — NPG
St Joseph, Prof. Keith — Pastel
Stacey, Rev. Nicholas

Stancliffe, Canoon Michael — Oil
Stancliffe, Michael S.
Stanley ? — Pastel
Stapleton, Captain Bryan
Staveley, Alan — Pastel
Stemp, Mr — Oil
Stemp, Leslie
Stephen, Virginia
Stephens, Sir David — Pastel
Stephens, Doreen
Stephenson, Admiral
  Sir Gilbert — Pastel
Stern, G.B.
Stern, Isaac — Pastel
Stern, Lady
Stevens, Cecil
Stewart, William — Oil
Stewart, Andrew
Stewart, Mrs Andrew
Stewart, Garry
Stewart, Sir Iain
Stewart, Very Rev. James Stuart
Stewart, William — Pastel
Stewart, ? — Child
Stirling, Colonel W.F.
Stoddard, Dr Alan — Oil
Stoddart, Michael Craig — Pastel
Storey, Lynette — Child
Storey, Michael — Child
Storey, ?
Stott, Mary — Pastel
Stravinsky, Igor
Sumsion, Dr Herbert
Swanborough, Baroness — Pastel
Switzer, J.F.Q.
Szeryng, Henryk

Tallents, Sir Stephen — NPG
Tansley, Lady
Taylor, Sandy
Tertis, Lionel
Thatcher, Margaret
Thesiger, Sir Wilfred
Thomas, Rt Hon. George — Pastel
Thomas, Nancy

Thompson, Colonel Digby — Oil
Thompson, Sir Harold — Pastel
Thompson, Sir Richard
Thorpe, Jeremy
Tinsley, Tom — Pastel
Tippett, Sir Michael — Oil NPG
Tobenhouse, Nina — Pastel
Todd, Lord (Alexander)
Tolmeyer, Richard Jonathan
Tookey, Geoffrey
Toomey, J.
Tortelier, Paul
Toynbee, Prof. Arnold — NPG
Trevelyan, G.M. — NPG
Trevor Roper, Prof. Hugh — NPG
Trowell, Brian
Tryon, Valerie
Tucker, Miss Elizabeth — Oil
Tucker, Miss
Tugwell, Simon — Oil
Tureck, Rosalyn
Turner, David
Turner, Theodora
Tweedsmuir, Lady
Twist, Miss M.

Upjohn, Lord

Vallier, John
van Beinum, Eduard
van der Post, Sir Laurens
Van der Welde
Van Gogh, Dr Vincent — Pastel
Vaughan Williams, Ralph (2)
  — Pastel NPG
Vian, Adm. Philip — Pastel NPG
Vickers, Joan
Vreeland, Frederick — Charcoal
Vyvyan, Jennifer

Waddilove, Father Deni (2)
Wadham, Justin — Pastel
Walker, Squadron Leader
Wallace, Miss Hazel Vint. — Oil

Wallis, Sir Barnes (2)
  — Oil + Pastel NPG
Ward, Sir Philip — Oil
Waugh, Evelyn
Way, W. — Oil
Weatherstone, Sir Duncan
Wedgwood, Veronica
Weisz, Victor
Welsch, Dr Robert
Wemyss & March, Countess of
Wemyss & March, Earl of
Wheeler, Michael — Oil
Wheeler, Tom
Wheeler-Bennett, Sir John
  — Pastel
Whettam, Graham
Whittington, Prof. Harry — Pastel
Wickens, Victoria and Virginia
Wickins, David
Widgery, Lord — NPG
Wilberforce, Squadron Leader
  Barbara — Oil
Wilberforce, Squadron Leader
  Barbara, and husband — Oil
Wilberforce, Lord
Wilkinson, Emma — Child
Wilkinson, James — Child
Wilkinson, Norman
Williams, Very Rev. H.C.N.
Williams, Leslie — Oil
Willis, Sir John — Oil
Wilsey, Captain John
Wilson, Prof. Dover
Wilson, Harold
Winn, Lord Justice
Wolfson, Sir Isaac
Wood, General George — Oil
Wood, Major General G.N.
Woodhouse, James — Oil
Wootton, Tony — Pastel
Wright, A. Dickson
Wyatt, R.E.S. — Oil

Yadin, Yigael

We are sorry if some sitters' names have not been listed.
Please send us all information and we'll add it in the next
edition.

Index

References to illustrations in the text are indicated in *italics*

Ada, maid in JP's family 15
Adrian, Max, Actor 54
Alanbrooke, Field Marshal Viscount *34*
Aldington, Lord, bank director 33
Alexandra, HRH Princess 40, *44*
Anderson, Miss Mabel, HRH Prince Andrew's Nurse 95
Andrew, HRH Prince 95-100, *96*
Annan, Lord, Master of King's College Cambridge 23
Anne, HRH Princess 95-96
Armstrong, Gordon, High Sheriff of Northumberland *34*
Armstrong, Louis, Musician 75, *80*
Armstrong-Jones, Antony, Photographer, married HRH
 Princess Margaret 71
Arnold, Stumpy, from Burpham, a rabbit catcher *8, 9*
Ashby, Sir Eric, Master of Clare College Cambridge 23, *47*
Ashcroft, Dame Peggy, Actress 55
Attlee, Lord, Clement, Prime Minister 70
Auchinleck, Field Marshal Sir Claude *33, 72*
Auden, WH, Poet *73*
Ayer, AJ, Professor of Logic, Oxford *23, 47*

Baden-Powell, Lady, founder of Girl Guides 28, *43*
Baden-Powell, Lord, son of the founder of Boy Scouts 43
Bader, Sir Douglas, Aviator 43
Barbirolli, Sir John, orchestra conductor 22, *75, 86*
Bardot, Brigitte, Film Star 54
Bardsley, Cuthbert, Bishop of Coventry 29
Barry, Father Patrick, headmaster of Ampleforth 28-29
Bartlett, Norman, Australian Press Attache 39
Beaton, Cecil, Photographer 94
Beatrix, HM Queen of the Netherlands 97, 100
Beatrix, Phoebe's pet mouse 71
Beckett, Arthur, Editor of the *Sussex County Magazine* *8, 9*
Bedells, Phyllis, ballerina and teacher 59
Beecham, Sir Thomas, conductor 22, 76
Bellew, Sir George, Garter King of Arms 42
Ben-Gurion, David, Israeli Prime Minister 65-67
Ben-Gurion, Mrs, wife of Israeli Prime Minister 67
Bennett, Ernest, Servant of the Royal Household 102
Beriosova, Svetlana, ballerina *58*
Bernstein, Leonard, Composer, Conductor *80*
Betjeman, Sir John, Poet Laureate 101
Bishop, Mrs, family servant 15
Blum, family from Vienna 12
Boam, Major General T.A. 35
Bobo, Maid to HM The Queen 100
Boult, Sir Adrian, orchestra conductor 22, *75, 77*
Bowley, EH, Cricketer 61
Bowra, Sir Maurice, Master of Wadham College, Oxford 23
Bradbury, Julia, Qantas Airlines public relations officer 37
Braden, Bernard, TV Personality 54
Brazier, William, war veteran *8*
Brice, William 13
Britten, Benjamin, Composer *75, 79*
Bruce, George, President, Royal Society of Portrait
 Painters *94*
Bryant, Lady 89
Bryant, Sir Arthur 89
Bryden, Beryl, Music Hall Singer *80*
Burnham, Lord, politician 42
Butler, Rt. Hon. RA, Chancellor of the Exchequer *71*

Cambridge Crew: Leggett, D.F.; Cooke, A.V.; Beckett, M.H.;
 Chewton, Viscount, President; De Rancourt, F.G.; Bevan,
 M.V.; Maasland, J.H.; Webb, P.J.; Jackson, D.B.R. *61*
Cameron, Basil, conductor 77
Campbell, Judy, actress *9*
Campbell, Sybil, Magistrate at Tower of London Courts 90
Canterbury, Archbishop of, 67
Carrington, Lord, Foreign Secretary *70*
Casals, Pablo, Cellist *79*
Cecil, Judge Henry, Justice and Writer *92*
Charles, HRH The Prince of Wales *8*, 74, 95, 100

Chataway, Chris, Olympic sprinter *60*
Chorley, Lord, politician 42
Churchill, Sir Winston 32, 48, *68*, 85
Cisek, Professor, well-known Austrian art master 12
Clark, Alan, Politician 68
Clarke, Stewart, surgeon 19
Cleaver, Robinson, Conductor 79
Cobb, family servant 15
Cockcroft, Sir John, Master of Churchill College,
 Cambridge 23, *47*
Cocteau, Jean, French poet, writer and film director *55*
Codling, Mrs, part-time cleaner 54, *71*
Coldstream, Sir George, Jurist *91*
Connaught, Duke and Duchess 95
Cope, Sir Zachary, Eminent Surgeon 30, 56-57
Cornford, Pat 'Titch', Cricketer *60*, 61
Coulson, David, Photographer 74
Courtney, Dame K, Suffragette 69
Cranmer, Peter, captain of the English rugby team 12
Cromwell, Oliver, Soldier and Statesman 35
Curzon, Clifford, Pianist 77

Dale, Sir Henry, Physiologist and Nobel Prize Winner 48
Daumier, Honore, Artist Front cover flap
Davis, Lord - Law Lord 87
De La Mare, Walter, Poet and Author *73*
De La Warr, Lord and Lady 38
De Lara, Adelina, Pianist 84
Delfont, Lord - Baron Bernard, theatre producer *46*, 96
Denning, Lady Joan *8*
Denning, Lord - Law Lord *87, 88*
Devas, Antony, Portrait Painter 72
Dixon Wright, Arthur. Surgeon 57
Dixon Wright, Clarissa, well-known TV cook 57
Dolin, Anton, Choreographer 58
Dolmetsch, Arnold, Musical Performer 81
Dolmetsch, Carl, Musical Performer 81
Dolmetsch, Family, Instrument Makers and Musicians *81*
Douglas-Home, Sir Alec, Prime Minister *69-71*
Dvorák, Antonin, Composer 84

Edward, HRH Prince *96-100*
Eggar, Thomas, Law Society Founder 90
Elizabeth II, HM The Queen 95-104, *100*
Elizabeth II, HM The Queen, and Juliet Pannett 103
Elizabeth, HM The Queen Mother 26
Elizabeth, HRH Princess, later HM Queen of England 26
Ellington, Duke, Composer, Conductor 75, *80*
Elliot, Bill, The Queen's Company of Archers 35
Elliot, George, cabbie *8*
Esther, JP's cousin 13
Fagin, Anthony, JP's former son-in-law,
 International Civil Servant 65
Farndale, General Sir Martin 33, *34*
Fauntleroy, Little Lord, Fictional Aristocratic Child 88
Fellowes, Robert, The Queen's Deputy Private Secretary
 97-102
Fischer, Annie, Pianist *84*
Fitzalan Howard, Lady Mary, Duke of Norfolk's daughter
 44
Fleming, Amaryllis, Cellist *84*
Fonteyn, Dame Margot, ballerina 59, *84*
Forsyth, Mr, JP's Heart Surgeon 6, 104
Fox, Mr, antique dealer 16
Fry, Christopher, Playwright *73*
Fuhrer, David, husband of JP's sister Leonore 14
Fulton, Lord, Master of the new University of Sussex 23

Gardiner, Lord - Lord High Chancellor of England 92
Genee, Dame Adeline, ballet dancer 30
George V, HM King 96, 100

Gilligan, Arthur, Captain of Cricket *61*
Ginnett, Louis, art master 7
Glubb, Sir John, 'Glubb Pasha,' Arab Legion Commander
 34, 72
Goddard, Lord - Lord Chief Justice *89*
Goossens, Leon, Eugene and Sidonie, Family of Musicians
 82
Gordon-Lennox, Admiral Sir Alexander *45*
Goyard, Amelie, JP's mother-in-law 17
Gray, Thelma (née Evans) Breeder of Corgis 101
Greenaway, Kate, 19 century children's illustrator 13
Griffith, John, Public Orator, Oxford *48*
Grimond, Jo, Leader of the Liberal Party *70*

Hailie Selassie, Emperor of Ethiopia *9*, 72
Hammond, WH, Cricketer 61
Harman, Lord Mayor of London *44*
Harman, Lord, High Court Judge 88
Harrison, Julius, Conductor *78*
Harrison, Sir Eric, Australian High Commissioner 41
Harry, HRH Prince 102
Hartnell, Norman, Dress Designer to the Queen 85
Hathaway, Anne, William Shakespeare's wife 13
Heath, Sir Edward, Prime Minister 71
Hermann, Luke, art editor 22
Herod, Biblical King 65
Heseltine, Michael, Deputy Prime Minister *71*
Heseltine, William, Private Secretary to The Queen 95-96
Hess, Dame Myra, Concert Pianist 28, *84*
Hitchcock, Sir Eldred, Tea Planter 27
Hitchens, Ivon, Artist *94*
Hochhauser, Victor, Rostropovich's manager *78*
Holland, Lady Eileen 92
Holland, Sir Milner, CBE, QC 30, 32, 92
Horrocks, Lieutenant-General Sir Brian, Black Rod 34-35, 42
Howard, Sir Edward, Lord Mayor of London *45*
Hoyle, Sir Fred, English astronomer and mathematician *73*
Hughes, T.G. 'Tiggie,' headmaster, Rose Hill School
 19-20, *59*
Hughes, Ted, Poet Laureate 101
Hume, Cardinal, Head of the English Catholic Church 28
Hume, Lady, wife of Sir Alec Douglas-Hume 69
Hussein, Saddam, Dictator of Iraq 33
Hustler, Tom, *Tatler* photographer 38
Hutchinson, Charley, JP's former fiancé *12*

Ingram, Hugh, nephew of Sir Bruce Ingram *23*
Ingram, Sir Bruce, Editor of the *Illustrated London News*
 22, 31, *47*
Innes, Malcolm, Lord Lyon, son of Sir Thomas Lerne *46*
Ireland, John, Composer *83*

Jackson, Dr. Francis, Organist at York Minster 82
James, Lord of Rusholme, Vice Chancellor of York
 University 48
Jeffreys, 17th- Century Judge 88
Jesus Christ 67
Job, Charles, JP's boyfriend *9, 10*
Job, Mrs, Mother of Charles Job 11
John the Baptist, Biblical Figure 65
John, Augustus, Painter 84
Jolly, Royal Corgi 100
Jones, Colonel 'H', VC *36*
Joyce, Eileen, Pianist *55, 85*
Juliet Pannett
 in Australia (with coala bear) *38*
 Monty's Double with JP *33*
 Mountbatten, Lord Louis, with JP *32*
 Willis, Sir John, being painted by JP *90*
Jumo, guard in village of Tabora *24*

Karmel, David, Jurist *91*
Karsavina, Tamara, Ballerina 30, *59*,

Kaye, Danny, Comedian and Film Star 67
Keith, Sir Arthur, Scottish surgeon and anthropologist 57
Kelly, Barbara, TV Personality, Bernard Braden's wife 54
Khachaturian, Aram Ilyich, Composer 96
Charles I, HM King 17
King, Col. Rodney, Yachtsman 61
Kitembe, tribal chief 24
Kitt, Eartha, Singer 102
Klemperer, Otto, Conductor 79
Knight, Dame Laura 7

Landseer, Sir Edwin, Victorian Painter 95
Laputa, Kenyan Portrait Painter 72
Large, R, Master, Worshipful Company of
    Painter Stainers 93
Lawson, Timothy, JP's Sitter 30
Lenton, Lilian, Suffragette 69
Leonardo Da Vinci, quotation 30
Lerney, Sir Thomas, Lord Lyon, King of Arms 46
Levy, Jacob, Guide 65-67
Lewis, CS, Oxford Don 23
Lewis, Flora, distinguished graphic artist 30
Liddell-Hart, Sir Basil, Military Historian 36
Lok Wan T, Chinese millionaire 39
Lonsdale, Dame Kathleen, Professor, London University 48
Lutyens, Elizabeth, Composer 84
Lyon, Lord (Lyon King of Arms), Chief Herald
    of Scotland 69
Lyons, Phoebe, JP's grandmother 13

Mackenzie, Sir Edward Montague Compton, Writer 69, 73
Mackie, John, writer 9
Magnus, Mr. Charles, Master of the Worshipful Company
    of Painter-Stainers 96
Mais, SPB, Author 74
Manas, Thai journalist 39-41
Mann, Mr, baptized JP 16
Marina, HRH Princess, Duchess of Kent 45
Marks, Baron Simon, Businessman 45
Mary, HM Queen, HM King George V's Wife 100-101
Maudling, Reginald, Chancellor of the Exchequer 71
McConnell, Neil, later husband of Vanessa Somers 52
Meir, Mrs Golda, Israeli Foreign Minister 65
Mendelssohn, Felix, Composer 96
Menuhin, Yehudi, Violinist 78, 82
Menzies, Sir Robert, Australian Prime Minister 38, 41
Mina, Lady van der Post's companion 74
Mitchell, George, Crookmaker 8
Mitchison, Lady Naomi, Poet-Novelist 73
Moiseiwitsch, Benno, Pianist 83
Monks begging on the Klongs of Thailand 40
Montgomery, Bernard Law, Viscount, Field-Marshal 33
Moore, Friar Gareth 29
Moore, Henry, sculptor 25
Morgan, Howard, Portrait Painter 97, 100
Morris, Lord, of Borth-y-Gest 45
Morrison, Jean, Headmistress of Christ's Hospital 47
Mott, Sir Nevill, Master, Gonville & Caius College,
    Cambridge 48
Mountbatten, Lord Louis, last Viceroy of India 32
Mountbatten, Pamela, daughter of
    Lord Louis Mountbatten 9
Mozart, Wolfgang Amadeus, Composer 77
Murray, Dr. Margaret 48
Mwajuma, Phoebe's house girl 24

Nahari, Mr, Portrait by JP 31
Nairne, Sandy, Director, National Portrait Gallery
    Back cover, 104
Napley, Sir David, President of the Law Society 89
Napoleon Bonaparte, French Emperor 54
Nerina, Nadia, Ballerina 59
Newsome, Dr. David, Master of Wellington College 47
Norfolk, Duke of, Earl Marshal 42, 44

Oistrakh, David and Igor, Father and son violinists 82
Osorio, Edwin, Master, Worshipful Company of Painter
    Stainers 93
Oxford Crew: Tennant, TW, President; Roff, PAV;
    Morton-Maskell, RA; Slailes, DDS; Morland, MQ;
    Morris, SR; Mead, RCT; Spencer, DC; Bevan, NV;
    Strong, CM 60
Oxton, Carolyn, Explorer 73

Pager, Paul, Oxford Fellow 48

Pannett, Denis, JP's son, artist 18-21, 62-63, 97-104
Pannett, Denis, and Elizabeth with JP and her MBE 103
Pannett, Elizabeth ('Lizzie'), JP's daughter, artist
    19-21, 62-63, 71
Pannett, Juliet Somers, at 17 17
Pannett, Maurice Richard Dalton ('Rick') 17, 16-21, 34,
    59, 62-63, 76, 89
Pannett, T.D., JP's father-in-law 17
Parker of Waddington, Lord Chief Justice 87
Parker, Lady, wife of Lord Chief Justice 87
Peacock, Lord GA, Jurist 91
Pearse, Captain Roger Gerard 36
Perry, Fred, Tennis player 61
Petrie, Sir Charles, historian 49
Phillip, HRH Prince, Duke of Edinburgh 26, 100-102
Piatigorsky, Gregor, Cellist 82
Pierotti, AM, Suffragette 69
Price, Nancy, Actress and author 54
Prince, Mary, art school friend 11

Quant, Mary,1960's fashion designer of the miniskirt 30

Rachmaninoff, Sergei, Composer 77
Radcliffe, T, Father, Prelate 28
Rambert, Madame Marie, ballerina and teacher 59
Reading, Lady, Head of Women's Voluntary Service,
    later Baroness Swanborough 30, 42
Reid, Miss, secretary to William Heseltine 95-100
Reid, Rt. Hon. Lord, Senior Judge, House of Lords 89
Relph, Lizzie 13
Rendell, Mr, Illustration Teacher 7
Riddell, Mr Victor, Eminent Surgeon 56
Robertson, Scott J., Publisher 73
Robinson, Leonard, Swanmaster, the Dyers' Company 43
Rodway, Jack, villager 19
Rogers, Ginger, Film star, dancer 55
Roope, Clover, ballerina 59
Rose, Grace, Suffragette 69
Rostropovich, Msitislav, Cellist 78
Rubens, Peter Paul 30
Rubenstein, Arthur, Pianist 81
Rundall, Jeremy, Author 73
Russell, Bertrand, Philosopher 73
Russell, Lord Justice 91

Salt, Dame Barbara, Foreign Office Official 46
Samang, Akaria, buddhist priest 40
Samuel, Lord, Herber Louis, Politician and Philosopher 49
Sargent, John Singer, Painter 30, 95
Sargent, Sir Malcolm, orchestra conductor 22, 76-77
Saxton, PG, Secretary General, The Chartered
    Insurance Institute 101
Scarman, Lord Leslie George, Jurist 91
Secombe, Harry, Comedian 54
Sellick, Phyllis, pianists, wife of Cyril Smith 79
Shackleton, Lord Ernest, Explorer 73
Shawcross, Lord 89
Shearer, Moira, ballerina 59
Shepherds, Sussex 7
Shostakovich, Dmitri, Composer 75, 83
Sinhji, Duleep, Cricketer 61
Sitwell, Dame Edith, Poet 73
Slim, Field Marshal Lord 33
Smeterlin, Jan, Pianist 82
Smith, Cyril, pianist, husband of Phyllis Sellick 79
Smith, Dennis 92
Smith, John, second master at St Paul's School 48
Sniffy, school butler 19
Socks, Royal Corgi 100
Solomon, Biblical King 66
Somers, Annie, JP's Aunt 13
Somers, Brice, JP's Brother 14-15, 18, 20
Somers, Charles, JP's Father 13-21
Somers, Claire-Lise, Brice Somers's wife 20
Somers, David, JP's Brother 15, 18, 21, 52, 83
Somers, Eileen, JP's Sister 14
Somers, George, JP's Uncle 13
Somers, Henry, JP's Uncle 13
Somers, Kate, JP's Aunt 13
Somers, Laurence, JP's Grandfather 13
Somers, Leonore, JP's Sister, Artist 14, 52
Somers, May, in JP's portrait 15
Somers, May, JP's Mother 13-21
Somers, Phoebe, JP's Sister, Artist 14-15, 18, 20,
    24-26, 35, 62, 71

Somers, Stanley, Brice Somers' christened name 14
Somers, Vanessa, Niece of JP Artist 18, 52, 80
Somers, Willie, JP's older brother 11, 14-15, 18,
Soraya, HSH Princess of Iran 45
Spencer, Earl, Princess Diana's Uncle 44
Stemp, Lord Leslie, Jurist 91
Stephen, Page to The Queen 102
Sterling, Col. WF, Lawrence of Arabia's Chief of Staff 30
Stern, GB, Author 73
Stewart Wilson, Col. Blair, Equerry to the Queen 102
Stewart, William, Master of Haileybury School 47
Stirling, Col. Walter F., Lawrence of Arabia's Staff Chief 36
Stravinsky, Igor, Composer 55, 75, 83
Summers, Juliet, [sic] in the Observer 9
Supper, Hilda, David Somers's first wife 12, 18
Supper, Hilda,(later wife of David Somers),
    Phoebe, Brice, Juliet and Leo 16
Sutherland, Joan, Soprano 84
Swanborough, Investiture of Baroness 42
Sydenham, Dr. Thomas, 17 Century Medical Doctor 57

Tallents, Sir Stephen, Order of St John of Malta 43
Tate, Maurice, Cricketer 60, 61
Taylor, Cice, Jock Taylor's wife 25
Taylor, J.H., Golfer 61
Taylor, Jock, JP's host in East Africa 25
Thatcher, Lady (Margaret), Prime Minister 71
Thesiger, Sir Wilfred, Explorer and Writer 72
Thomas, Lord 87
Thompson, Col. Digby, Inns of Court and City Yeomanry 35
Thorpe, Jeremy, Liberal MP 70, 89
Tiepolo, Italian 17th-Century Painter 72
Timberley, Joe, champion boomerang thrower 38
Timms, Mr, Deputy Master of the Queen's household 102
Tippett, Sir Michael, Composer 86
Titian (Tiziano, Vecellio), Painter 30
Todd, Lord, Professor of Organic Chemistry, Cambridge 48
Topolski, Feliks, Artist Back cover
Toulouse Lautrec, Henri de, Artist, JP visits collection 21
Toynbee, Arnold Joseph, Historian 49
Trevelyan, GM, Master of Trinity College, Cambridge 49
Trevor Roper, Hugh, Lord Dacre, historian, Oxford 49
Truman, Christine, Tennis player 61
Tugwell, Biddy Hutchinson, JP's childhood friend Foreword
Tugwell, Revd Dr Simon, OP 28, 29

van der Post, Lady 74
van der Post, Sir Laurens, Explorer and Writer 74
Van Gogh, Dr Vincent, nephew of Vincent 62, 63
Van Gogh, Vincent, JP visits house 21
Vaughan Williams, Ralph, English composer 49, 82, 82
Victoria, HM Queen 88, 95
Vreeland, Frederick ('Freck'), U.S. Ambassador 63
Vreeland, Vanessa Somers, Niece of JP, Artist Foreword, 63

Walpole, Lucy, Portrait of JP 7
Walsh, Dr John, JP's old friend 48
Walton, Lady, wife of Sir William Walton 82
Walton, Sir William, composer 82
Warner, Plum, Middlesex Cricket Club President 61
Watson, Clare Kathleen, May Somers's sister 13
Waugh, Evelyn, Author 73
Wedgwood Benn, Tony, Labour MP 70
Westminster, Duke of 99
Widgery, Lord Chief Justice 35, 90
Wilberforce, Squadron Leader Barbara 35
Wilberforce, Lord 89
Willis (Murray-Willis), Betty 12, 17-18
Willis, Sir John 92
Wilmott, Chester, Australian journalist 40
Wilsey, Captain John 36
Wilsey, General Sir John 63, 104
Wilson, Sir Harold, Prime Minister 70
Winterhalter, Franz, Painter 95
Wogan, Terry, Comedian 95
Wolfson, Sir Isaac 44
Wood, Major General GN 36
Wood, Major General GN, Devonshire & Dorset
    Regiment 36

Yadin, Professor Yigael 65, 66
York, Archbishop of 67

Zoffany, John, Portraitist 76

RALLY LIBRARY 1

GRAHAM
ROBSON

CW00685086

Audi QUATTRO

MOTOR RACING PUBLICATIONS

MOTOR RACING PUBLICATIONS LTD
32 Devonshire Road, Chiswick, London W4 2HD, England

ISBN 0 900549 88 2
First published 1984

Printed in Great Britain by Netherwood, Dalton & Co. Ltd.,
Bradley Mills, Huddersfield, West Yorkshire

Contents

Introduction and acknowledgements   3

Chapter 1   AUDI'S SPORTING HERITAGE   5
               Grand Prix cars and front-drive rallying

Chapter 2   FOUR-WHEEL DRIVE   7
               Breakthrough with the Quattro

Chapter 3   OVERTURE AND BEGINNERS   15
               1980 and 1981: The fight for reliability

Chapter 4   1982: TRIUMPH AT LAST   25
               Quattro wins the World Championship

Chapter 5   MIKKOLA THE 1983 CHAMPION   45
               But Blomqvist the fastest of all?

Chapter 6   QUATTROS ROUND THE WORLD   59
               Progress of the ex-works cars

Appendix A   SPECIFICATIONS   65
               Quattro rally and road cars

Appendix B   QUATTRO RALLY RECORD   67
               The works cars, 1981 to 1983

Introduction

There is no need to qualify the next statement in any way: The Audi Quattro has completely changed the face of rallying. The reason for this is very simple. In the years BQ (Before Quattro), a world-class rally car usually had a front-mounted engine and rear-wheel drive, but AQ (After Quattro), to be competitive it needed not only four-wheel drive, but also a massively powerful turbocharged engine. Yet when the new Quattro was first rumoured to be on its way, a few pundits (including, I have to admit, myself) thought that four-wheel drive could never be made to work properly at such speeds.

This, then, is my chance to admit that I was wrong, and for me to chronicle the story of the concept, development and early rallying career of the Quattro. Not only have I been enthralled by the way that Audi came to grips with their new competition car (with very little previous experience of top-level competition), but I have also been fascinated to see how Hannu Mikkola, Michele Mouton, Stig Blomqvist and several other drivers have all mastered the Quattro's habits, and were able to find grip and acceleration where every other rally car in the world would be floundering.

The Quattro's biggest leap forward from the 'norm' of the late 1970s, of course, was not just that it had four-wheel drive, but that the installation was very sophisticated indeed. Its most important built-in problem, not at all sorted out in the works cars, was that the engine was mounted too far forward for ideal chassis weight distribution. On the other hand, the rally cars have always been able to call up a great deal of sheer brute horsepower and torque, which has usually been able to make up for other deficiencies.

Perhaps the Quattro could not have been turned into a rally car so quickly, let alone into a potential winner, by any other organization. To win a World Championship event second time out, and a mere six weeks after homologation had been achieved, was a triumph of Teutonic application over a lack of experience, for Audi's own works team had only been founded, in a very small way, in 1978.

Perhaps, in a few years, we may look back on the Quattro

merely as the first, and the crudest, of the four-wheel-drive rallying Super Cars, but that will not mean that it was an ill-conceived machine in the first place. Later there may be rallying 'specials', with engines behind the driver, with glass-fibre bodywork, and with ever more sophisticated drivelines, but they will always be recognized as such — built in tiny numbers to creep around the regulations. Thousands of Quattro road cars are already in use, offering a remarkable blend of style, refinement, high performance and great security of roadholding to their lucky owners, their sophistication having increased at the start of each successive model year. The appearance of a short-wheelbase Quattro towards the end of 1983 reminded me that the whole Audi four-wheel-drive philosophy may still be only in its infancy.

In assembling the facts, figures and illustrations for this book I am grateful to several people for helping me, not least Laura Warren and Don Hume, of VAG (United Kingdom) Ltd; Ray Hutton and Nigel Fryatt, of Britain's most prestigious motoring magazine, *Autocar;* David Sutton, who runs the very successful rallying Quattros in the UK; Neil Eason-Gibson, for advice on homologation; Hugh Bishop, for offering pictures from his collection; Jeremy Walton, for his expertise on all things German; and Martin Holmes, for his archives and wonderful memory.

To all the readers of this book, finally, an apology. Inevitably, this can only be 'The Story So Far', for the Quattros look like piling up success upon success in the years to come.

GRAHAM ROBSON

December 1983

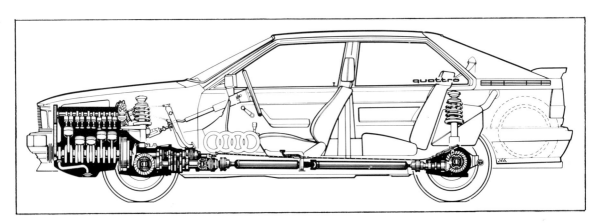

The basis of the Quattro was the four-wheel-drive installation from the VW Iltis. The 4WD was permanently engaged, there was a five-speed gearbox, lockable front and rear differentials and a tiny but effective third differential at the rear of the main gearbox.

CHAPTER 1

Audi's sporting heritage
Grand Prix cars and front-drive rallying

It all seemed to happen very quickly, for Audi did not even start entering cars at international level until 1978, yet they had rally-prepared Quattros ready to take on the world before the end of 1980. Once Hannu Mikkola's car had won the Swedish Rally early in 1981 the World Championship bandwagon began to roll. But there was more to it than this. Perhaps not at Audi, but in companies connected with Audi, there was a long and successful history of works-sponsored motor sport.

I have to go back to 1932 for a significant date. Audi had been building cars since 1910, but at the beginning of the 1930s the effects of the depression made the company decide to merge with three other German concerns — DKW,, Horch and Wanderer. The result was Auto-Union.

From 1934 to 1939, helped along initially by a design from Dr Ferdinand Porsche, Auto-Union raced a series of ferocious mid-engined Grand Prix cars, which had precarious handling characteristics and were not always able to match the pace of the more conventionally engineered Mercedes-Benz models. The Second World War then put a stop to all that, the cars and most of the expertise being lost, permanently, behind the Iron Curtain.

Although Auto-Union eventually recovered from the holocaust, the cars produced were mainly badged as DKWs at first, all with two-stroke engines and front-wheel drive. Genealogists will want to be reminded that the original Saabs were DKW copies, and that the Saabs also gained an impressive rallying record in due course!

The European Rally Championship (for drivers) was founded in 1953, won for the first time by Helmuth Polensky driving a Porsche, then, the following year, most unexpectedly by Walter Schluter in a little DKW. The fact that he did this with one outright win and only three class successes merely shows that competition was not so fierce in those days.

For the next few years, factory-assisted DKWs and Auto-Unions appeared in many European events, but unless the handicapping was favourable they could not be expected to win much with sub-1,000cc engines, however highly tuned. There was one famous near-miss on the 1959 RAC Rally when Wolfgang Levy's Auto-Union 1000 Coupe was denied outright victory by a freak snowstorm in the Braemar region of the Scottish Highlands. His navigator was an intensely professional young man called Stuart Turner . . .

But still there were no Audis, for the name was still in cold storage. Mercedes-Benz became the major shareholder in Auto-Union in the mid-1950s, and found time to style a new and larger bodyshell, as well as to inspire the birth of new water-cooled engines, before selling out completely to VW in 1964. The birth of a new Audi, thereafter, was not long delayed, for the marque name was revived in 1965, and gradually became more and more important to the VW group.

From the beginning of the 1970s, VW's marketing policy developed considerably as the old rear-engined air-cooled cars were progressively ditched, planning of new Audi and VW models proceeded in concert, and Audi gradually became the more prestigious of the cars built by the West German colossus. New generations of cars flooded on to the market, first the 80 of 1973, then the little 50 of 1975, and finally the advanced and (in some versions) five-cylinder-engined 100 of 1976; it wasn't the world's first five-cylinder engine, not by many years, but it *was* the first such conventional petrol engine to be put into production.

By this time Audi's management was marketing its cars in every way they could, and

In the early 1930s Audi merged with three other German car manufacturers to form Auto-Union, which means that the company's competitions heritage embraces those mighty rear-engined Grand Prix cars, including this 1936 Auto Union Type C, whose battles with the rival Mercedes-Benz team became such a feature of the international motor racing scene prior to the Second World War.

although their first move into big-time rallying was tentative, they soon saw that success could be promoted well.

Jurgen Stockmar started a more serious competition programme, using the 'small' Audi, the fuel-injected 80, in 1978. At first, the pundits could not see that it was a serious prelude to greater things, especially as few believed that a front-wheel-drive car like the 80 could ever achieve outright victories, but once the rumours of four-wheel-drive coupes began to circulate, the reason for such modest beginnings became clear.

Even in 1978, Joachim Knollman put his works 80 into the top 10 positions of European Championship events on four occasions in Germany — fifth on the Sachs Winter (first time out, no less!), eighth on the Saarland, sixth on the Hunsruck and eighth on the Baltic. For such an inexperienced department, it was a very good show.

For 1979 there was not only a new 80 model on the market, with a longer wheelbase and new styling, and still with front-wheel drive, but a new Group 4 rally car was developed from it. Audi elected to use a two-door saloon version of the new style, which had a 1.6-litre four-cylinder engine producing about 160bhp with the aid of fuel injection. Reinhard Rode took over team management while Freddy Kottulinsky and Harald Demuth were the contracted drivers.

The cars could still not be totally competitive, but since it was now known that the Quattro was on the way (and that the world's fastest rally driver, Hannu Mikkola, had been invited to sample a prototype!), more attention was centred on the team's preparation and on their approach to rallying.

Even so, it was an encouraging season, for Harald Demuth finished second overall in the Austrian Arbo and OASC events (behind a Porsche 911 and a Fiat 131 Abarth, respectively), while Walter Smolej took third in the Saarland, and Demuth was fourth in the Sachs Winter Rally. Three cars were sent to the UK for the Lombard-RAC Rally, where Demuth again shone by winning his class. The most outstanding performance of all, however, was in the Group 4 car's first World Championship event, the Portuguese round, where Demuth finished sixth overall and Kottulinsky was seventh.

Audi did not contest World Championship events again in 1980, but concentrated instead on German and Austrian rounds of the European Championship. Franz Wittmann heartened everyone by winning the Janner Rally outright — this was Audi's first victory, in only their third year of competition — and there were other excellent results, such as Wittmann's third in the Arbo, Demuth's third in the Sachs Winter and the same driver's fourth place in the Hessen Rally.

By the autumn, however, Audi themselves were beginning to lose interest in the front-wheel-drive 80s, for their workshops were filling up with more exciting projects. The four-wheel-drive Quattro was on the way and with it a new chapter in rallying!

CHAPTER 2

Four-wheel drive

Breakthrough with the Quattro

The story of the world-famous Audi Quattro actually began in the mid-1970s with a Germany military requirement. Agreed, there is a world of difference between light cross-country military vehicles and a dominant Group B rally car, but the connection is there, all the same. The *real* connection, of course, is four-wheel drive.

For many years after the Second World War the German army was dependent on the United States for much of its hardware. By the 1970s, however, the West German 'economic miracle' had evolved, and for a new generation of cross-country vehicles to replace the DKW Munga the army turned to its own industry for help. It is said that Daimler-Benz also tried very hard for this contract, but that their contender turned out to be too expensive — now, of course, their 4 × 4 is also on sale to the civilian customer as the Gelandewagen.

To develop a vehicle for this requirement, the Volkswagen combine appointed Ferdinand Piech, Audi's Research and Development Director, to take charge, and his team produced a relatively conventional (by four-wheel-drive standards) vehicle with all-independent suspension and a 1.7-litre four-cylinder overhead-camshaft petrol engine, which was effectively a long-stroke version of that used in the VW Passat and Audi 80 passenger cars.

More important, even, was that the main gearbox/front-drive transaxle was that of the Audi 80/Passat car, modified so that drive was taken by open propeller shaft to the rear wheels.

The new machine was christened Iltis (which is German for Polecat), and was first shown to the public at the Amsterdam Motor Show in February 1979, by which time large orders had already been received, not only from the West German, but also from the Dutch army. A civilian version of the Iltis was launched shortly afterwards, when the quoted peak power output of the engine was 75bhp and the unladen weight was a solid 1,550kg/3,420lb. With a claimed top speed of only 80mph, the Iltis was clearly not intended to be a high-performance machine.

By this time, one of Audi's senior project managers, Walter Treser, had bucked the system (not an easy thing to do in a German motor car company, where strict adherence to rules and guidelines usually applies); not only had he decided that there might be a future for a fast Audi car having a modified version of this four-wheel drive system, but he had actually had a prototype built, *without permission,* to prove it!

Working in secret, and keeping the project well under wraps, away from his superiors, Treser installed the Iltis' transmission under the bodyshell of an Audi 80 saloon, which normally, of course, would have had front-wheel drive only. Treser used his own initiative and years of experience (he had raced and rallied himself, had spent years running the test department of Pirelli Veith, and was now Audi's Advance Development Manager, at Ingolstadt, north of Munich), completed the car and had it tested on difficult terrain before even inviting his Chairman to drive it. He prepared a steeply sloping lawn by soaking the ground with water, then put a front-wheel-drive Audi 80, a rear-drive car of another make and the four-wheel-drive prototype at the Chairman's disposal. The result, thank goodness for Treser, was that the Chairman was impressed, and before long it had become an officially blessed Audi project.

But at this point (1977) there was still no immediate thought of designing a rallying Super Car, quite simply because the rules forbade such machines. Under existing Appendix J homologation regulations, cars could only have two wheels driven. However,

The four-wheel-drive VW Iltis from which the Quattro's drive line was derived . . .

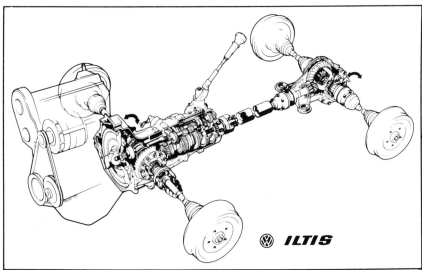

VW ILTIS

. . . and a schematic drawing of the Iltis' four-wheel-drive installation. In many respects, however, the Iltis 4WD system was different from that of the Quattro, as comparison with Quattro drawings published elsewhere in this book will confirm.

discreet lobbying by the West Germans at FIA and FISA meetings eventually saw the ban lifted. The 1979 FIA Year Book (the 'yellow book') had new wording no longer banning four-wheel drive, but few people thought this important, as their idea of such vehicles for rallying might include crazy people entering a Range Rover in a rough-road event, or something equally unsuitable as a Chevrolet Blazer in a North American international event.

Even so, four-wheel drive was only one of the important facets of new technology which would eventually come together to form the Quattro. During the mid-1970s and late 1970s, Audi were working steadily towards the building of new and updated cars. Their original four-cylinder front-drive 80s had been launched in 1972, and the smoothly-styled second-generation 100s in 1976, both with front-wheel drive and longitudinally-positioned engines ahead of the gearbox/transaxle assembly. For the latest 100s, they had taken the very important step of developing in-line five-cylinder engines, something done many years earlier by diesel engine builders, but never before used in petrol-engine guise in passenger cars.

The next generation of new cars would start with the 80s, launched in the summer of 1978, with a longer wheelbase than before and a more roomy engine bay. At first, only four-cylinder engines and saloon car styles were on offer, but it was widely expected that more sporting derivatives, and the five-cylinder engine, would be announced as well. In the event, the five-cylinder engine and the much-rumoured fastback coupe style both arrived in September 1980 – but by this time the Quattro's secret had been blown and had overshadowed everything.

Formal project work to develop a new four-wheel-drive coupe began in May 1978 under Treser, and although it was always meant to be (and was, as subsequent events proved) a practical road car, the four-wheel-drive coupe was also meant to be a serious competitor in international rallies. The rally-winning standards of the day included Ford's conventionally-engineered 250bhp, 2-litre Escort RS and the 270bhp, 2.4-litre, transverse mid-engined special, the Lancia Stratos. Clearly, if Audi were to produce a winner, they would need to provide more traction *and* a better power-to-weight ratio.

That, for sure, explains why the Quattro needed a turbocharged engine. The Ford and the Lancia both weighed about 1,000kg in rally trim, and since all the signs were that the Quattro would be considerably heavier, it was as well to aim for at least 300bhp right away. The entire range of Audi 80s and 100s was built around a family of inclined, single-cam, four- and five-cylinder engines, the largest of which was a 2,144cc unit producing 136bhp with the aid of Bosch fuel injection. No further engine stretching was possible, so Audi *had* to turbocharge the unit to become competitive. In the same way that Saab had already done, they found this to be a very practical and effective way of designing a 'larger' engine.

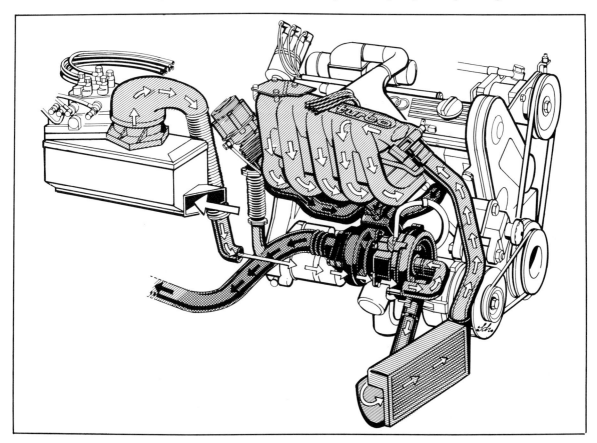

The turbocharging 'plumbing' system of the Quattro road car. The air intake and the fuel injection installation are to the left (towards the rear of the engine bay), the turbocharger is under the five-port inlet manifold, and the intercooler is low down to the right.

The new four-wheel-drive road car, therefore, came together like this. Because it was to be something of a high-prestige and very high-performance machine, even in standard form, it was decided to base it on the bodyshell of the Audi Coupe, which was already on the way. This car used the standard-wheelbase underpan, 'chassis' and normal front-wheel-drive mechanical layout of the 80 saloon, but had an entirely different superstructure and two-door (*not* three-door hatchback) four-seater fastback body style, crisply shaped, with four rectangular headlamps.

For the new four-wheel-drive derivative, however, it would be necessary to make major changes to that floorpan to accommodate the propeller shaft running to the rear, the rear final-drive assembly (lifted from the Iltis cross-country vehicle) and the new rear suspension instead of the Coupe's simple 'dead' axle

beam. Audi's design chief for the Quattro project, Herr Benzinger, chose to match the MacPherson-strut front end with a very similar type of MacPherson-strut rear. All in all, the 'chassis' of the Quattro was a masterpiece of improvization, for the basic five-speed gearbox was that of the 200 saloon (for which a turbocharged engine was also to be listed), front and rear MacPherson struts were both from the front of the 200, while the rear suspension subframe mounting was really that from the front suspension, turned right round, with standard front wishbones and hubs being used.

Nor was the rest of the bodyshell exactly like that of the new 80 coupe, for there was a unique rear lower skirt under the bumper (to match the standard one at the front on both types), and both front and rear wings had subtle but definite wheelarch flares to allow wider wheel rims to be standardized. [It was not until the 80

Audi issued this cutaway drawing when the Quattro road car was launched in 1980, confirming that it was, in effect, a modified 80 Coupe body style, with the Iltis-type four-wheel-drive system grafted in underneath.

The unmodified Quattro road car, complete with flared wheelarches and special insignia, plus distinctive alloy road wheels. One way to recognize a Quattro on the road was by the front and rear underbody 'skirts'.

The Quattro road cars had a deep under-bumper spoiler added to the flared front and rear wings to make them distinctive. Note the twinned rectangular headlamps, which were not used on the rally cars when they had properly been developed.

Coupe was launched, six months after the Quattro, that we realized that the original Coupe body style had not included such flares, which the Coupes lack.]

Four-wheel disc brakes were from the 200 Turbo, which had been announced in September 1979, six months before the Quattro, though in that case the engine was rated at a mere 170bhp (DIN) at 5,300rpm, and the same car also provided the multi-spoke alloy wheels.

The *raison d'etre* − the entire point − of the new Super Car, of course, was its four-wheel-drive transmission, something not quite a worldwide 'first' (Bugatti had built a four-wheel-drive racing car in 1932, and Jensen had put the Chrysler-engined FF road car on sale in 1966, to say nothing of BL's lofty, but prestigious, Range Rover), but a definite advance on any previous system. It needed to be because competitions experience with previous four-wheel-drive cars had not been successful.

In *Autocar,* on October 13, 1979 (five months before the Quattro was actually launched), I suggested that the new Audi might not be competitive, not entirely, I hasten to add, because the transmission would not be satisfactory, but because the whole car might be too heavy. I was wrong, of course, but I had strong memories of the late 1960s, when a fashion for four-wheel-drive Grand Prix cars

suddenly swept around the racing business, a fashion lasting for about one season only, when not a single car proved to be as fast as the rear-wheel-drive types they were supposed to supersede. There were basic differences, of course, which only became apparent after the Quattro was launched. My supposition had been made in referring to the performance of those racing cars *on tarmac;* in that respect, I was right, for the Quattro is still not (at the time of writing, at the end of 1983) demonstrably faster on sealed asphalt or concrete stages.

Audi engineers, however, were so convinced that they had cracked the problem, not only by using the latest in tyre technology, but also by designing and developing a very effective, grapefruit-sized, centre differential (so small, in fact, that it was accommodated in the rear extension of the gearbox itself), that they invited rally driver Hannu Mikkola to drive a prototype. This, incidentally, was in 1979, when Hannu was still fully committed to a determined Ford assault on the rallying World Championship in their last year in big-time rallying.

Hannu's first experience of five-cylinder turbocharged power, allied to four-wheel drive, was in a suitably prepared converted Audi 80:

'It was a 'phone call from Jurgen Stockmar,' Hannu said some time later. 'He asked me to

The first Quattro rally car publicity pictures of 1980, showing a very early test car liveried for the 1981 season. Four headlamps were still fitted.

Three-quarter rear view of the early Quattro rally car from Ingolstadt, showing the spoiler hiding three small oil cooler radiators. This would be enlarged considerably within a year. Note the standard wheels.

come and talk . . . I said I had already decided what I was doing in 1980.' [In fact, he was committed to a World Championship programme split between driving for Daimler-Benz and the Rothmans-David Sutton team of Ford Escort RSs.] 'He carried on, asked me to come for a couple of days to Munich and Ingolstadt, and intimated I would have a chance to drive a four-wheel-drive turbo car. Wouldn't that be interesting?'

In September 1979, therefore, Hannu drove the converted Audi 80 for half an hour — driving so fast, incidentally, that Stockmar asked if he could get out of the car and let Hannu go on playing alone!

After 30 minutes, Hannu could see the possibilities of the new installation. He could

not drive such a car in major rallies in 1980 (there was no guarantee, in fact, that it would be ready and homologated by then), but he was ready to sign a testing contract, and took out an option for 1981 . . . Much of that testing was to take place in co-operation with Freddie Kottulinsky, the German who was a principal member of Audi's rally team at the time, and it was Kottulinsky, in fact, who gave Audi an early four-wheel-drive success when he set best 'car' performance in the 1980 Paris-Dakar *raid*, driving an Iltis.

It was difficult for momentous news like that to be kept quiet. Early in January, before Mikkola's 1980 season had begun, and still before the Quattro had been launched, Audi confirmed that they would be producing such a car during 1980. The car, they said, would be of 'totally new design', and they hoped to have it homologated by August 1, 1980. Hannu Mikkola was contracted to help with the development of the car, and there were plans to tackle at least three events later in the year. There was more. 'For 1981,' Audi went on, 'we will embark on a full programme of World Championship rounds, and have already signed Hannu Mikkola and Arne Hertz.'

The Quattro was finally launched just in time to be the star of the Geneva Motor Show in March 1980, and selected journalists were invited to drive early examples in suitably snowy conditions in the Alps. Without exception, every writer was dumbfounded by the Quattro's performance and its tenacious grip on the most slippery of surfaces. Perhaps Gordon Wilkins, the doyen of all British scribes, summed it up best in *Autocar* when he wrote:

'Skiers stopped and gaped open-mouthed as the car flashed by in a cloud of snow at 80mph ... I felt like a visitor from another planet for whom the laws of nature have been suspended. I was on ordinary summer tyres, but the car stormed up the steep snowbound slopes on full throttle, then slowed swiftly in a straight line as hard braking pinned it down.'

For the Quattro, incidentally, the engineers had specified an intercooler to help the efficiency of the engine, such that even the

road car produced a peak of 200bhp (DIN) at 5,500rpm, with a maximum boost from the KKK exhaust-driven turbocharger of 12.1psi. This was 30bhp more than the similar engine in the 200 Turbo saloon, and 64bhp (or 47 per cent) more than the normally-aspirated 2.2-litre engine in the 100 saloon.

One secret of the Quattro's success, which the engineers only discovered part-way through the programme, was that the permanent four-wheel drive actually gave slightly better fuel consumption and performance than an equivalent two-wheel-drive machine would produce. The transmission, of course, produced slightly more friction in four-wheel-drive form, but diligent testing showed that the tyres were having an easier time, and the result was a small, but definite (0.9 per cent) overall advantage for four-wheel drive.

There was never going to be much problem in producing sufficient power — 285bhp was already available in the first rally 'mule' which Hannu and Kottulinsky drove, with 300bhp seen on testbed engines even before the road car was announced — but there was also no doubt that the Quattro was going to be a difficult car to drive really hard. To this day, there are good drivers, and good Quattro drivers — it is not easy even for a competent rally driver to convert without a great deal of practice. Audi

The official Audi Sport cutaway drawing of the original Quattro rally car when it still had four headlamps and the small-size rear spoiler and coolers. By this time, special rallying wheels had been fitted. Compared with the standard car, the turbocharger and the intercooler had been relocated. A comparison with the colour cutaway drawing of the 1982 VAG-UK Quattro on page 41 makes clear the development changes which were still to come.

Sport built the first proper Quattro rally car prototype by April 1980, and others soon followed. In an *Autosport* column in May 1980, Hannu said: 'I'm having to learn a new technique because you know it's not only four-wheel drive but also turbo and, when you don't know the road beforehand, then the lag can be a problem . . . The only thing that I can say about the handling is that you can drive it sideways but it's very undramatic.'

By the autumn of 1980, Audi and Walter Treser knew that the new Quattro was already competitive, and they thought it might even be an early winner. Certainly they were confident enough to confirm that a full 1981 programme was in prospect, and to look around (reputedly, offering large sums of money) for a team of drivers.

Treser, it is known, talked to Walter Rohrl, the talented but lugubrious German, whose home was not far from Ingolstadt and who was well on the way to becoming rallying's World Champion after his third year with Fiat. Rohrl, however, chose to sign for Daimler-Benz instead, which proved to be a big (but unavoidable) mistake as Daimler-Benz withdrew from the sport even before Rohrl could get his hands on a car in competition.

On reflection, Rohrl's refusal to drive for Audi gave the company a wonderful opportunity, whose benefits it is still reaping. In addition to signing one of the world's most successful rally drivers to lead the team — Hannu Mikkola — they then went out to capture the best lady driver in the business — Michele Mouton. For 1981, therefore, Audi had all the potential for a publicity coup — the world's best rally car, with the world's best male *and* female rally drivers in the team!

By any standards, in fact, Michele Mouton was an outstanding competitor. For many years, it seemed, there had been lots of lady drivers, but only one Pat Moss, whose talents were never even approached by her rivals. Then, along came Michele, years after the famous Miss Moss had married Erik Carlsson and retired to become a mother.

Michele first came into rallying when she was 22 years old, and her first events, in her native France, were as a co-driver. Soon her father helped her take the big step to becoming a driver by buying her a rear-engined Alpine-Renault and it was in one of those cars that she became French Ladies' Champion in 1974. In due course she began to drive for Fiat-France, won the Tour de France in 1978 in a 131 Abarth, and on three consecutive occasions finished seventh in the Monte Carlo Rally (twice in Fiats, once in a Chardonnet Stratos). Before 1980, she had not had an outright win in a World Championship rally, but Audi were prepared to gamble on their hope that she could come to terms with the Quattro, and do just that.

The line-up for 1981 — Quattro, Mikkola and Mouton — was announced in November 1980, just before the Quattro went on general sale in West Germany. The launch had been slightly premature, in that production had not begun in March 1980, but well over the required number of cars had already been built to ensure homologation, and the demand was such that Audi were projecting the building of 2,000 Quattro road cars in the first full year.

Now it was up to the rally team.

CHAPTER 3

Overture and beginners

1980 and 1981: The fight for reliability

Audi approached their rallying programme for the Quattro in a typically Teutonic way — by planning, organizing and testing well before they even sent a car out to tackle a rally of any sort. As 1980 progressed, Hannu Mikkola assessed cars which were further developed, faster and more completely prepared on every occasion. Homologation was planned for January 1, 1981, and before then at least six full-specification rally cars were to be made ready, two of them for Hannu Mikkola and Michele Mouton to use in the Monte Carlo Rally, one for Franz Wittmann to debut in the Austrian Janner Rally and a test car for Mikkola to take to the Algarve before the end of the year.

The Quattro's homologation papers, when published, showed just how much work Audi Sport had already carried out, and how many special fittings had already been developed. In addition to the basic papers, there were nine additional sheets of information, listing parts as different as heavy-duty suspension subframes, hydraulic handbrakes, a dry-sump lubrication kit, light-alloy brake calipers and larger brake discs, an oil-cooler/modified rear spoiler kit, a larger fuel tank, modified front end without fog lamps, a propeller shaft made from a synthetic plastic material, Perspex side and rear window 'glass', extra final-drive ratios, plastic and aluminium skin panels, and much more. If there was going to be an homologation race, Audi planned to be in it, right away.

Since Walter Treser knew that the eyes of the sporting world would be on his new team in Monte Carlo, in January 1981, he decided to 'blood' the design on minor events before that. However, since the Quattro would not be homologated until January 1, 1981, it could not officially enter international rallies before then. Its first public appearance, therefore, was in the Algarve Rally, in Portugal, in October 1980, where Hannu Mikkola and Arne Hertz took an

early rally car as the '00' course car, yet drove at rally speeds throughout.

The Algarve was a European Championship qualifier (the only one of the year on the Portuguese mainland), and attracted a mediocre entry, with only two A-priority drivers, but in such an event, where practice was allowed, drivers like Bernard Beguin (Porsche 911) and Antonio Zanini (Escort RS) were no pushover. As it happened, Mikkola's performance, running at the head of the field, was nothing short of sensational, for he set fastest time on 24 of the 30 stages. His quote, after the finish, was that the traction and handling of the Quattro (IN-NE-3) was incredible, and that the only places where it did not compare with the Escorts he was used to driving was on very twisty sections, or into hairpins.

Just before the end of the year, too, a couple of Quattros were 'entered' in the final round of the Finnish rally series, the Northern Lights, for Michele Mouton and Freddie Kottulinsky to use as course cars, and the results, once again, were encouraging. It all boded well for 1981.

The first official works Quattro entry in an international event, however, came early in January 1981, when Franz Wittmann (already hoping to do several German events for Audi during the season) was sent on the opening European Championship round of the year, the Janner, held in Austria. Once again, it was not the most scintillating competition, with the only A-priority driver being Shekhar Mehta (an East African resident with virtually no ice driving experience!), but Wittman put in a workmanlike display to win easily in a car destined for use by Mikkola in Sweden the following month (IN-NV-90).

The event for which everyone had been waiting, however, was the Monte Carlo Rally, in which the two works Quattros started from Bad

Hombourg in West Germany and from Paris, and faced other factory teams from Renault, Talbot, Opel, Fiat, Datsun and Rothmans-Ford Escort, and several fancied private Porsche and Lancia Stratos entries.

As Rupert Saunders commented when writing about the rally in *Autosport:* 'Never can the debut of a car have been watched with quite such interest.' Audi produced two cars with identical mechanical specifications — claiming 310bhp at 6,000rpm with Pierburg fuel injection and using the contracted Kleber tyres — with Mikkola's machine in Audi Sport colours and Michele Mouton's liveried for BP, her French oil company sponsor.

For Audi, the good news was that there was plenty of snow and ice on the six stages leading down to Monaco, but the bad news was that later stages were much clearer. Mikkola instantly stamped his authority on the event, being fastest on all six opening stages and leading by almost six *minutes.* Poor Michele Mouton, on the other hand, was forced out even before reaching a stage when dirt contaminated the fuel injection system of her car.

As soon as the *Route Commun* (Monaco to Monaco — 1,600kms with a further 18 stages)

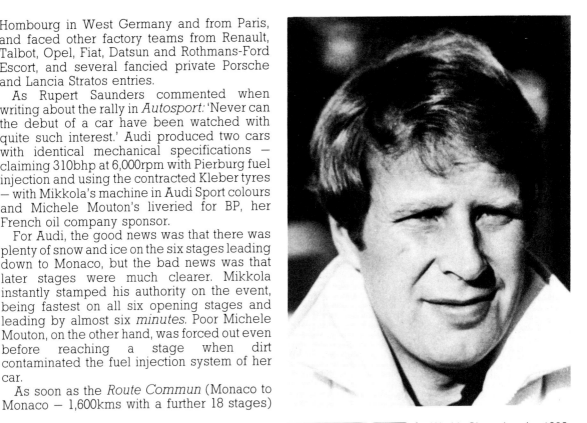

World Champion in 1983, officially, but by my reckoning one of the best three rally drivers in the world for the last 15 years — Hannu Mikkola of Finland. He was the first driver to be captivated by the Quattro, and the first to give it a World Championship win.

Arne Hertz, Hannu Mikkola's regular co-driver, and one of the true gentlemen of rally-ing, here looking just a little less smooth than usual . . .

began, Mikkola hit trouble, first when his alternator belt broke and then when he crashed the car, wiping off a complete front strut. Thereafter it was always a struggle to get the car right again, and when the steering rack was changed a mechanic omitted to lock one of the bolts and the car lost its steering in mid-stage. The end came on the final night when Mikkola's brakes failed on the horrifyingly fast Col de Couillole stage and he crashed the car very badly. That particular machine was never used again . . .

It was an entirely different story on the Swedish Rally, which followed just two weeks later. While the mechanics at Ingolstadt slaved away to produce two new cars for Portugal (the original intention had been to use the Monte cars, reprepared), Mikkola took along the ex-Wittmann/Janner car to tackle the snow-covered forestry tracks of central Sweden.

Michele Mouton, that very fast lady of rallying from France, who started driving for Audi in 1981. Right away she proved to be completely 'on the pace', and her first World Championship victory was at Sanremo later that year.

Michele Mouton was a famous lady rally driver before she even joined Audi for 1981, but when teamed with the Quattro she rapidly became a superstar. Her 'stance' in the car — with head forward and a slight crouch — was readily recognizable, as was her sheer pace.

Quattro premiere — on the Algarve Rally of 1980, where Hannu Mikkola and Arne Hertz took out IN-NE-3 as a non-homologated course car and set fastest time on all the stages! For Audi's rivals, it was an ominous debut.

This time there was no mistake, as Mikkola rewrote the history books, not only by taking a Quattro to the first World Championship victory for a four-wheel-drive car, but by being the first-ever non-Swedish driver to win the Swedish Rally! The event, based on Karlstad, saw Mikkola give a copybook performance, setting fastest times on no fewer than 15 of the 25 long special stages and never being lower than fifth fastest on any of them. Nor was it an easy victory, for Mikkola won by 1 minute 53 seconds from other world-class drivers like Ari Vatanen, Pentti Airikkala, Anders Kullang and Stig Blomqvist. It was interesting to hear comments from experienced photographers on this event, that whereas it was easy to catch an Escort or an Opel Ascona in an exciting-looking 'sideways' posture, the Quattro just seemed to motor round the corners as if on rails, whether they were clear or snow-covered. The real excitement of Quattro motoring was its sheer unobtrusive pace, and the spumes of snow propelled from all four driven wheels.

It was in Portugal, in March, however, where Audi Sport received their first real test, not just because the competition was strong, but because there were high-speed tarmac and gravel stages in abundance. It was here, the pundits suggested, that we would learn if the four-wheel-drive system really worked and had the endurance.

It was to be a bitter-sweet weekend for the German team, for although Mikkola and Ms Mouton dominated the stages when their cars were running well, it was Markku Alen who won the event outright in an old-style Fiat 131 Abarth, with two other 'conventional' two-wheel-drive cars — a Talbot Sunbeam-Lotus and a Toyota Celica GT — behind him. Michele was rewarded with fourth place, but Hannu Mikkola had to retire.

The pace of Audi's programme, however, was becoming obvious — two cars had already been written-off on the way home from events, and Michele's Portugal car was the 13th which the hard-working mechanics at Ingolstadt had

Fabrizia Pons, from Italy, became Michele Mouton's co-driver in the Quattro team in 1981, and shared in three World Championship victories during 1982. She claims to be shy, which may be true, but she is nevertheless a very effective co-driver.

After Walter Treser left the Audi Sport competitions department in Ingolstadt, Reinhard Rode became the team's Competitions Manager, and saw the Quattro develop from a superfast failure to a formidable winner in many events.

already prepared. The engines for Portugal were running with more boost than before (up to 1.8 bar/26psi) and with different camshaft profiles, so that up to 340bhp was available. Perhaps that was a mistake, for after showing remarkable pace, setting more fastest stage times than any other competitor — 1981 was going to be that sort of a year — and leading the rally until half-distance, Mikkola's engine suddenly stopped and seized with a dropped valve. Michele, still going well, also had a long delay in the middle of a stage when her car's fuel injection control box failed. Eventually she finished fourth, more than 22 minutes behind Alen's old Fiat.

There was no more luck for the Quattros in the Tour de Corse, where the narrow, slow and twisty tarmac roads could hardly have been said to favour the big four-wheel-drive cars in any case. Further development had seen larger (Porsche 935-type) brakes fitted to harness the considerable bulk of the cars, and the engines were as powerful as they had been in Portugal. It was all too much, for both cars were broken after eight stages, Mikkola's with a piston failure and Mouton's with a broken camshaft. Heat, under-bonnet heat in particular, was proving to be a real problem.

All of us in what might be called the 'rallying media' had now discovered that the Audi Sport/Quattro operation might be German, and

it might be very formalized in several ways, but it was never boring. The Acropolis Rally of May 1981 turned out to be one of those events where there was real controversy, caused by Team Manager Walter Treser's determination to keep the highly-stressed Quattro engines in one piece. Not only that, but along the way he nearly got himself incinerated at a service point!

Audi turned up in Greece for one of the toughest and hottest events of the year, with two more new cars (bringing the total, in less than a year, to nearly 20 different machines). Compared with Corsica and Portugal, the engines had been detuned, approximately back to Monte Carlo levels, but there was another change which caused a great deal of comment. The inner pair of headlamps had been removed from each car, and in their place were lightweight flaps, closed when the cars were at rest, but blown open by the wind when the car was moving, and thus allowing more fresh air to enter the engine bay to cool it down.

The story of the rally is quickly told, for all three cars (there was a works entry for Franz Wittmann, in one of the older Quattros), were right on the pace from the start, but they suffered their usual troubles and dramas. Michele's Quattro lost its left-side rear suspension at one point, such that she had to drag the car through a stage with the tail down and only three wheels on the car driving. At the very next service point, Walter Treser crawled under the back of Mikkola's car to see that everything was in order at the very moment when a mechanic spilt petrol on the hot exhaust pipes and the Quattro burst into flames. Fortunately, Arne Hertz had the presence of mind to leap into the car, start it up and drive it to safety, though Treser was burnt around the face and hands and took weeks to recover. Later, Mikkola's car broke its rear differential, and had to be rallied for a time as a front-wheel-drive machine.

At half-distance, Mikkola was leading the event, but after the rest halt at Lagonissi, all three cars were summarily excluded from the event because of the auxiliary air inlets (instead of the headlamps), and in addition the team was fined for sending cars into the *parc fermé* with auxiliary batteries in the passenger compartment, intended to aid hot restarts later in the day. A close reading of the regulations, Audi said, allowed them to modify their cars like that, but the organizers disagreed and, eventually, were upheld. The disqualifications stood.

At this point, make no mistake, the Quattro rallying project was in crisis, and the whole question of continued participation was discussed at Audi Board level. Almost as much in West Germany as in Japan, there was the question of 'loss of face' to be considered, especially as the attitude of the German press was hostile to Audi at this time.

[It has often been said that an important reason for Daimler-Benz's abrupt withdrawal from rallying at the end of 1980 was that they were getting nowhere with the West German media, who were unsympathetic to their general lack of success.]

Changes had to be made, and unhappily for Walter Treser, the 'father' of the whole Quattro project, he was smartly removed from his position in Audi Sport and moved back into the research and development department. At this point, in fact, Treser fades out of our story, for shortly afterwards he left Audi's employment altogether, setting up his own business for the manufacture of special vehicles, some based on the Quattro road car.

You can even get a four-wheel-drive Quattro sideways, as Michele Cinotto demonstrated in the Costa Smeralda Rally. Cinotto used a works-prepared car on many events during the Quattro's first three years as a competition car, and joined the official factory team on several occasions.

A famous accident, on the way to a famous victory. In the Lombard-RAC Rally of 1981, Hannu Mikkola rolled his Quattro when a corner loomed up unexpectedly in the fog, but he lost little time and eventually won the event outright. He repeated the win, but not the roll, in 1982.

Some rallying gossip columns considered that Treser had been made the scapegoat for all the controversy surrounding this new team, which was true enough, even if he had not always been responsible for the pantomimes. In any case, his replacement was Reinhard Rode, once of VW Motorsport, but latterly operating under Jurgen Stockmar and then under Treser himself.

On the non-championship Mille Pistes event in France, in July, Michele Mouton competed with a modified Quattro in which a different type of two-headlamp Quattro grille was tried, and for the 1000 Lakes in Finland, at the end of August, three new cars (once again, there was a car for Franz Wittmann) turned up with this grille. Homologated from July 1, it was wider and further forward, covering the areas previously occupied by the inner pair of lamps (and allowing cooling area through in exactly the same way...) and also allowing more space in the engine bay for enlarged intercoolers and repositioned components. The new cooling arrangements had apparently been checked out in no less hot a place than the middle of the Sahara desert! The cars were now running at a weight of about 1,170kg/2,580lb, and engine power was quoted as 320bhp. Rode was running the team, and his newly-appointed Development Engineer was a bearded man called Roland Gumpert.

Even so, things did not go entirely well, for although Mikkola was as dominant as usual (29 fastest stage times out of 47 stages in total), he could only finish third, behind an Escort RS and a Fiat 131 Abarth, while Michele Mouton

managed 13th place in her first attempt on this specialized rally and Wittmann retired. Tragically, Wittmann's car overshot the end of an early stage, ploughing into a group of people in the control area and gravely injuring the President of the Finnish Automobile Federation, Raul Falin, who later died. Naturally, Wittmann's car was later withdrawn, but it was yet another incident to add to the Quattro's controversial first season.

Michele Mouton finished pluckily, still rather out of her depth on this very fast rally, but Mikkola's aggressive run was slowed when his engine developed serious trouble and needed a camshaft change and a new cam follower to restore it to health; much time was lost, he dropped to fifth place, and spent the rest of the rally struggling back into third place, three minutes behind the winning Escort of Ari Vatanen.

It was beginning to look as if the works Quattro team would never be able to merely turn up at the start of a rally, put in a workmanlike performance, then go home with whatever awards they had earned, and even in Sanremo, in October, there was the usual share of West German drama. Three works Quattros appeared, one of them — actually the car used by Wittmann in Finland — being for Michele Cinotto of the Italian Audi team, and all of them not only sported the revised front grille, but had a new and much larger oil cooler kit mounted under the spoiler on the tailgate. At first glance, the spoiler itself appeared to be new, whereas a very simple piece of homologation on October 1 had specified spacer blocks

Michele Mouton achieved a most outstanding victory in the Sanremo Rally of 1981, becoming the first lady ever to win an official World Championship rally. Her co-driver, as so often, was Fabrizia Pons.

between the spoiler and the boot lid itself to deepen the space in between. In most other respects, except for the provision of 'tarmac' and 'forest' settings for an event which had two definite characters, the cars were much as before.

Cinotto, the local hero, startled everyone by taking the lead after the first eight special stages and holding it to almost half-distance before crashing out of the running, while Hannu Mikkola suffered a very depressing start to the event, with seemingly untraceable engine trouble, causing a severe lack of power, which saw him lying 56th (out of 59 runners!) after the first few tarmac stages. Once cured, by the drastic expedient of changing everything possible in the fuel injection and electrical systems, Mikkola began to go like the wind, and spent the rest of the 59-stage rally climbing the leader board. Statistically, it was the usual story, for he set 30 fastest times and 14 second-fastests — but could only finish fourth overall, nearly 13 minutes adrift.

To everyone's joy, however, it was Michele Mouton's turn to be lucky — for luck had eluded her most of the year so far. After 18 stages, at the Pisa halt, Michele was second, just 32 seconds behind the mercurial Cinotto, and after he had crashed his Quattro not once, but twice, she took the lead and never lost it again. By the Siena control she led Rohrl's Porsche 911SC by 3 minutes 25 seconds and Vatanen's Rothmans Escort by a further second. At Sanremo, with only six tarmac stages to go, Rohrl's gearbox had broken and Vatanen had closed to within 34 seconds, mainly due to a stone which had flown up at one point, breaking

a front drive shaft and brake caliper on Mouton's car.

In one last desperate effort, Vatanen tried to overhaul the Quattro, but crashed against a hidden rock in the verge and plunged to seventh place, leaving the delightful French girl to win, from Henri Toivonen's Talbot Sunbeam-Lotus, by a comfortable 3 minutes 25 seconds. Not only was it Michele's first World Championship victory, and Audi's first in the Makes series (Sweden had only counted for the Drivers' Championship), but it was the first ever by a lady in a World Championship rally — though in the 1960s, of course, before such things were thought of, the redoubtable Pat Moss had achieved similar miracles in Big Healeys and BMC Mini-Coopers.

Thus encouraged, and amid a great wave of goodwill from the media, who had come to respect the cars and the team more and more as this trouble-strewn season progressed, Audi Sport sent their usual pair of drivers to tackle the Lombard-RAC Rally, the last event of the season. Hannu Mikkola had already won the event twice before, in Escort RSs (1978 and 1979), so the 'secret stages' format held no terrors for him, but Michele Mouton had never seen a British forest stage before and did not normally tackle any rally without a lot of diligent training. According to the registration numbers they carried (which are not always reliable where a works team with a fleet of rally cars is concerned), both drivers retained the cars they had used at Sanremo, six weeks earlier.

Even before the rally started from Chester, Hannu Mikkola (with a little help from Grand Prix driver Alan Jones) demoralized his

The car is filthy, due to ploughing through British Forestry Commission mud — but this was Michele Mouton in the Lombard-RAC Rally of 1981, where the icy roads of North Wales finally caught out the Quattro. A year later, she returned to the RAC and took second place, behind Hannu Mikkola's sister car.

opposition by winning the Donington TV Rallysprint event while driving on a punctured tyre. There had also been time to indulge in some pre-event testing in the Nant-yr-Hwch forest in South Wales in the car Hannu was to use at Donington a week later. One of the testing objects was to assess a new engine tune, with camshaft and turbo settings designed to give more torque lower down the range and a more flexible response, but even so the 2.14-litre unit was still good for 320bhp — more than any of its competitors in world-class rallying.

On the event itself, which encompassed 65 stages, there was never much doubt that Mikkola was going to win, to make it three victories in four years, even though he was able to indulge in a most uncharacteristic accident and roll-over in the foggy depths of the Lake District. Apart from the immediate consequences of that roll, when he ceded the lead to Tony Pond's Chevette HSR for a few stages, he led throughout, eventually winning, easing up, by a comfortable 11 minutes from Ari Vatanen's Rothmans-Escort. Ari, for his part, was satisfied, for he had therefore confirmed

The Quattro front view which offended the scrutineers at the Acropolis Rally in 1981, when the car's inner head-lamps had been removed, and easily movable flaps allowed extra air to enter the engine bay for cooling pur-poses. All the team cars were disqualified and the Quattros never appeared in that form again.

his Driver's World Championship victory.

Even so, the surprise of the event was Michele Mouton's pace in the second Quattro on an event she had never even started before. Until she was finally caught out by an icy section in North Wales, plunging off the track and not being able to get back, four-wheel drive or not, she was always in the top few positions. At the half-way halt in Chester she lay third behind Vatanen's Escort, and no other car looked like catching her before the finish. After such a showing, the likeable French lady with the flashing brown eyes had become very popular indeed with British crowds.

On this event, as on so many others in 1981, one only needed to read a few statistics to see that Mikkola was considerably quicker than anyone else when he felt like it. Overall, he set 29 fastest times and nine second-fastests — which was more than half of all the stages in the event. By half-distance, back at Chester after 38 hours in Northern England and South Scotland, he already led by 10 minutes and had stopped pressing. For the rest of the rally, in fact, he was being 'paced', or controlled, very firmly and expertly by his long-time co-driver, Arne Hertz.

But even in a performance like this, which made all Quattro-watchers realize that the traditional mould of rallying had now been smashed, perhaps for ever, there was time for the usual Quattro dramas. Apart from Mikkola's slow roll (which necessitated much panel-beating and a new windscreen to be taped into place), Michele's engine gave trouble, with more turbo lag than usual, and in Brecon the mechanics were forced to consider a complete gearbox/front transaxle change against the clock on her car. The gearbox itself was giving trouble, but nevertheless Michele had to leave for the next batch of stages without front drive shafts (in other words, this was the world's first rear-drive Quattro!) and with only first and fourth gears working in the defective box. At the next opportunity, the box itself was changed, in 49 minutes — a record for the mechanics at this time — and four-wheel drive was restored! But that was not all, for the hastily renewed box was wrongly installed, another drive shaft broke, and the courageous French girl completed more stages in rear-wheel drive only. It was no wonder that, later in the night,

she fell foul of the awful weather conditions for which studded tyres were not allowed.

All in all, however, it was a successful end to a season which had turned out to be more headline-producing, but more troubled, than Audi's management could ever have feared. The Quattros had only tackled eight of the 12 World Championship events, and had managed to finish fifth in the Makes series (behind Talbot, Datsun, Ford and Opel), while Hannu Mikkola himself had finished third in the Driver's series, well behind Ari Vatanen of Rothmans-Ford and Guy Frequelin of Talbot. No fewer than 20 full works rally cars had been built — many events being started with brand-new cars — and several others were already on the way for 1982.

Before the Lombard-RAC Rally of 1981, my journalistic colleague Jeremy Walton paid a visit to Ingolstadt and talked to Rode and his engineer, Roland Gumpert, to get a feel for the Audi operation. Even at this point it was becoming clear that Gumpert was the rising star and that — as with Erich Waxenberger at Daimler-Benz in 1980 — none of the German mechanics would initiate work of their own unless Gumpert approved and asked them to do so. The engine tuning genius was Thomas Ammerschlager, and the whole team seemed to be working more closely with mainstream Audi engineering than ever before.

One problem, Gumpert admitted, was that almost every modification they made tended to increase the weight of the Quattro, for they were still fighting to get back below the 1,200kg/2,645lb mark. Engine tuning, they thought, was not a matter of producing enough horsepower (350bhp, they thought, was easy enough to find), but of finding the right sort of flexibility and torque delivery. Handling, they claimed, was now perfectly acceptable in the loose, or on snow and ice, but more work was needed for dry tarmac stages.

As far as the opposition was concerned, however, the most ominous remarks concerned the 1982 programme — with more events to be tackled by the works teams and more works-blessed, but privately-operated, Quattros appearing overseas. Was no event, and no country, safe from the fabulous four-wheel-drive cars?

CHAPTER 4

1982: Triumph at last

Quattro wins the World Championship

As Audi Sport faced up to 1982, everything seemed to be coming right for them. They had a successful and increasingly reliable car, a team of mechanics gaining experience with every event they tackled, and the most charismatic team of drivers in the world. More than this, Hannu Mikkola was quite determined to make up for the disappointments of 1981 by winning a *lot* of rallies in 1982.

As to the cars themselves, there would only be one important change, for a light-alloy cylinder block (worth, perhaps, 22kg/48lb in weight-saving) had been homologated on December 1, 1981. It was certainly no homologation fiddle, either, for we soon learned that Audi had built a goodly batch of these blocks, and phased them into production-line cars at the appropriate moment. Every little helps — and this weight-saving, hung out at the front, ahead of the front wheels, would improve the weight distribution and handling balance into the bargain. No further homologation changes were made to the existing Group 4 Quattro for the rest of its life, and the 1982 cars were only improved in development detail. That was quite enough, however, for 1982 was an interim year, in which Ford's new Group B RS1700T failed to appear, the new mid-engined Lancia Rally proved to be fragile and unreliable at first, and several obsolescent Group 4 cars gradually faded away.

Audi, incidentally, were also determined not to sell their success to other interests, to sponsors wanting only to ride on the crest of their hoped-for success. For 1982, they decided, the entire rally programme (which must have been costing upwards of £2.5 million/10 million DM for the season) was to be funded in-house. In the autumn of 1981, a very generous offer from Rothmans, who were ending a three-year link with Ford and the Escort RS, was turned down, and the Rothmans money eventually went to Opel for 1982 and 1983.

As Ferdinand Piech once said: '90 per cent of all our work in 1981-82 was concerned with increasing the reliability of the car. For 1982 our car was up to 100kg/220lb lighter in competition form, partly because of the aluminium block which makes a difference of 22kg/48lb, but also because of the different materials we use elsewhere.' Those different materials mainly encompassed Kevlar bonnet, wings, boot lid and wheelarch extensions — in 1981 the boot lid had been of glass-fibre, the other panels of light-alloy. There was still a great span of different weights, for a truly lightweight Ingolstadt car weighed 1,120kg/2,470lb, whereas the 1982 Audi UK machine, driven by Hannu Mikkola and using the original iron block, weighed 1,262kg/2,783lb.

In Monte Carlo, at the beginning of the season, Hannu Mikkola came near, but not very near, to winning the event, for it was run in most unseasonably mild weather on mainly dry roads, so that the Opel Ascona 400s were not put at a disadvantage. In particular, Walter Rohrl's Opel had the legs of the Quattro whenever he needed to go flat-out, and Hannu could finish no higher than second.

In fact there were three works Quattros in the Monte, two new cars for Mikkola and Mouton, and a third example for Michele Cinotto, said to be the 1981 Mikkola/Corsica car, but carrying a different identity. Even though Mikkola did so well, incidentally, he still had to drive the whole of one test on a puncture, and suffered a broken drive shaft on another (three-wheel drive must have been very exciting!). Cinotto never even made it to the end of the *Classement* stages into Monaco, for his old Quattro punctured and he subsequently went off with a lack of grip, while Michele Mouton (who had less excuse, as she

The business cockpit of a left-hand-drive Quattro rally car, complete with extra floorboard for the co-driver, electronic rally computer and two-way radio installation. Note that the standard steering wheel has been retained.

Quattro engine bay, full of power — more than 300bhp of it — and other fittings. The big trunking across the top of the camshaft cover is leading air from the intercooler to the inlet manifold.

lives in Grasse, not far from the site), put her Quattro very firmly off the road on ice in Pont de Miolans, hitting a house hard, and badly shaking herself and co-driver Fabrizia Pons.

In Sweden, three weeks later, everything went right for Audi — and everything went wrong. For sure, a Quattro won the event (as in 1982), and all the factory cars finished — the problem was that they should really have achieved 1-2-3 for an impressive demonstration, whereas the factory cars actually crashed into each other on the same special stage, and the winning car was driven by Stig Blomqvist and owned by the Audi Swedish importers!

Of the three cars, Hannu's was his Monte machine, speedily refurbished, while Michele Mouton had an older model, actually that used by Hannu in the Acropolis, when it had been disqualified. Blomqvist's Quattro, looking most unusual in the colours of Sanyo (the Japanese makers of electronic equipment), was that which Hannu Mikkola had used to win the recent Lombard-RAC Rally. The time of building brand new cars for most events, it seemed, had already passed at Ingolstadt!

There was definitely no evidence of team orders in this three-car assault, with Blomqvist not only driving to win, but with Swedish Championship points in mind. By 1981 Audi standards, the event was incident-free until the closing stages, when the cars were in a firm 1-2-3 position, Mikkola leading Stig Blomqvist, with Michele Mouton behind them, securely ahead of Ari Vatanen's Ford Escort RS, which had lost a front wheel at one point.

On the last section of the event, which encompassed only six stages, it so nearly went wrong for Audi. Perhaps the leader, Hannu Mikkola, was not concentrating completely (this is not my supposition, for he offered this as a thought, after the event), for he understeered his Quattro into a snow bank, and moments later Michele Mouton arrived, could not avoid him completely and thumped him yet more firmly into the hole. She also went off, and spent a couple of minutes struggling to get out of trouble again.

The result was that the phlegmatic Blomqvist cruised past to win (from Vatanen's Escort) by 2 minutes 36 seconds, with Mouton down in fifth place and Mikkola a dejected 16th.

In Portugal, Audi clocked up another victory, but once again it did not all go according to plan. Three cars started, two finished, but it was team leader Hannu Mikkola who crashed, and

This is what happens to steering tie rods on Quattros when the car is jumped too high and the rod is hit by the transmission casing as the machine crashes down again. The 'model', of course, is David Sutton, and the offending rod came off Bjorn Waldegaard's Quattro on the Welsh Rally of 1982. But it still won the event!

the lovely lady who carved her way through to victory — her second Quattro win in six months. The good news for Audi was that yet another event was completed without a retirement being caused by mechanical failure — the last time this had happened had been in the Tour de Corse, in April 1981, more than 10 months earlier. Mechanically, the most important feature of this Quattro entry was that the light-alloy cylinder block had still not been used in a rally car starting an event, even though it had been homologated since December 1981. The front-line cars, in fact, were brand-new, while Franz Wittmann had 'Old No 9', the car which Michele Mouton had used to win at Sanremo and had dropped off the road in the Lombard-RAC Rally in 1981.

Audi, as usual, started well, but Hannu Mikkola crashed on the 11th stage, rolling his Quattro in thick fog, but Ms Mouton not only

Harald Demuth rallied a works Quattro in Germany and on other events with great success before journeying to the UK to tackle the 1982 Lombard-RAC Rally. In a splendid performance (having had very little 'blind' forestry-driving experience) he took fifth place — and there were two other Quattros ahead of him! John Buffum (below) who used to wrestle with V8-engined Triumph TR7s in North American rallying, switched to a Quattro for 1982, won eight events outright, the USA Rally Championship and set fastest time in the Pikes Peak hill-climb.

Britain's young hope for the 1980s, Malcolm Wilson, had driven Ford Escorts for several years before he was offered the VAG-UK Quattro (ex-Mikkola) for the Lombard-RAC Rally of 1982. Still learning how to extract the best from the car at the finish of the event, he nevertheless managed 10th place.

carried on, but led from that point. No-one got near her, and she subsequently won by no less than 13 minutes, while Franz Wittmann, having started slowly, gradually crept up through the field and took third place, 28 minutes behind Michele.

On the Tour de Corse, the aluminium-block engines were finally pressed into service, for all three cars in the event were as close to being 'lightweight tarmac specials' as was possible with such a bulky car. Two of the three cars entered were to retire, but this was nothing to compare with the stupid events which occurred before the start, when Hannu Mikkola's new car was written-off by a mechanic 36 hours before it had to be presented at scrutineering. At such short notice, the only possible course was to reprepare Michele Mouton's practice car, using as many components from the crashed car as possible, even including the registration plates! [Historians like me have problems, even at two years' notice. Pity the poor archivist, 20 years hence . . . The third car, driven by Wittmann, carried a different number, but was nevertheless the one that he had used in Portugal, as IN-NL-88.]

Having run for a year, since Corsica the previous year, without terminal mechanical breakdown, Audi Sport blotted their copybook in 1982. Hannu Mikkola's car, so hastily built before the start, broke its transmission on the very first stage, while Wittmann's engine (the old cast-iron block type) blew up six stages later. Michele Mouton, if not on home ground, at least on French-speaking territory, plugged on, never in the first few runners and suffering less serious breakages, but she must have been relieved to reach the finish after her car's seat mounting broke away. Seventh, after such a weekend, was something of a relief.

There was no better 'batting average' of car problems in Greece at the end of May, for the two regular team members were joined by Michele Cinotto as a works driver, while Franz Wittmann also started as a private Audi-Austria entry. Hannu's and Michele's heavy-duty cars were new, while Cinotto's R6-sponsored Quattro was the rebuilt Mikkola Portugal machine — if, that is, one can believe the registration plate . . .? Wittmann's Quattro was as in Corsica, running with an Austrian identity, and was the only one of the four cars to have the original iron-block engine. An important point for this event, traditionally very hot and demanding, was that the cars were using larger intercooler radiators, like those seen in Corsica for the first time.

Hannu Mikkola once again disappeared at a very early stage — running out of time after a front strut top mounting broke away *without* him hitting anything to make it do so, and Cinotto soon retired with electrical trouble. Franz Wittmann's car retired with damaged steering, and it was left to the French girl to keep Audi hopes alive. She did so in the most emphatic way — leading almost from the start, and finally winning from Walter Rohrl's Rothmans-Opel by an impressive 14 minutes.

At mid-season, therefore, Audi were winning more regularly than they had in 1981, but there was still a great deal of bad luck about. Hannu Mikkola, if he had not been an immensely experienced rally driver, would have been near despair, for this was his third successive retirement, and he had not won a World Championship event since the previous November. For Michele Mouton, on the other hand, the most exciting prospects were

In the winter of 1981-82, David Sutton was attracted to the Audi camp after running Ford Escort RSs for many years. His mechanics built this car in a matter of weeks, after which it dominated the Rothmans-RAC Open Championship in Hannu Mikkola's capable hands. Pirelli and Duckhams were major sponsors, and right from the start this car used the big rear spoiler and oil coolers.

On its very first event, the Audi Sport UK Quattro, built at Ingolstadt by David Sutton's mechanics and driven by Hannu Mikkola, won the Mintex International Rally outright. LYV 4X became a very famous vehicle identity that year.

opening up, for she was catching up with Walter Rohrl in the Driver's series, a process which was evidently rattling the West German, who was heard to suggest that the Quattro was so good that even a monkey could drive one to victory. Fighting talk, which the charming French girl could not be expected to enjoy.

For Audi, however, there was worse fortune to come. Three victories in the last four events they had tackled was suddenly to be balanced by a long, vastly expensive and completely wasted trip to New Zealand for the Motogard rally. Two cars had been flown out to the other side of the world, and reregistered with local identities. Hannu's car had last been seen in Michele Mouton's hands in Sweden (carrying IN-NU-81), while Michele's was new, actually being the 30th chassis built by Audi Sport at Ingolstadt. Both were to the latest specification for loose surface events, which is to say that they had alloy engines, big intercoolers, but small turbochargers for enhanced mid-range

torque. The real innovation, however, was that David Sutton had been invited to manage the team, with only a handful of mechanics from Germany — David had been running a Quattro for Hannu Mikkola and Bjorn Waldegaard in the UK on behalf of the importers, VAG (UK) Ltd.

It was almost a rerun of 1981, in general, for the Quattros were demonstrably faster than any other car in the event, Hannu Mikkola set most fastest stage times — but neither car finished the rally. Michele's fell out after 14 stages, when leading, with a broken engine oil pipe and a ruined engine. Hannu suffered from an early engine problem, traced to fuel injection malfunction, fought his way back up towards the lead, lost six minutes with a detached distributor lead, then stopped with broken steering. It did not help Michele's World Championship chances that Walter Rohrl finished third behind the two Toyotas of Bjorn Waldegaard and Per Eklund.

The Quattros were not ideally suited to tarmac events, even by 1982, and the result was that Hannu Mikkola's UK car was struggling to stay on terms in the Circuit of Ireland. It was not so much a lack of handling as the car's heavy weight which handicapped it.

This is an unfamiliar aspect of the Quattro's works profile, which shows off how deep the rear spoiler is, and the way the factory colour scheme is carried across the rear of the roof.

Hannu Mikkola could not drive the UK Quattro in the Welsh Rally of 1982, so his place was taken by Bjorn Waldegaard, once his team-mate at Ford. Bjorn had no previous four-wheel-drive experience, but he took to the Quattro with great aplomb . . . and won outright.

After New Zealand, however, the tide suddenly turned in favour of Audi. They tackled five more World Championship events before the end of the season, winning four of them and morally deserving to win the fifth as well. On the very last event of the season, the Lombard-RAC, they won the 1982 Championship for Makes, and Michele Mouton came very close indeed to winning the Drivers' series, but eventually had to give best to Walter Rohrl, who was rather ungracious about the whole affair.

After New Zealand, Audi decided to enter two cars for the Rallye do Brasil, which had been elevated to the Makes series following the cancellation of the Argentine Rally. Argentina had been involved in a more momentous contest in the South Atlantic earlier in the year (the Falklands war) and the event had been cancelled while this conflict was still raging.

As a world-class contest, Brazil was something of a non-starter, for there were only five A-priority drivers in the event (Mikkola and Mouton for Audi, Rohrl and Shekhar Mehta in Opel and Datsun cars, respectively and De Vitta in a Escort RS2000) and, in addition, there

was organizational strife a few days before the start when the popular Clerk of the Course, Fransisco Santos, was sacked. The event itself, which only attracted 55 starters, all but four of them from the South American continent, turned into a real shambles, for only eight crews were left running after the first sector of eight special stages, and only five at half-distance. At the finish there were just four — with first and fourth being separated by penalties of 3 hours 25 minutes!

Audi exported both Quattros from New Zealand, originally planning to use them in Brazil, but in the end only Michele Mouton did that (in a reregistered machine), while Hannu had Mouton's Acropolis-winning car rebuilt and flown out to Brazil to join the team. As in New Zealand, David Sutton managed the team, which included five British mechanics as well as German staff.

The rally started and finished in Sao Paulo, the headquarters of the organizing club (and, so they say, the world's fastest growing city). Out in the countryside, however, conditions were awfully slippery, and the timing arrangements were in chaos, so it was not

In the British TV Rallysprint of 1982, the UK-prepared Quattro carried cameras (see the fitting on the front of the car) to capture the spectacle for the viewers. There is another camera on the facia roll, facing the driver.

surprising that the European crews were soon disenchanted with the whole scene, and that the retirements soon piled up. Hannu Mikkola, in fact, put his Quattro off the track on the fourth stage, took more than two hours to get it out of a ditch, and was out of contention before the rally had really begun. In general, however, it was much easier for Michele's Quattro to find grip than for the Opel to do the same, and even though she spent one stage with rear-wheel drive only, she was still leading the event for a time.

For the next two days there was a spine-tingling battle between the surviving Quattro and Rohrl in his Rothmans-Opel. Rohrl, who had been driving for points rather than with fire for much of the season, turned on one of those performances we so rarely saw in 1982, and fought Mouton every inch of the way. At the end of the first leg Rohrl led by 1 minute 54 seconds, and at the end of the third leg it was still 34 seconds, as the Quattro could only close the gap by fractions. The last leg, from Rio de Janiero back to Sao Paulo, encompassed eight stages, but after two of them Mouton had regained the lead, shortly afterwards Rohrl clipped a rock and broke the steering of his

Opel, and the battle was over. The German still led the Driver's series, but the gap was slowly closing.

It had all been very strange, on the other side of the world, so Audi and Roland Gumpert must have been relieved to get back to something approaching normality in Finland, for the 1000 Lakes Rally. Three cars were entered — with a fourth older car for Bjorn Waldegaard to use at the head of the field as a 'camera' car — those for the regular team drivers being new, and that for Stig Blomqvist being 'NK-54', as used (and nearly incinerated) by Mikkola on the Acropolis. It was an event where Audi's main competition seemed to come from the new mid-engined Lancia Rally of Markku Alen and the Opel of Henri Toivonen. Walter Rohrl did not choose to appear, as he dislikes the 1000 Lakes format.

After Alen's Lancia broke its engine, the only real Quattro competition came from Toivonen's Opel, but this disappeared after the young Finn suffered a high-speed accident and destroyed the front of his Ascona 400. Michele Mouton performed very well until the middle of the event, then she jumped her Quattro too high over one of the notorious Finnish brows,

Four driving wheels, but only two of them spewing out dust and rocks in this shot — Hannu Mikkola on his way to victory in the Scottish Rally of 1982.

smashed the front differential, lost drive to the front wheels, then oversteered off at the next fast corner with her 'conventional' Quattro and rolled out of fifth place.

Thereafter, the battle — and the controversy — was between Mikkola's Kleber-shod car and Blomqvist's Michelin-shod sister model. There seemed to be no doubt that the Blomqvist-Michelin combination was the faster, but team orders had to be obeyed, such that Hannu Mikkola won the event (it was his first finish, never mind victory, for Ingolstadt since February, so everyone was relieved), and Blomqvist finished second, just 28 seconds behind him. Neither Blomqvist, nor his fans in the Swedish press, were amused . . .

Five weeks later, however, there were no team orders for the Quattro drivers in the six-day Sanremo Rally in which a positive fleet of Audis appeared. No fewer than six works-linked Quattros took the start, Mikkola, Mouton and Blomqvist in the official team, with Harald Demuth (Germany), Michele Cinotto (Italy) and Franz Wittmann (Austria) backing them up. The specification of the cars was now virtually settled for the rest of the season, which meant that Mikkola and Blomqvist turned up with their

1000 Lakes cars, but since Michele had up-ended her car in Finland she had a new one here in Italy. The tyre controversy was still raging, and on this Italian event, Audi tended to use Italian Pirelli rubber on many special stages.

In spite of spirited drives from Markku Alen (Lancia Rally) and the two Opel team drivers (Rohrl and Toivonen), Sanremo in 1982 was really the stage for a monumental battle between the Quattros. Two of the semi-private cars (those of Wittmann and Demuth) fell out before the end, but the other four all finished in the top six, only being split by the Rothmans-Opels. The two fastest Quattro drivers, as in Finland, were Mikkola and Blomqvist, but Mikkola was always in trouble, not only with penalties, but with other competitors' dust, after a front differential broke and dropped him temporarily to tenth place.

Because the Audi mechanics were having to look after three cars, all running closely together on the road, and because no mechanic would take an initiative without the word from Gumpert, the whole support operation nearly broke down on several occasions, with Hannu Mikkola having to take an unaccustomed place as third favourite in the 'pecking order'. It was almost, if not quite, 1981 all over again, as the Quattros variously suffered from worn-out (unchecked) brake pads, loose front suspension struts, collapsed seats, broken exhaust systems, broken rear differentials and a lot of aggravation. Only the massive power of the cars, and the patient professionalism of their drivers, saw them through. The fact was, however, that Audi did not seem to be able to handle a big team, or keep the cars running, unless the 'conductor of the orchestra', Roland Gumpert, was giving the orders.

After Sanremo, the position in the two World Championships was both exciting and intriguing. Audi led Opel by two points in the Makes series, while Michele (who had finished fourth on the Sanremo) was still second to Walter Rohrl. There was a mathematical chance that she could win the Driver's series by doing well in the Ivory Coast and the Lombard-RAC Rallies; Audi, who had not wanted to enter their cars for the lottery of a long-distance African marathon, suddenly found that they had to go to the Ivory Coast. So much money and effort had already been put into the season that it would have been insane to back out at this stage.

Whereas the Safari is an adventure everyone seems to enjoy, the Ivory Coast event is one they all love to hate. The country is not nearly as civilized, the wild life is more dangerous, and

By the time the Quattro reached the 1982 Manx Rally, its tarmac handling was competitive and it flew straight and level over the bumps, too! Even though it was using wide racing tyres, the wheels still fitted inside the wheelarches, which had extra screwed-on eyebrows at front and rear.

Both works Quattros in the 1982 Rallye Cote d'Ivoire (Ivory Coast to the British-speakers among us), wore Marlboro (cigarette) sponsorship. On this event, Hannu Mikkola (in car No 5) carried team chief Roland Gumpert as his co-driver, to provide 'flying service' support for Michele Mouton (in car No 2), who aimed to clinch the World Championship. The ploy failed — Gumpert was most unwell inside the car, while Michele crashed her Quattro and had to retire.

36

the predictability of the route, other traffic and the result almost non-existent. Reluctantly, but very bravely, therefore, Audi entered two cars — one a serious entry for Michele Mouton and Fabrizia Pons, the other really a 'chase' car for Michele, to be crewed by Hannu Mikkola and team chief Roland Gumpert. Opel, for their part, entered a single (ex-Safari) car for Walter Rohrl. One way or another, it seemed, the Championships would be settled on the mud and in the heat of the Ivory Coast.

Michele's car was a heavyweight 'rough road' Quattro — the very machine she had used to win the Acropolis, and which Mikkola had briefly used in Brazil, earlier in the year, while Mikkola's 'chase' car, carrying extra spares, was 'NU-38' with which Michele had won in

Brazil. In addition to these two cars, Stig Blomqvist (partnered by Arne Hertz) was used as a 'course-opener' ahead of the official entries, 'NU 81' being an old car which had not been used in a rally for many months. For the first and only time in 1982, the two team cars carried major commercial sponsorship, by Marlboro, who were also sponsoring the rally itself.

There were only 51 starters, and after the first 16 long sections (no special stages were needed to establish a result in this awfully primitive going!) only 16 cars were still running. By this time, Mikkola's function as 'chase' car to Mouton was suffering because he had had to keep slowing down as Roland Gumpert became unwell and was physically sick;

Stig Blomqvist might well have won the 1000 Lakes in 1982, but in the end was narrowly beaten by Mikkola. In this car he made no mistake, a few weeks later, by winning the Sanremo Rally, in Italy, with Bjorn Cederberg as his co-driver.

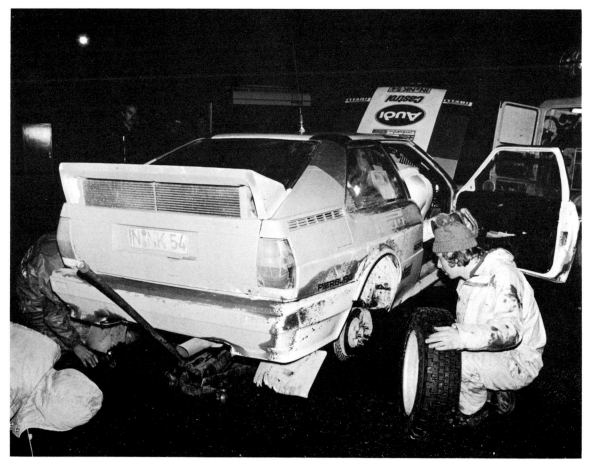

It is not always obvious that the 'big' rear spoiler of the rally Quattros is merely the standard spoiler pushed up on spacer blocks. The joint is just visible in this picture. This is Harald Demuth's car during the 1982 Lombard-RAC Rally.

nevertheless, he was second to Michele and well ahead of Walter Rohrl's Opel.

Five more cars retired on the second leg, one of them being Mikkola's back-up Quattro, out of time after first the rear differential, then the front differential, broke up and had to be repaired by Gumpert at the side of the road. On the other hand, Ms Mouton now led Rohrl by 59 minutes, and the mathematicians were working their calculators overtime. On the third leg the positions were nearly reversed when the surviving Quattro broke a drive shaft and later needed a gearbox change. On the fourth leg it all finally went wrong for her for, mentally and physically under stress (and, by now, overhauled by the German), she rolled her Quattro into retirement.

For Michele, the World Championship chase was over, for her rival, Walter Rohrl, went on to win the Ivory Coast event (protesting, the while, that he had not been driving fast at any point in the event), and moved into an unassailable points position. For Audi, however, nothing had changed for the Ivory Coast event had not qualified for the Makes series. Now, it all depended on the Lombard-RAC Rally.

In every way, in the end, the Lombard-RAC Rally of 1982 was a triumph for Audi, for the two regular team drivers took first and second places, Harald Demuth's works-backed example was fifth, two more Quattros for Malcolm Wilson — in the Audi (UK) car which Hannu Mikkola had been using all season — and John Buffum, over from North America in his ex-Mouton Portugal-winning car (then registered as 'NH-42') were well-placed, and only one competitive machine, the David Sutton-built example driven by Lasse Lampi, retired. The team cars from Ingolstadt used Michelin and Kleber rubber while continuing to carry Kleber decals on their bodywork, though Buffum was contracted to BF Goodrich, and the

Quattros carrying this registration number — IN-NK-54 — competed in Greece in 1982 (Mikkola — retired), 1000 Lakes in 1982 (Blomqvist — second), and Sanremo in 1982 (Blomqvist — won outright), before Harald Demuth brought this car to the UK to finish fifth in the 1982 Lombard-RAC Rally.

Audi (UK) car was on Pirellis — a cosmopolitan choice of tyres!

For this event, Mikkola's car was brand-new, while Michele used the 1000 Lakes-winning/ Sanremo second-place car, while Demuth was allocated the car Blomqvist had used to finish second in Finland and win at Sanremo. Life at Ingolstadt, as indeed at Boreham, Turin, or Russelsheim, was now extremely complex!

Before the start, the big sensation was not that Markku Alen turned up in a mid-engined Lancia Rally (was it really going to be suitable for this sort of motoring?), but that the new World Champion, Walter Rohrl, was sacked the night before the start, his car being taken over by Jochi Kleint! Throughout the season, Opel and their sponsors, Rothmans, had become more and more exasperated by the German's unco-operative moods, and when they found his heart was not in the idea of tackling a

'secret' rally at the end of the season, they sent him packing. It was difficult to find anyone in York who was sorry about this . . .

Even though there were more factory teams on the event than at any other time during the season, Audi only had to worry about two other marques — Opel and Lancia — and after Alen's fragile Italian car had dropped back with minor engine problems and Vatanen's Opel had gone hedging-and-ditching, it was really all over. Audi had been so confident about their cars' supremacy, by the way, that they had fitted Mikkola's car with a clutch control fixed into the gear lever itself, so that left-foot braking would be even easier for him than usual, and for the final night, with so many Quattros still running, Roland Gumpert turned up the boost on Michele's car so that she could catch up with Henri Toivonen's Opel.

In many ways, it was a copybook

performance. Mikkola, almost as expected, swished to his second consecutive RAC/Quattro win, and his record-breaking fourth victory in the event, while Michele Mouton not only survived the horrors of Kielder and North Yorkshire, but caught and passed Toivonen to finish second, 4 minutes 17 seconds behind her team-mate. Hannu was quoted, after it was all over, as saying: 'I think she will give me a real headache, because this is only her second time here and she finished number-two. If she goes on improving like that, I might as well go home!'

[Where was Blomqvist, incidentally? Contracted to drive for Talbot in Britain in 1982, he drove the obsolete Sunbeam-Lotus into an outclassed eighth place.]

The outcome of the Lombard-RAC, too, was that Audi finally clinched the Makes series, with 116 points to Opel's 104, and five wins (the last three in consecutive qualifying events) against just one by Opel. But then, if Audi had not won at the end of such an ambitious season, which encompassed 11 major rallies, they would have had embarrassing questions to answer when they faced up to the Audi Board back home.

Ambitious, did I say? 1983 was going to be even more so!

Overleaf — artistry in action. This reproduction of Stig Blomqvist, the 1983 British Open Rally Champion, driving his Quattro to victory in the Scottish Rally, is from an original painting by Graham Turner. High-quality fine art prints of this picture (measuring 17 × 24 inches overall) are available at £5.95 each, or £6.70 by post, from Connoisseur Carbooks, 32 Devonshire Road, Chiswick, London W4 2HD.

Audi's Quattro technology laid bare. This was the original 1982 car, as prepared by David Sutton's mechanics for Hannu Mikkola to drive.

Stig Blomqvist — the Quattro star performer of 1983 — has his car under perfect control in the snow above Monte Carlo as he heads for third place. *(Hugh Bishop)*

The pundits said that four-wheel drive would mean that rally cars would no longer look exciting. Judge for yourselves . . . *(Hugh Bishop)*

First rally and first win. The British Quattro, imported by VAG (United Kingdom) Ltd and driven by Hannu Mikkola, on the finishing ramp at the end of the 1982 Mintex Rally.

CHAPTER 5

Mikkola the 1983 champion

But Blomqvist the fastest of all?

In 1983, Audi's World Championship programme was the most massive ever mounted by a manufacturer; even compared with 1982, it was bigger, better and more extensive. Not only did the team enter at least two cars in every one of the 12 qualifying rounds (they notched up 38 car-starts during the season), but they homologated the Quattro in Group B, produced an important evolution of that car later in the season, and even found time to show a short-wheelbase prototype during an intensely busy year.

Sport or business? Sport it certainly was, but it was also obvious that Audi were trying to operate in a very businesslike manner as well. That they were sometimes thwarted in this aim was because it often proved difficult to control more than two cars at a time — and in 1983 Hannu Mikkola and Michele Mouton had been joined by a formidable additional team member, Stig Blomqvist of Sweden. There were at least three works Quattros on 10 events, and it showed! Perhaps Audi did not inherit the title of 'Team Shambles', but they came close to it on several occasions.

For 1983, FISA decreed that in order to score World Championship points, all cars must be of Groups N, A or B, which meant that Audi had to rehomologate their Quattro as a Group B contender. Even though they had to convince the authorities and their rivals that more than 200 examples of a high-specification Quattro had been built, they had no trouble with this, and from January 1 the Group B Quattro came into existence, not having lost any of the equipment so faithfully and painstakingly developed in the previous two years. There was still a wide choice of transmission gearing, body materials, wheels, brakes and engine tuning parts. But that was only the start, for the Quattro homologated under Form B229 in January became the 'new', then the 'evolution'

Quattro under B242/B243 in May 1983. The important difference was that it was homologated with a slightly *smaller* engine which, because of the turbocharging multiplication factor, meant that the latest car could run as an under-3-litre Group B car, and could therefore be built down to lower weight limits. The reduction in engine capacity was from 2,145cc to 2,135cc (achieved by using a 79.3mm cylinder bore instead of a 79.5mm bore), and the effect on power potential was negligible.

In addition to this, the 'new' Group B Quattro had enlarged wheelarch flares and a moulded scoop arrangement ahead of the rear wheels which could, where regulations allowed, be opened up to feed more fresh air to the rear brakes.

The team was enhanced, for 1983, by the addition of Stig Blomqvist (and his long-time co-driver Bjorn Cederberg) to the driving strength. Compared with the gentlemanly Mikkola and the very Latin Ms Mouton, Stig was a taciturn Nordic character, who could nevertheless drive a Quattro like the wind. For years, in the 1970s, he had been faithful to Saab and front-wheel-drive cars, then had suddenly driven a mid-engined/rear-drive Lancia Stratos (just once) and front-engined rear-drive Talbot Sunbeam-Lotus hatchbacks to prove his versatility. A splendid 1982 Quattro season, not only in the 1000 Lakes and Sanremo events, but at home in Sweden too, convinced the free-spending Audi management that they could afford three drivers in 1983. As it happened, only Hannu Mikkola started in all 12 rallies, with Mouton present on 11 and Blomqvist on nine occasions (one of them actually in a non-turbocharged 80 Quattro saloon).

Audi's aim in 1983, quite simply, was domination, to be achieved in a typically Germanic manner, by weight of numbers. They

An interesting, though under-powered, offshoot of the Quattro was the 80 Quattro, which used the bodyshell of the standard four-door saloon instead of the coupe, and was driven by the 2.2-litre five-cylinder engine in non-turbocharged form.

had won the Makes series in 1982, but had failed to provide a suitable platform for either regular driver. In 1983 they intended to win both series if they could, their leading driver being nominated as the season progressed and a pattern emerged. To do this, they planned to match their Quattros against the wilderness of the Safari for the first time, to go back to the Ivory Coast and to visit Argentina in the chase for points and glory.

The play, however, did not unfold according to the plot, for the massed Quattro presence in mid-season (three cars in Greece and New Zealand, five in Argentina and Finland and four

in Sanremo) always threatened to reduce the service back-up to chaos, and there was something of a spate of breakdowns. Though Audi got their act back together by the autumn, they had been out-fumbled by the ever-inventive and resourceful Lancia team of mid-engined Rally coupes. Lancia went on to win the Makes series, while Hannu Mikkola finally overcame misfortune to win the Driver's Championship in a season which included four victories and three second places. It was no wonder that, at the end of the year, Hannu seemed happy to accept a less intensive role for 1984 . . .

David Sutton's team built
another car for 1983 and, in
place of Hannu Mikkola, Stig
Blomqvist was hired to drive
it. The new registration
number was MVV 44Y, and
the car was just as com-
petitive. Blomqvist won the
Mintex International, first time
out. Notice the newly homologated rear wheelarch air
scoops.

John Buffum has dominated
United States rallying for
some time in Quattros,
initially prepared by the
factory at Ingolstadt. His cars
always use tyres made in the
United States by BF
Goodrich, who are one of his
major sponsors.

Stig Blomqvist, however, was the star of the
year, and as he took more and more of the
limelight, he also became more and more
talkative. The motoring press, having
despaired of more than two polite words from
the Swede, now found that they could get
coherent interviews for the very first time. *Don't*
some things change?

If, however, Audi wanted to get their 1983
season off with a win at once, in Monte Carlo
they were disappointed, for it was the driest

winter classic on record, with virtually no snow
anywhere. In such conditions the mid-engined
Lancias looked, and were, ideal, with the new
World Champion, Walter Rohrl, winning his
first event for a new team, and his colleague
Markku Alen finishing right behind him. Stig
Blomqvist was nearly 12 minutes off the pace
after 31 stages, and Hannu Mikkola finished
behind him, fourth. Poor Michele Mouton
crashed her Quattro at an early stage, just as
she had in 1982, which was a pity, for her Monte

Duck to water? No — Quattro to watersplash, with Michele Mouton on her way to winning the aptly-named Audi National Rally of 1983 in Wales . . .

. . . where she was equally as fast and impressive on loose going as well.

car and that of Mikkola had been brand-new for 1983, while Stig's was Mikkola's 1982 Lombard-RAC-winning machine, rebuilt for the occasion.

Technically, the most important Quattro changes were to Michelin tyres, for which Audi were contracted for 1983, and the fact that there was no sign of the gear lever knob-operated clutch which Mikkola had used in 1982; Gumpert had received an opinion from the sport's administrators in Paris that this was not legal according to the rules, so they were omitted from the specification. But Audi's

defeat, in the winter sun of the Mediterranean, was so decisive that *Autosport's* Peter Foubister, summing up his view of the rally, wrote: '. .. everyone else was left to question whether four-wheel drive really was the way to go. Certainly the last sight I had of Audi Sport boss Roland Gumpert, he was sitting alone quietly in Monte Carlo, head in his hands, gazing at the beautifully sunny blue sky.'

Peter should have saved his typewriter ribbon, for in Sweden just a few weeks later, where there was a lot more snow, Audi finished

1-2-3-4, with Hannu Mikkola winning the event, Stig Blomqvist taking a remarkable second place in the newly-homologated 80 Quattro (which had a mere 190bhp from its non-turbocharged engine), Lasse Lampi third in a private Quattro and Michele Mouton on the second works Quattro in fourth place. The only driver to set a stage fastest time, apart from in a Quattro, was Ari Vatanen (Opel Ascona 400), and he achieved this just once.

Audi Sport were well into their car-shuffling antics for the season, for Mikkola's winning car had been used by Michele in the Lombard-RAC, and Michele's was her Sanremo car, both from 1982. Lampi's was the David Sutton-built machine he had used on the Lombard-RAC, itself a recreation of IN-ND-21 which Ms Mouton had crashed on the 1982 Monte Carlo...

In some ways it was a 'business as usual' performance for Audi, as Michele had to fight her way back up the order from one terrible stage time after her throttle linkage came adrift, but their general mechanical performance was much better than usual. Was Audi going to be able to manage to run three cars efficiently after all?

In Portugal, it almost looked as if they could, for Hannu won yet again, Michele Mouton finishing second less than four minutes behind

him, and a fleet of Lancias struggling to stay on terms, but Blomqvist's car broke its transmission after hitting a rock at the side of a stage, ran for some time with front-wheel drive only and eventually ran out of time after having the front transmission fail as well. All three cars, incidentally, had been used by the same driving teams on the Monte Carlo in January, which at least made it easy for all the chassis number charters to follow!

To take a team of Quattros to the Safari, at Eastertime, was a big gamble, even though Hannu Mikkola had won the event (for Ford) way back in 1972 and Vic Preston Junior, given the third car, was a Kenyan resident with an impressive, if not Safari-winning, record. Nonetheless, Audi made a gargantuan effort, befitting such a professional team. Just about every team member, spare part and resource, it seemed, was sent to East Africa for Easter. Like Datsun, Audi employed a light aeroplane for communications and radio relay work, but they added to this the use of chase cars and they employed a helicopter as well, the total fleet being three rally cars, three chase cars (rebuilt practice cars), three Iltis 4 × 4 vehicles, four 'mud' cars, six VW service minibuses and the two flying machines!

It was quite an operation, with three brand-

By winning the 1983 Welsh Rally, Stig Blomqvist established a lead in the Rothmans-RAC series that he was not to lose for the rest of the year. Lasse Lampi's Quattro finished third in that event.

Stig Blomqvist (left) and Harald Demuth at the start of the 1983 Audi season, which was to prove such a successful one.

new cars, which so nearly succeeded, in dry and impossibly-targeted driving conditions. The cars were 'heavyweights', in the Ivory Coast/Lombard-RAC tradition, with the maximum boost rolled back from 1.7 bar to 1.5 bar (24psi to 21psi) in a effort to improve reliability without losing too much peak power, which was still quoted at 310bhp. Another special feature, apart from the obvious 'roo bars, were the enormous 200-litre/44-gallon fuel tanks, which seemed to fill most of the rear of the passenger compartment. These were not homologated, as special regulations allowed long-range tanks in Kenya.

Early in the event, Mikkola's car had a water pump fail, but Gumpert's magic helicopter produced a new pump and mechanics, in the middle of nowhere, so that the car could be repaired with the big loss of 1 hour 50 minutes. By the end of the first leg, therefore, 'Junior' Preston led the event from Timo Salonen's Datsun, with Michele Mouton's Quattro third and Mikkola catching up rapidly, in 11th place.

After the second leg, running north from Nairobi and including the traditional run around Mount Kenya, 'Junior' still led the Safari from Salonen and Mouton, but Mikkola was now up to sixth, though 2 hours 9 minutes behind 'Junior'; all the Quattros were now running at the front of the event, a great advantage in a 'dry' year, especially with a spotter helicopter to warn of hazards ahead.

The third and final leg — nearly 2,000kms up towards Lake Victoria and the Ugandan border and back — was a real endurance test in which almost everything seemed to happen. Mikkola and Ari Vatanen (Opel Ascona 400) were charging up through the field, but soon Preston's Quattro faltered with a broken turbocharger (which the Audi service team managed to change), while Michele's car needed its fuel injection system changed.

Soon, however, the retirements began to pile up — Aaltonen's oil pump failing and Salonen's Datsun breaking its engine. Then Preston crashed the Quattro in a dust cloud, putting himself out of the rally, while Michele's car lost a rear wheel for the second time on this rally and lost an hour having the damage repaired. Suddenly, at Nakuru, the last major halt in the event, a delighted Vatanen found himself leading, by only seven minutes from Mikkola (what a tragedy his water pump had failed early in the event!), with the ladies' Quattro third. And so it was, at the finish in Nairobi, except that Mikkola had clawed back a further minute. So near, and yet so far!

After the Safari (or, who knows, perhaps *because* of the effort put into the Safari?) everything started to go wrong for Audi. In the next three months, only one car of the eight starting the next three World Championship events actually made it to the finish, and the jibes about 'Team Shambles' began to surface once again. It would not be until Audi mounted a truly massive attack on the Argentine Rally, in

July, that things began to come right again.

In the Tour de Corse, the entirely new type of Quattro, which Audi Sport had newly homologated, and then produced an evolution of it straight away, appeared. Outwardly, of course, it was the Quattro as before, but there were many mechanical changes, including the use of the smaller-capacity (2,135cc) engine in a higher state of tune (about 360bhp was mentioned), a more compact transmission in which the central differential had been omitted, a profusion of Kevlar body panels, and brake-cooling ducts in the rear wings. Although the gearlever-mounted clutch control was now officially homologated, it was not featured on these new cars. As a '3-litre' Group B car, the latest Quattro could weigh as little as 960kg, but in fact weighed about 1,000kg/2,205lb, a remarkable achievement compared with the heavyweights of 1981!

Blomqvist won the 1983 Scottish Rally, despite going off the road at one point during the last night. Why else would he be carrying No 1?

Pirelli provided so much grip from their tarmac racing tyres that Blomqvist's UK Quattro was able to lift wheels at times.

51

Stig Blomqvist (holding trophy) and Bjorn Cederberg, the Swedish superstars who were able to match Hannu Mikkola's pace in Quattros in 1982 and 1983.

There should have been three Quattros on the startline, but Bernard Darniche suffered foot injuries in a practice crash (Darniche is a Tour de Corse specialist), so only the usual two team members started. Both were completely outclassed by the nimble Lancias in the narrow Corsican lanes, with Mikkola never higher than fourth. On the last sector of the event, however, the Finn crashed and wrecked the rear suspension of his Quattro, while Ms Mouton's car suffered a serious engine fire and was also forced out.

Things went only a little better for the team in Greece, where Michele Mouton had so pluckily won in 1982, for of the three cars, only Blomqvist's made it to the finish, in third place, behind Rohrl and Alen in the surprisingly strong Lancias. It was Monte Carlo all over again, this time with heat and dust to add to the challenge. All three cars were new — Ingolstadt was in the middle of one of its most productive periods again — and all three had the latest, rather peaky engines, and this time the hand-controlled clutch was also being used.

It all went wrong, right at the start, when Michele Mouton rolled her car on the very first stage. Later in the event, Mikkola took the lead for the very first time, then Blomqvist had a small fire when petrol leaked from a tank whose cap had not been replaced, then his steering broke . . . but Mikkola still led at the Lagonissi halt, with Blomqvist fifth. Before the final sector, the race was really on (for the Lancias were close), the boost controls were turned up and some over-optimistic soul spoke of 420bhp being available! For the very first time, perhaps, Hannu Mikkola might actually finish an Acropolis Rally.

But he didn't. Towards the end his Quattro's boot lid hinge broke, the lid came adrift and with it the oil pipe to the rear-mounted cooler. No oil meant no engine oil pressure, and no pressure meant — seizure.

New Zealand, which followed, was, to put it bluntly, a complete team disaster in which Blomqvist's disqualification soon after starting the event was merely the salt being rubbed into the wound. It was a complicated little story, where the reader needs to know his rally regulations very well, but basically Audi had only entered Mikkola and Mouton when the entry lists closed, then added Blomqvist some days later, the organizers being delighted to have three Quattros instead of two on their event. But Lancia, who were as keen on winning the World Championship as Audi, protested this decision, and after a discussion the rally stewards were obliged to exclude him after all.

The David Sutton workshops in 1983, showing three Quattros and the VAG-UK 80 Quattro in various stages of prepara-tion. The car with the open passenger door and without front wings is Stig Blomqvist's rally car and the one behind it looks suspiciously like an exhibition replica . . .

All three Quattros, reregistered in New Zealand as in 1982, were the ex-Safari cars, which is to say that they had the heavyweight/heavy-duty structures and suspensions, but before the start they were fitted with the latest small-capacity engines and the electrically-actuated clutch controls. All the service vans, too, were brought from Kenya.

Although Michele Mouton led much of the way, Hannu's car was often in trouble. On the very first special stage a water pump pulley broke and displaced the camshaft drive belt; the Gumpert helicopter rescue trick got him going again in last place. After getting back up to fourth place, his engine then suffered a fire due to a fuel leak from the injection system, which put him out for good. Michele's rally lasted for eight more stages when, still in the lead and with a mere six stages to complete, her engine failed abruptly. For Michele, it was not turning out to be a happy year.

Afterwards 'Harry Milne' (a pseudonym for a well-known rallying personality), wrote this in *Autosport's* Backstage column: 'What *are* we going to do with Audi? By now they should have been light years ahead in the World Championship, but they still muddle along to disaster . . . Why they tried to push Blomqvist into the rally is a mystery. It showed something

worrying about their philosophy . . . It has taken the Lancia team 15 years to reach their standard of competence, and nobody can little wonder they get irate when newcomers think that corners in the rules are there for cutting . . . In the middle of the crisis that the Blomqvist affair created, Audi personnel were openly admitting they would send four cars to Argentina, without noticing they do not seem to be capable of running three, or even two cars.' Few observers would disagree with those sentiments.

In Argentina, thank goodness for Gumpert and Audi, it all came right in the end. Not four, but five (yes — five) Quattros started the rally, being faced by only two other competitive machines, a pair of Lancia Rally 037s for Alen and Vudafieri, so there was no excuse if they did not win this time. There were three brand new 1983½ models for Mikkola, Mouton and Blomqvist, and two practice cars, refurbished for use by 'guest' drivers Shekhar Mehta and Luis Di Palma. Audi needed to finish in the top three positions to keep Lancia out of an unassailable lead in the Makes series, for after New Zealand they had 86 points to Audi's 62.

It might have been high summer in Europe, but it was winter in the mountains of Argentina, so the Quattros revelled in snowy conditions. Only Di Palma, the local hero, had problems,

The underside of a Quattro rally car, complete with plastic sump shield, showing the battering that it receives. The whole of the engine and gearbox/front transaxle are protected by this shield.

rolling his Quattro into retirement, otherwise the Quattros were in complete control, for Blomqvist led after the first leg, Mikkola after the second, and — to his undisguised joy — Mikkola at the finish as well.

Not only did this restore Audi's confidence in their cars and their own technical abilities, but it suddenly made the Championship chase very interesting again. In the Makes series, Audi now had 80 points to Lancia's 96 (and one victory was worth 18 points), while in the Driver's series, Hannu Mikkola had 85 points compared with Walter Rohrl's 87 (and in this case victory was worth 20 points an event). With four events still to come in 1983, outright victory in both categories looked possible again, whereas in May it had all begun to look out of reach.

With that in mind, Audi Sport mounted another massive five-car team entry in the Finnish 1000 Lakes, for they were sure that it was an ideal event for them, and all their drivers (even Michele Mouton, who had crashed in the 1982 event) were well suited to the fast sweeps and high-speed jumps of the Finnish forests. The major opposition came from Lancia, Toyota (with the new Celica Turbo)· and Opel, with Markku Alen as usual expected to be very rapid indeed. The good news for Mikkola was that Walter Rohrl was not competing, so any good result would put Hannu at the head of the table in the Driver's Championship.

During the season there had been much evidence that the Quattro's transmission was highly stressed in fully-tuned rally car form, and this was proved yet again in Finland when Mikkola's Quattro broke its front differential on the very first jump of the very first stage! A complete gearbox change was needed at the next service point, which put Hannu down into 143rd place; with a repaired car, he suddenly had everything to do!

At the end of the first leg, of 11 stages, Alen's Lancia was leading and Blomqvist's Quattro was second, but the other German cars were all running strongly. After the second leg,

Looking like new, all dressed up, and ready to go rallying — there is about 320bhp of turbocharged power here. This was Michele Mouton's car for the Audi National Rally of 1983, in which Fleet Street journalist Sue Baker was her co-driver. Points to note include the high-mounted alternator, the position of the water radiator on the left side of the compartment (right in this picture, taken from the front), and the location of the turbocharger, which is hidden beneath the 'Turbo' manifold.

Blomqvist led from Alen, and Mikkola was back up to fourth place, 1 minute 17 seconds behind the leading Audi. Soon afterwards, however, Michele Mouton's car developed a fuel leak and the engine caught fire. The girls emptied their fire extinguishers into the blaze, without much effect (TV film cameras caught Hannu Mikkola advising Michele, on the two-way radio, to 'Drive the car into a lake, there must be one somewhere nearby!'), before spectators eventually doused the flames with water; Michele lost 23 minutes and eventually finished only 16th. By the end of the third leg, Mikkola quite suddenly found himself leading again by one second. During the last hours, the Quattros confirmed their positions, and Mikkola eventually won by 21 seconds, though as Blomqvist had been slower by 16 seconds on the last four-minute stage many felt that Gumpert had stage-managed the finish to suit his superstar and the World Championship positions.

In Sanremo, Lancia turned the tables on their rivals, even though Audi's regular team drivers were joined by Bernard Darniche in the ex-Blomqvist/1000 Lakes machine. The other three cars were brand-new (Blomqvist's car carrying Competitions chassis number 50, which showed just how hard Ingolstadt had been working in three years), with stronger transmissions and redesigned fuel pipe layouts. However, on this truly mixed-surface Italian rally, the Lancias were always in control and Audi were always in trouble. Mikkola's new car was completely gutted by a fire at the rear, while Darniche's car also suffered a fire due to leaking power steering fluid, then later caught fire again, while Blomqvist (who had been as high as third at one point) had a low-speed accident which destroyed his car. Michele Mouton eventually finished seventh, 24 minutes behind Alen's winning Lancia.

Mikkola now led Rohrl by just three points in the Driver's series, which meant that Audi had to go to the Ivory Coast to glean every possible point, as only this event and the Lombard-RAC now remained. To save on costs and complication, however, only Hannu Mikkola (of the regular drivers) was entered, in Mouton's ex-1000 Lakes car, while Lasse Lampi (with mechanic Otto Harsch) drove a back-up car, really in the 'chase' function carried out by Hannu Mikkola and Gumpert in 1982. In addition, John Buffum, from North America, was also in attendance, not actually competing, but driving another Quattro 'chase' car.

The Ivory Coast in 1983 was a very 'thin' event, with only four A-priority drivers starting, a mere 50 cars in all driving off the starting ramp and only 17 of them reaching the first rest halt after 360 miles of rallying. The Quattros started from numbers 1 and 2, which meant that Mikkola had no dust to contend with until and unless he was overhauled by another car. Naturally, Mikkola led at the first halt, with Lampi (and a most unhappy and unwell mechanic) fourth, but Waldegaard's Toyota Celica Turbo was second, and looking good.

Soon afterwards, Lampi's car was withdrawn, so that he and John Buffum could take turns to run proper (non-competing) 'chase' cars, which left Mikkola on his own to fight the Toyotas. His troubles started in the bush when he hit a tree

trunk, which had thoughtfully been placed across the road, round a corner, at night (Waldegaard hit the same tree, put back by natives after Mikkola had moved it!), and it needed Buffum's flying-mechanic service to repair the deranged steering. Audi lost their lead in the rally at that point, but regained it a day later when the Toyota struck transmission trouble.

Nine cars started the fourth leg, where Mikkola held on to a slender seven-minute lead, but on the last leg, from San Pedro back to Abidjan, Hannu lost the rally by sliding off the road when a pacenote was misread, damaging the rear of the car quite seriously and taking a 15-minute penalty to have it patched up. Waldegaard, in the turbocharged Toyota, won the Ivory Coast Rally by just 11 minutes.

But if it was disappointment for Audi, it was fulfilment for Hannu, whose lead over Walter Rohrl had been stretched to 20 points. Because Rohrl was not starting the final round (nor was Alen, two points further adrift), this confirmed Hannu as the World Driver's Champion for 1983.

However, the Ivory Coast event had not counted for Manufacturer's points, which meant that Lancia was already confirmed as the 1983 Champion marque, and because they had

A characteristic flame emerges from the exhaust of Stig Blomqvist's Quattro as the Swedish driver brakes hard on the approach to a tight corner on one of the early stages of the 1983 Lombard-RAC Rally.

One wheel is off the deck, but both right-side Pirellis are working hard as Blomqvist balances his VAG-UK Quattro on the way to his clear-cut victory in the same event. Six auxiliary lights are ready to lighten the approaching darkness.

already overspent their budget for the year they decided not to enter cars for the Lombard-RAC Rally. Markku Alen, who loves the event, even though he is convinced that Kielder Forest has a jinx on him, was so anxious to start that he was reputedly trying to get a drive in a spare Quattro, but this came to nothing.

By the rest of Audi Sport's 1983 standards, their entry in the British event, the last of the season, was rather a restrained affair. David Sutton's UK-based mechanics spent weeks in Germany building a new car for Stig Blomqvist to drive in the event; registered 44 CMN in the Isle of Man (to circumvent British Type Approval regulation problems), it was to replace the very successful 'A1' type he had used in the UK throughout the season. The other two cars, for Mikkola and Mouton, both carried new identities.

Although the Lombard-RAC was expected to favour the Quattros, they had to face determined opposition from teams like Opel and Toyota. Even so, from the very first stage

(on tarmac in the Stately Home surroundings of Longleat) the Quattros led the field. It was not until the 11th stage than anything other than a Quattro set fastest time on a stage, and after 27 stages, at the Carlisle control, Henry Toivonen's Opel Manta 400 had been fastest twice and all other FTDs had been shared by Stig Blomqvist and Hannu Mikkola.

As in 1981, Britain was not kind to Michele Mouton. After the Sutton Park stage a mechanic inadvertently filled her petrol tank with pure water, which speedily put the fire out in the engine (a complete drain-down was needed to restore it to health), and in the forests of North Yorkshire she put her Quattro off the track and could not retrieve it. Later, very disgruntled, she drove an otherwise undamaged Quattro into a Middlesborough car park and abandoned it to the mechanics.

For Hannu Mikkola, too, there was to be no chance of a 1983 victory and a straight hat-trick, for in Knowsley Park, near Liverpool, he clipped a pile of logs just off the route of the

Wheels barely touching the ground, mud-spattered bodywork, low winter sunlight against a background of dense Forestry Commission land — all the atmosphere of the Lombard-RAC Rally is contained in this three-quarter rear picture of Blomqvist and Cederberg as they head for victory in the 1983 event.

stage and broke the front suspension so badly that the wheel had to be removed, co-driver Arne Hertz had to sit on the corner of the boot lid to give counterbalance, and the car had to be sledged out of the stage on three wheels and a brake disc. This cost Mikkola more than five minutes, which he was never to recover.

The rest of the event, indeed the whole event, belonged to Blomqvist's 'UK' Quattro — a car serviced entirely by the David Sutton team's mechanics — for he pulled gradually and inexorably away from everyone else, Mikkola included. Hannu soon picked up his lost places, if not his lost time, and at the half-way rest halt in Windermere, Blomqvist's lead over his team-mate was 8 minutes 9 seconds. Thereafter he did not have to try so hard, winning at something of a strolling pace, by 9 minutes 53 seconds. Lasse Lampi, driving his own (Sutton-built) Quattro, finished fourth overall, and John Buffum took sixth place in yet another impressive Quattro 'squadron' performance on the British secret-stages event.

At the end of the third year, therefore, Audi had still not managed to win the Makes *and* the Driver's series in the same year, but by all the plans they made public at the time they had every intention of doing so in the future. Not only was there to be a reshuffle of drivers, but there was the likelihood of the new 'short' Quattro also being brought into service during the 1984 season.

Hannu Mikkola, having at last won his World Driver's Championship at 41 years of age, was looking forward to spending more time at home with his family, and would only do six major events in 1984. Team boss Roland Gumpert had already taken the decision to hire Walter Rohrl to join the team (Rohrl disgraced himself by destroying a rally car on his first public appearance for Audi . . .) while retaining Stig Blomqvist and Michele Mouton as regular drivers.

Even in 1983, Audi Sport employed up to 60 people in the 'Supermarket' headquarters in Ingolstadt, and by the end of that year they had completed their 60th Quattro rally car chassis. Nonetheless, for 1984, Gumpert promised a bigger department with more staff, continued work on the 20-valve, 300bhp (road-car tune) short-wheelbase Quattro Sport, and hoped to see it in production, and homologated, by the middle of 1984.

And if a short-wheelbase, lightweight, Sport Quattro with up to 450bhp is rally-ready by then, what other car can possibly beat it?

CHAPTER 6

Quattros round the world

Progress of the ex-works cars

As I hope I have made clear throughout this book, the Quattro is no mere 'homologation special'. Whereas Lancia built just 200 road-car versions of the Rally 037 to satisfy the Group B requirement (and Opel had great difficulty in convincing the authorities that so many Manta 400s were actually constructed...), Audi put the Quattro into series production in the autumn of 1980, were soon building 10 cars a day, and have been doing so ever since. They never caused anyone to doubt that more than 400 Group 4 (and — later — 200 Group B) machines had been produced. In any case, any factory which can build 60 different *competition* Quattros in three years *has* to be taken seriously.

Once the Quattro had been established, both as a road car and as a serious rally car, Audi Sport were ready to start talking about the supply of replicas, or of encouraging various concessionaires to set up their own teams. This explains how David Sutton Motorsport came to cut their links with Ford (and Rothmans) at the end of 1981, how Michele Cinotto spent a year in the Audi-Italy Quattro, and how John Buffum moved smartly over from Triumph TR7 V8s to a Quattro in the USA in 1982. In almost every country where the Quattros have been prepared properly, they have been successful.

There is little space in this chapter to describe every programme in detail (the information, in any case, would soon go out of date), but I should make mention of the very successful Quattro entries from VAG (UK), through their Audi Sport UK operation. Even at the beginning of 1981, Audi at Ingolstadt were interested in supplying cars to a Briton, and Russell Brookes went a long way down the negotiating road (so much so that two new cars were in build, for a time, with his name on the job sheets), before policy was reversed.

For 1982, however, the UK importers hired David Sutton and his experienced mechanics to run a British Quattro rally car. In a matter of weeks, between New Year and the first event of the season, Ron Lumley's team learned all about Quattros and built up a new car, which they registered LYV 4X, for Hannu Mikkola to drive.

Apart from the Welsh Rally (which the car won, though Bjorn Waldegaard was driving instead of Mikkola, who was otherwise engaged on the Tour de Corse), Mikkola drove it to victory in the Mintex and Scottish events, finished sixth on the Circuit of Ireland and retired from the Manx with engine trouble, as well as providing *Autocar's* Peter Windsor with the drive of his life in a TV Rallysprint spectacular as well. Since Mikkola had an Ingolstadt car for the Lombard-RAC Rally of 1982, LYV 4X was driven by Malcolm Wilson, who spent most of the event coming to terms with left-hand drive and four-wheel drive, but still finished in 10th place.

Darryl Weidner then bought the car for 1983, and using it and another Sutton-built Quattro, won the Shell Oils-*Autosport* national series. His top-10 placing in the Lombard-RAC was also assured until an engine fire (Audi had a lot of those in 1983 . . .) forced him to retire.

For 1983, the David Sutton team produced a new car (MVV 44Y) for Stig Blomqvist to drive, in which he won the Mintex, Welsh, Scottish and Ulster rounds of the Rothmans-RAC Open series, but broke the gearbox in the Circuit of Ireland and had the engine blow up in the Manx event.

[There was also a vain attempt to make an 80 Quattro competitive in the 1983 Rothmans-RAC series, but this was not helped when driver Harald Demuth had a heavy accident in Ireland and later hurt himself severely in a testing accident at home.]

Over in North America, John Buffum drove

Steve Bagnall of VAG (UK) Ltd handing over a Quattro model to Darryl Weidner, who won the British Shell Oils-*Autosport* National Championship of 1983 in his own Quattro. David Sutton looks on, and Phil Short is behind Sutton's shoulder.

conventional front-drive Audi 80/4000s several times in the 1981 USA (SCCA) Championship, then took over Michele Mouton's ex-Portugal '82 Quattro, and started winning events all over the continent. His first outright victory came in April and was the beginning of seven straight wins, all of which helped him win the national title in the USA. He brought the car to the UK for the Lombard-RAC Rally of 1982, finishing 12th after a steady run. It was the same success story in 1983, with spice added by a sparkling run up the famous Pike's Peak hill-climb course (where Audi four-wheel drive reigned supreme), and on this occasion his visit to the Lombard-RAC Rally was rewarded with sixth place behind three other Quattros and two conventional GM products.

Although Franz Wittmann won the Austrian Janner Rally in January 1981 in a Quattro, he was not dominant for the rest of the year. In 1982 he started the season by winning the Janner again, but had to wait until November, and the Semperit, for his next Austrian victory; he ran as an official, or semi-works entry in various other rallies during the year.

Stig Blomqvist, of course, burst on to the Quattro scene in 1982 with his Swedish and Sanremo World Championship victories, but he also won five of the other six qualifying events in the Swedish calendar to become the Swedish Champion by an overwhelming margin, also finding time to win the Finnish Hankiralli and South Swedish international events along the way. No wonder the Swede became positively talkative as his Quattro

season commenced! Naturally, there were similar victories in 1983, though he was also heavily committed to the David Sutton/UK programme into the bargain.

Since some of the European Championship rounds were held on tarmac roads, where practice was allowed, the bulky Quattros did not always shine, but a skim through the results shows Cinotto (Audi-Italy) winning the Costa Smeralda and Harald Demuth in the Saarland and the Hunsruck. Demuth, in fact, won so often in West Germany that he easily defeated Kleint's Opel Ascona 400 for the German Championship, which must have made the patriotic Audi workers very happy indeed.

In 1983, as ex-works cars began to be sold to lucky (and wealthy!) private teams, Quattro victories proliferated. Apart from John Buffum's continued dominance in North America (which augmented a win in the German Sachs Winter Rally, immediately after he had picked up a new car to take home), Sarel Van Der Merwe completely obliterated all opposition in South Africa, Franz Wittmann kept on winning in Austria, Lasse Lampi beat the field in Finland on several occasions and Marc Duez used a Quattro with success in Belgium and neighbouring territories.

And yet, after three years, the Quattro bandwagon, worldwide, had only just got itself into top gear. Other four-wheel-drive rally cars will certainly appear to challenge it in the future, but will the Quattro be *the* rally car of the 1980s? Only time will be able to answer that, but Audi certainly hope so.

An historic occasion — the two best lady rally drivers the world has ever known meet for a chat about past and present cars. Pat Moss-Carlsson talked to Michele Mouton, and the two of them sampled each other's Quattro and Austin-Healey 3000 during 1983.

Darryl Weidner's 'other' Quattro (the second one he used in 1983 after crashing the ex-Mikkola car earlier in the season), spitting flame on the over-run, in the characteristic way of all turbocharged Quattros. Clearlite is Weidner's sponsor (he actually owns the firm).

Quattro routine service — no rush and no panics at this point. That is a *real* bonnetful of engine!

The dashboard/instrument layout of the Quattro is very stark, but very purposeful. On this particular car, the accelerator pedal is covered by a large mesh plate. Note, also, the very large footrest alongside the clutch pedal.

In vivid contrast, the Quattro road car has a nicely equipped and neatly styled facia and a discreet message in the centre of the steering wheel as a reminder of the power on tap.

This rally car interior shot proves that they are not all identical. This example has a different fuse layout (they are all grouped above the transmission tunnel) while the gear lever extension is exposed on its run from the lever to the gearbox proper. Life in a works rally car is not luxurious, for sure.

On to 1984! A new colour scheme, signifying sponsorship by the HB tobacco company, was to identify the Audi Sport cars for their fourth full season of competition. This is Stig Blomqvist's car, a few days before making its debut in the Monte Carlo Rally.

Second-generation Quattro, the Quattro Sport, announced in 1983 for production in 1984. The mechanical layout is basically the same as before, but the wheelbase is considerably shorter, and a four-valve-per-cylinder engine of 300bhp is standardized. Note, too, the rear wheel brake cooling ducts, the reshaped nose and bonnet panels and the cooling grilles in the bonnet itself.

APPENDIX A

Specifications

Quattro rally and road cars

Right from the start, it was always intended that the four-wheel-drive Quattro would be used as the works rally car, so the specification of the road car was settled with an eye to the best possible homologation in Group 4 trim. Although the Quattro was only announced in the spring of 1980, and homologated as a Group 4 car on January 1, 1981 (Recognition No 671), a lot of development took place in the first few years. These are the basic details of Quattros rallied, and used on the road, from 1980 to 1983:

1981 Quattro rally car

Basic equipment: 2.1-litre five-cylinder turbocharged engine, with three differentials, a five-speed gearbox and all-independent suspension. Front engine and permanent four-wheel drive.

Structure: Based on floorpan and superstructure of front-wheel-drive Audi Coupe, itself based on floorpan of Audi 80 saloon, but with extended wheelarches, front and rear spoilers and additional lower rear bodywork. From autumn 1981, big rear boot lid spoiler incorporated engine oil cooler matrix. Wheelbase 8ft 3.4in, tracks (front) 4ft 9.7in, (rear) 4ft 11.1in, depending on wheels and tyres used.

Engine: Five-cylinder unit, installed at 20 degrees to left side of engine bay. In-line valves, two per cylinder, operated by single overhead camshaft arrangement. 79.5 × 86.4mm, 2,145cc (equivalent to 3,003cc, because of turbocharging factor of 1.4:1 in motor sport). Bosch or Pierburg fuel injection, with KKK turbocharger and intercooler. Approx 320/330bhp (nett) at 6,500rpm; peak torque about 300lb/ft at 3,500rpm. Dry-sump lubrication.

Transmission: Single-plate diaphragm-spring clutch and five-speed, all-indirect, all-synchromesh, gearbox. Internal ratios 1.040, 1.217, 1.500, 2.000, 3.000 and reverse 3.500:1. Alternative (road-car) ratios 0.778, 0.967, 1.360, 2.125, 3.600 and reverse 3.500:1. Front and rear hypoid-bevel final-drive units, 3.889:1 or 4.11:1 ratios, plus central torque-splitting differential. Also homologated from January 1, 1981 were the following final-drive ratios: 3.222, 3.444, 3.556, 3.700, 4.300, 4.375, 4.556, 4.625, 4.778, 4.875:1.

Suspension and brakes: Independent front, by coil springs, MacPherson struts, lower wishbones, telescopic dampers and anti-roll bar; independent rear, by coil springs, MacPherson struts, lower wishbones and telescopic dampers. Power-assisted rack-and-pinion steering.

Ventilated 11in front disc brakes and 9.6in solid rear disc brakes, with divided hydraulic circuits and vacuum servo assistance. [From April 1981, 11.97in ventilated front and rear discs with alloy calipers were homologated.]

Forged aluminium alloy five-bolt road wheels, various rim widths, 15in rim diameter. Radial-ply tyres at first by Kleber Colombes on works cars. 6J or 7J rim width normal for loose-surface tyres, up to 10J for racing tyres.

Other dimensions: Overall length 14ft 5.4in. Weight (in rally trim) approx 2,625lb/1,190kg. Fuel tank capacity 26.4 gallons/120 litres.

Development changes

During 1981 many extra items were homologated, including heavy-duty chassis parts, larger brake calipers, the positioning of oil coolers under the rear spoiler, lightweight body panels (aluminium or plastic material) and an engine dry-sump lubrication kit.

From July 1, 1981, a modified grille was homologated, allowing for single headlamps and for more space for turbocharging intercooler installation.

From October 1, 1981, a kit was homologated to raise the rear spoiler on blocks to allow a larger full-width engine oil cooler to be mounted under it.

From December 1, 1981, a light-alloy cylinder block, saving 48lb/22kg, was homologated.

The Group B process

Groups A and B came into force on January 1, 1982, though the old Groups (which, in the case of the Quattro, meant Group 4) were still eligible for international rallying. From the start of 1983, however, either new cars had to be homologated, or older models had to be transferred. Accordingly, from January 1, 1983, the Quattro was rehomologated as a Group B car under Approval No B-229. The basic specification was as for the Group 4 Quattro except for:

Transmission: Gearbox ratios as before, but standard final-drive ratio now quoted as 4.375:1, with 4.571:1 and 4.625:1 as options.

Other dimensions: Overall width became 6ft 0.3in due to reprofiled wheelarch extensions incorporating, at the rear, a moulded scoop facility ahead of the rear wheels (normally not pierced). Weight (approx) 2,485lb/1,130kg. Additional optional fuel tank capacity of 19.8 gallons/90 litres.

This specification was usually known as A1 by Audi personnel and was effectively the first 'evolution model' of 20 cars.

A2 followed, from May 1, 1983, when the following changes were approved:

Engine: 79.3 × 86.4mm, 2,135cc (equivalent to 2,989cc because of the turbocharging factor of 1.4:1). Pierburg fuel injection with KKK turbocharger. Approximately 340bhp at 6,000rpm; peak torque about 305lb/ft at 3,600rpm.

Transmission: Optional final-drive ratios became 4.571:1 and 4.857:1. Close-ratio gear set became 0.962, 1.174, 1.500, 2.000, 3.000, reverse 3.500:1, with original close-ratio set continued and road-car wide-ratio set discarded.

Bodyshell: Rear wheelarches with pierced brake cooling scoops.

This was formalized under Approval No B-243.

Road cars

There was never any question of the Quattro being rushed into rallying before the necessary 400 production cars had been built. The production car was revealed at the Geneva Motor Show in March 1980, and the planned output of 10 cars a day (about 2,000 cars a year allowing for holiday breaks) was soon being achieved, though right-hand-drive derivatives were not available until the autumn of 1982. This was the specification of the production car:

1980 Quattro road car

Basic equipment: As 1981 rally car.

Structure: As 1981 rally car, except tracks (front) 4ft 7.9in, (rear) 4ft 9.4in.

Engine: As 1981 rally car, except for Bosch fuel injection.

200bhp (DIN) at 5,500rpm; peak torque 210lb/ft at 3,500rpm. Wet-sump lubrication.

Transmission: As 1981 rally car except for: Internal ratios 0.778, 0.967, 1.360, 2.125, 3.600, reverse 3.500:1. Final-drive ratios, front and rear, 3.889:1.

Suspension and brakes: As 1981 rally car except for 11.02in front disc brakes, 9.7in solid rear disc brakes. Cast-alloy road wheels with 6in rim width and 15in rim diameter. Radial-ply tyres, 205/60VR—15in.

Other dimensions: Overall length 14ft 5.4in. Weight approx 2,838lb/1,290kg. Fuel tank capacity 20.0 gallons/90.8 litres.

1983 Quattro Sport road car

This was based on the running gear and bodyshell of the Quattro road car, but with shorter wheelbase, four-valves-per-cylinder engine and very marginal 2+2 seating. Details:

Structure: Wheelbase 7ft 2.8in.

Engine: Five-cylinder unit with 20 valves (four valves per cylinder). Power output 300bhp (nett) at 6,500rpm, peak torque 243lb/ft at 4,500rpm using 'small' 2,135cc engine derivative (as 1983 A2 rally car).

Suspension and brakes: ABS (anti-lock) braking system standard (to be fitted to all 1984-model Quattros).

Other dimensions: Overall length 13ft 7.9in.

Quattro rally record

The works cars, 1981 to 1983

Even though the Quattro had only been rallying for three years when this book went to press, the works cars from Audi Sport at Ingolstadt had already chalked up an impressive record.

Below I have tabled their activities in World Championship events only. I have tried to be as precise as possible over the vexed question of individual vehicle identities, though I should point out that in West Germany a registration number does not necessarily live with one car throughout its life.

Year and event	Drivers	Car identity	Result
1980			
Algarve	Mikkola/ Hertz	IN-NE-3	Fastest — running as course car
(Non-World Championship event)			
1981			
Monte Carlo	Mikkola/ Hertz	IN-NP-50	DNF (Accident)
	Mouton/ Arrii	IN-NP-60	DNF (Fuel block)
Sweden	Mikkola/ Hertz	IN-NV-90	1st
Portugal	Mikkola/ Hertz	IN-NR-87	DNF (Engine)
	Mouton/ Pons	IN-NV-90	4th
Tour de Corse	Mikkola/ Hertz	IN-NJ-40	DNF (Engine)
	Mouton/ Pons	IN-NR-87	DNF (Engine)
Acropolis	Mikkola/ Hertz	IN-NU-81	All disqualified — homologation reasons
	Mouton/ Pons	IN-NP-40	
	Wittmann/ Nestinger	IN-NJ-10	
1000 Lakes	Mikkola/ Hertz	IN-NL-88	3rd
	Mouton/ Pons	IN-NV-66	13th
	Wittmann/ Nestinger	IN-NL-77	DNF (Withdrawn)

Sanremo	Mikkola/ Hertz	IN-NM-61	4th
	Mouton/ Pons	IN-NL-88	1st
	Cinotto/ Radaelli	IN-NL-77	DNF (Accident)
Lombard-RAC	Mikkola/ Hertz	IN-NM-61	1st
	Mouton/ Pons	IN-NL-88	DNF (Accident)

In the World Championship for Makes, Audi finished in fifth place, while in the Driver's Championship, Hannu Mikkola finished third.

1982			
Monte Carlo	Mikkola/ Hertz	IN-ND-78	2nd
	Mouton/ Pons	IN-ND-21	DNF (Accident)
	Cinotto/ Radaelli	IN-NP-40	DNF (Accident)
Sweden	Mikkola/ Hertz	IN-ND-78	16th
	Mouton/ Pons	IN-NU-81	5th
	Blomqvist/ Cederberg	N-DC-163	1st
Portugal	Mikkola/ Hertz	IN-NK-79	DNF (Accident)
	Mouton/ Pons	IN-NH-42	1st
	Wittmann/ Diekmann	IN-NL-88	3rd
Tour de Corse	Mikkola/ Hertz	IN-NU-81	DNF (Transmission)
	Mouton/ Pons	IN-NU-38	7th
	Wittmann/ Diekmann	651-Z7959 (ex IN-NL-88)	DNF (Engine)
Acropolis	Mikkola/ Hertz	IN-NK-54	DNF (Suspension)
	Mouton/ Pons	IN-NU-40	1st
	Cinotto/ Radaelli	IN-NK-79	DNF (Electrics)
New Zealand	Mikkola/ Hertz	KJ9030 (NZ number ex-IN-NU-81)	DNF (Steering)

Event	Crew	Number	Result
Brazil	Mouton/Pons	KJ9029 (NZ number)	DNF (Oil pipe)
	Mikkola/Hertz	IN-NU-40	DNF (Out of time)
	Mouton/Pons	IN-NU-38 (ex KJ9029)	1st
1000 Lakes	Mikkola/Hertz	IN-NN-82	1st
	Mouton/Pons	IN-NK-84	DNF (Accident)
	Blomqvist/Cederberg	IN-NK-54	2nd
Sanremo	Mikkola/Hertz	IN-NN-82	2nd
	Mouton/Pons	IN-NU-84	4th
	Blomqvist/Cederberg	IN-NK-54	1st
	Cinotto/Radaelli	IN-NP-40	6th
	Demuth/Fischer	IN-ND-37	DNF (Engine)
Ivory Coast	Mouton/Pons	IN-NU-40	DNF (Accident)
	Mikkola/Gumpert	IN-NU-38	DNF (Out of time)
Lombard-RAC	Mikkola/Hertz	IN-NV-84	1st
	Mouton/Pons	IN-NN-82	2nd
	Demuth/Daniels	IN-NK-54	5th

In the World Championship for Makes, Audi finished first, while in the Driver's Championship, Michele Mouton finished second, Hannu Mikkola third and Stig Blomqvist fourth.

1983

Event	Crew	Number	Result
Monte Carlo	Mikkola/Hertz	IN-NM-62	4th
	Mouton/Pons	IN-NM-82	DNF (Accident)
	Blomqvist/Cederberg	IN-NV-84	3rd
Sweden	Mikkola/Hertz	IN-NN-82	1st
	Mouton/Pons	IN-NU-84	4th
(Plus:	Blomqvist/Cederberg	IN-NJ-41 [80 Quattro]	2nd)
Portugal	Mikkola/Hertz	IN-NM-62	1st
	Mouton/Pons	IN-NM-82	2nd
	Blomqvist/Cederberg	IN-NV-84	DNF (Transmission)
Safari	Mikkola/Hertz	IN-YC-17	2nd
	Mouton/Pons	IN-YC-19	3rd
Tour de Corse	Preston/Lyall	IN-YC-18	DNF (Accident)
	Mikkola/Hertz	IN-NL-67	DNF (Accident)
	Mouton/Pons	IN-NT-49	DNF (Engine fire)
Acropolis	Mikkola/Hertz	IN-NM-27	DNF (Engine)
	Mouton/Pons	IN-NN-86	DNF (Accident)
	Blomqvist/Cederberg	IN-NN-17	3rd
New Zealand	Mikkola/Hertz	LB7800 (NZ number)	DNF (Engine)
	Mouton/Pons	LB7802 (NZ number)	DNF (Engine)
	Blomqvist/Cederberg	LB7801 (NZ number)	Withdrawn — eligibility problems
Argentina	Mikkola/Hertz	IN-NH-26	1st
	Mouton/Pons	IN-NH-75	3rd
	Blomqvist/Cederberg	IN-NH-74	2nd
	Mehta/Mrs Mehta	IN-NW-72	4th
	Luis Di Palma/Straimel	IN-NL-62	DNF (Accident)
1000 Lakes	Mikkola/Hertz	IN-NL-12	1st
	Mouton/Pons	IN-NL-67	16th
	Blomqvist/Cederberg	IN-YA-34	2nd
	Eklund/Spjuth	IN-NN-17	4th
	Lampi/Kuukkala	IN-NM-27	7th
Sanremo	Mikkola/Hertz	IN-NX-99	DNF (Fire)
	Mouton/Pons	IN-NL-12	7th
	Darniche/Mahé	IN-YA-34	9th
	Blomqvist/Cederberg	IN-ND-1	DNF (Accident)
Ivory Coast	Mikkola/Hertz	IN-NL-67	2nd
	Lampi/Harsch	IN-NN-17	DNF (Withdrawn)
Lombard-RAC	Blomqvist/Cederberg	44 CMN (IoM-registered)	1st
	Mikkola/Hertz	IN-NV-3	2nd
	Mouton/Pons	IN-NE-8	DNF (Accident)